BLAH

RAV IZEN

(GRAPHIC) NOVEL (ENGLISH)
RIGHTS ALL RESERVED
FIRST EDITION NOV 2024

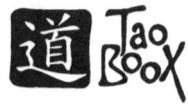

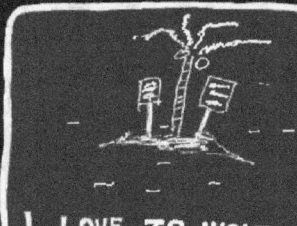

I LOVE TO VISIT THE ISLE CALLED SOLITAIRE ONCE IN A WHILE.

ANSWEAR

As I swore earlier
and again I
would be dying
before 33 that is
in a moon
or so that means
the fellow now standing
in this mist here
would be just
fading out soon

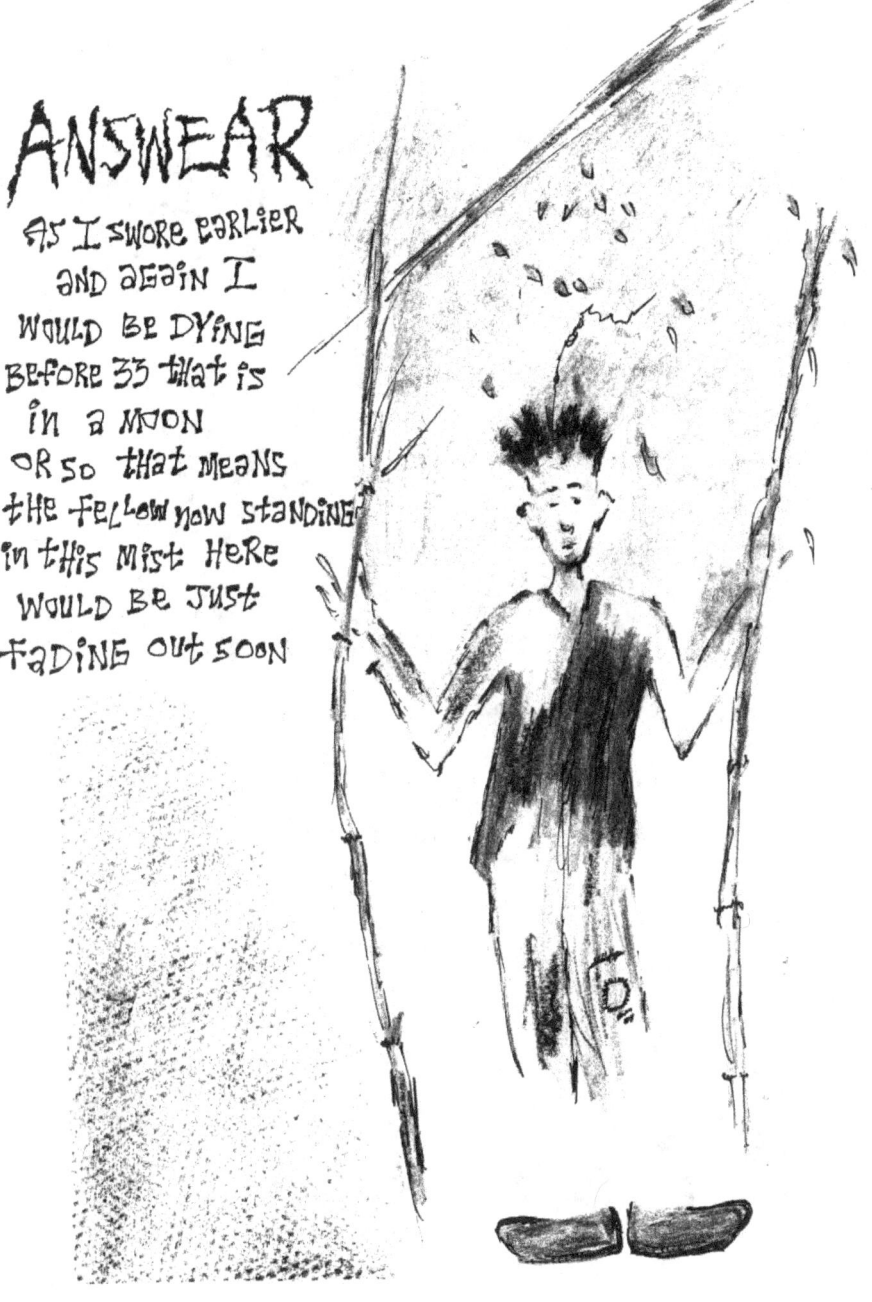

ANSWER THIS DUDE:
the thingy that looks like a beautiful lily blushing and moist with morning dew

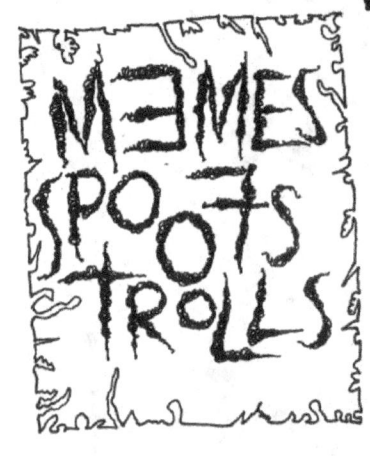

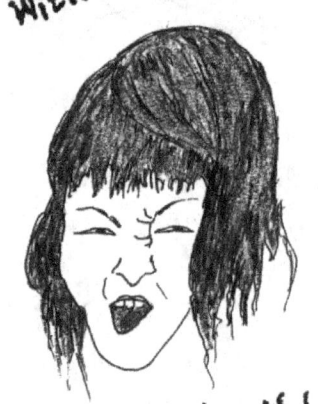

BEFORE SEX and a Bulldog after eating a Bowl of Mayonnaise... answer fast, no clues!

— xes ziuq

is that funny nuf

So someone tell me what is humor

Half joking it is id est 33% sarcasm 33% serious 33% WTF
[actually 33.33% each]

Mind you, everybody!

All stuff isnt sarcasm

— from classic tweets

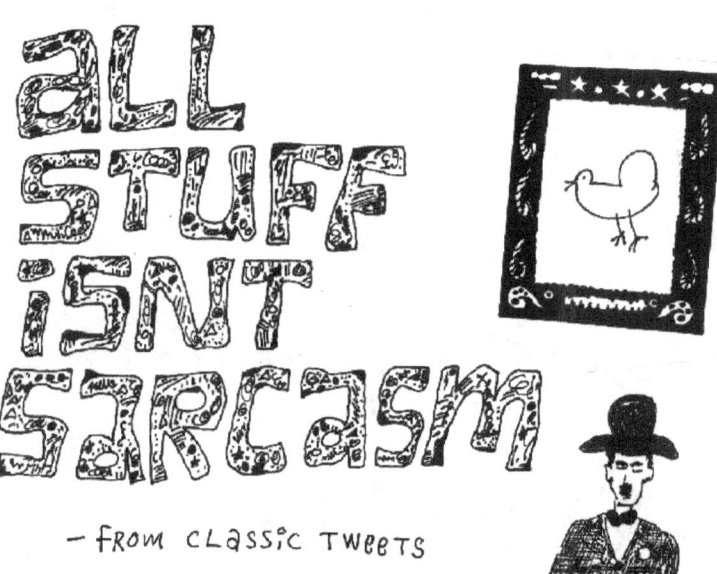

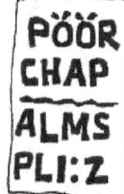

POOR CHAP
———
ALMS
PLI:Z

LET MASQUERADERS RULE FOR A WHILE NOW THEM GENERATE THE BEST PHILOSOPHY

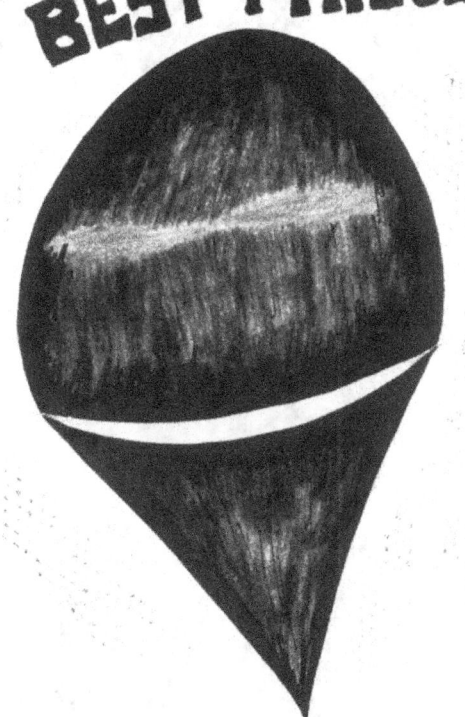

HALF JOKINGLY THOUGH

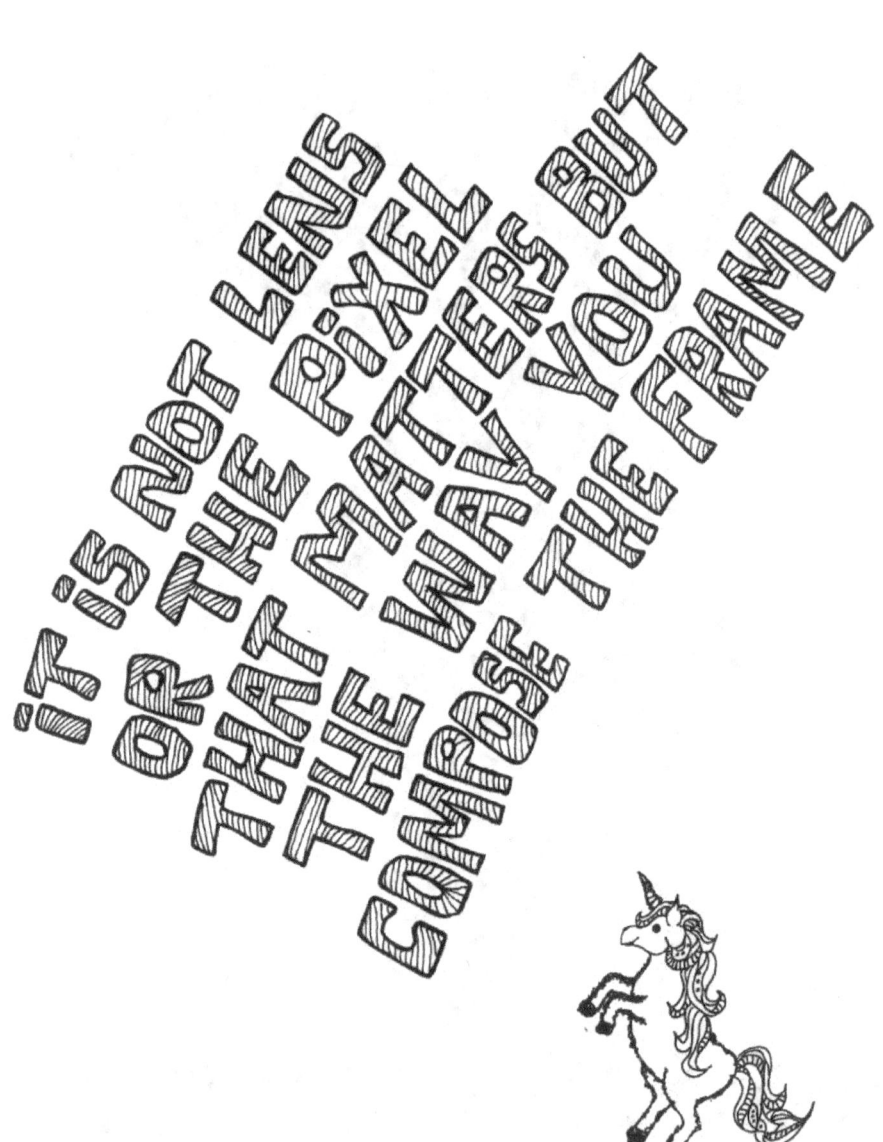

The Overestimated Reaper

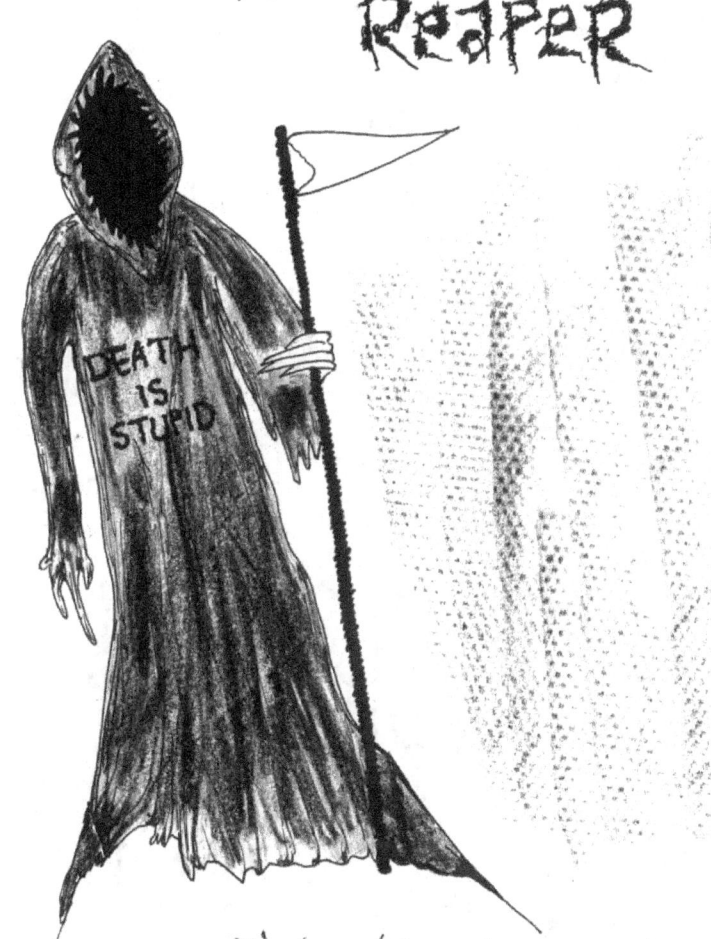

Grim Fairy Tales Contd

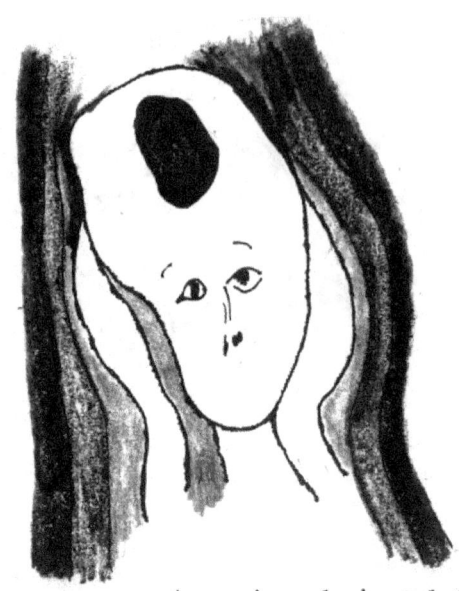

DONT KNOW WHO SLASHED MY TONGUE
WHO SLICED MY BALLS

AND I CAN ONLY SLANG
WHEN YOU MUGGLES
DO ME SOME FAVOUR

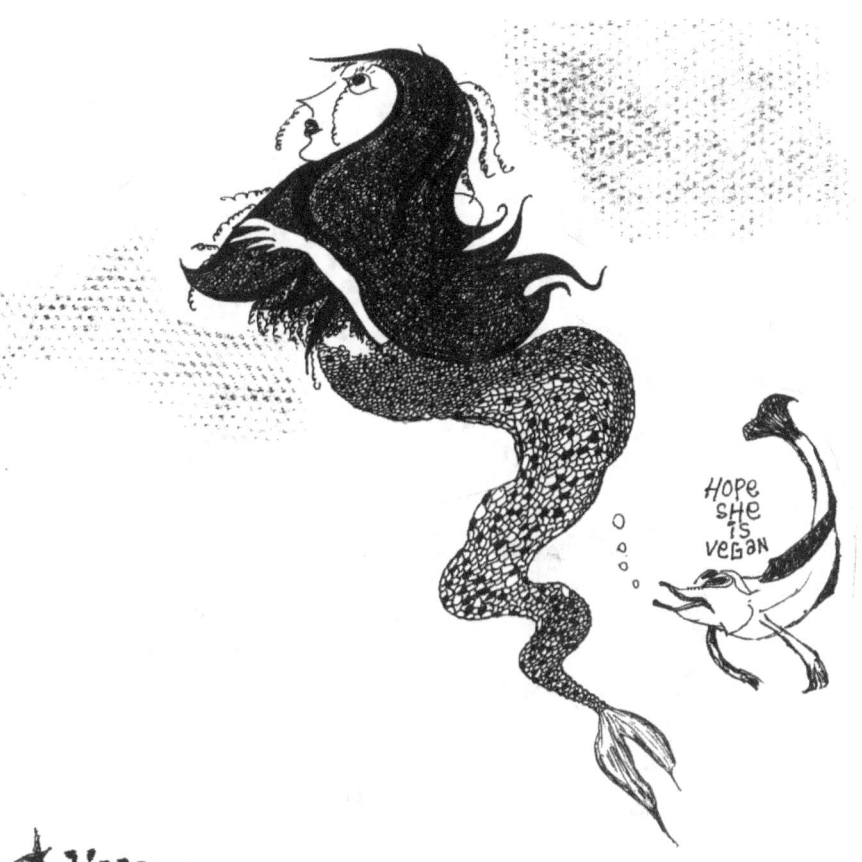

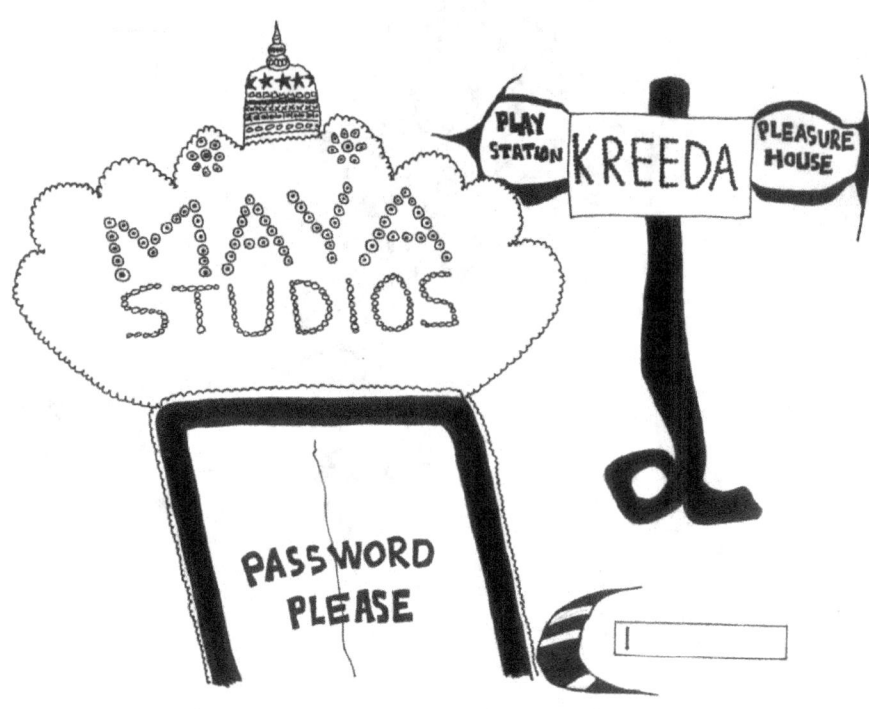

ABOUT FOLKS WHO ARE TOO PROUD OF THEIR ANCESTORS

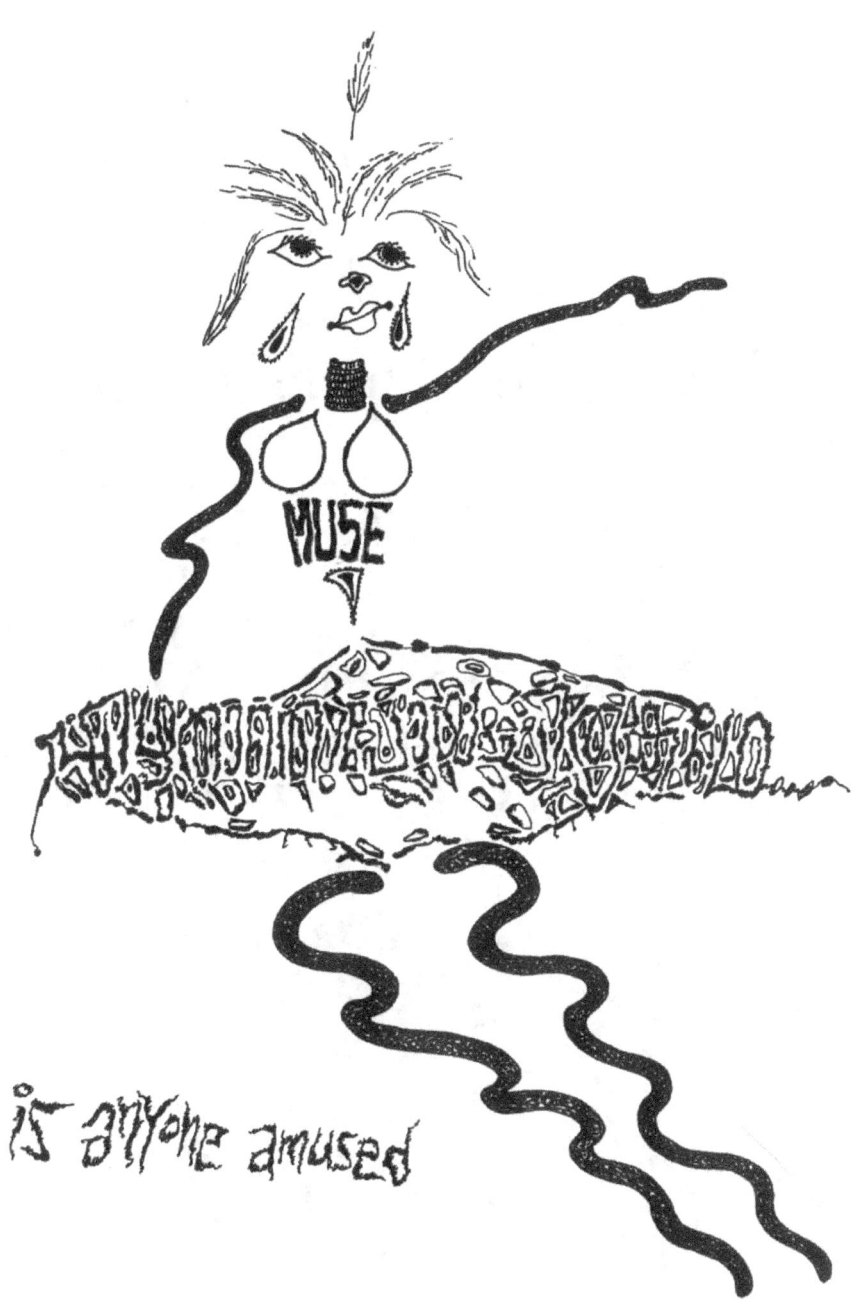

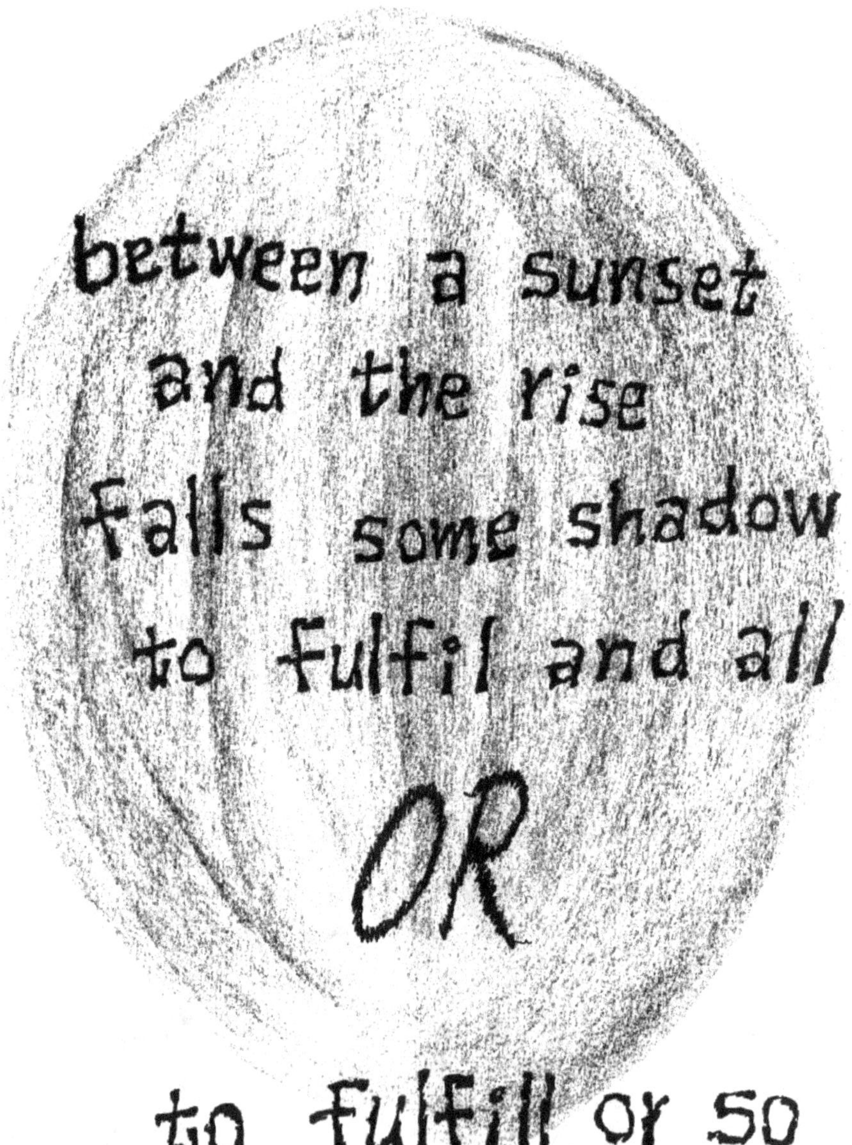

between a sunset
and the rise
Falls some shadow
to fulfil and all

OR

to fulfill or so

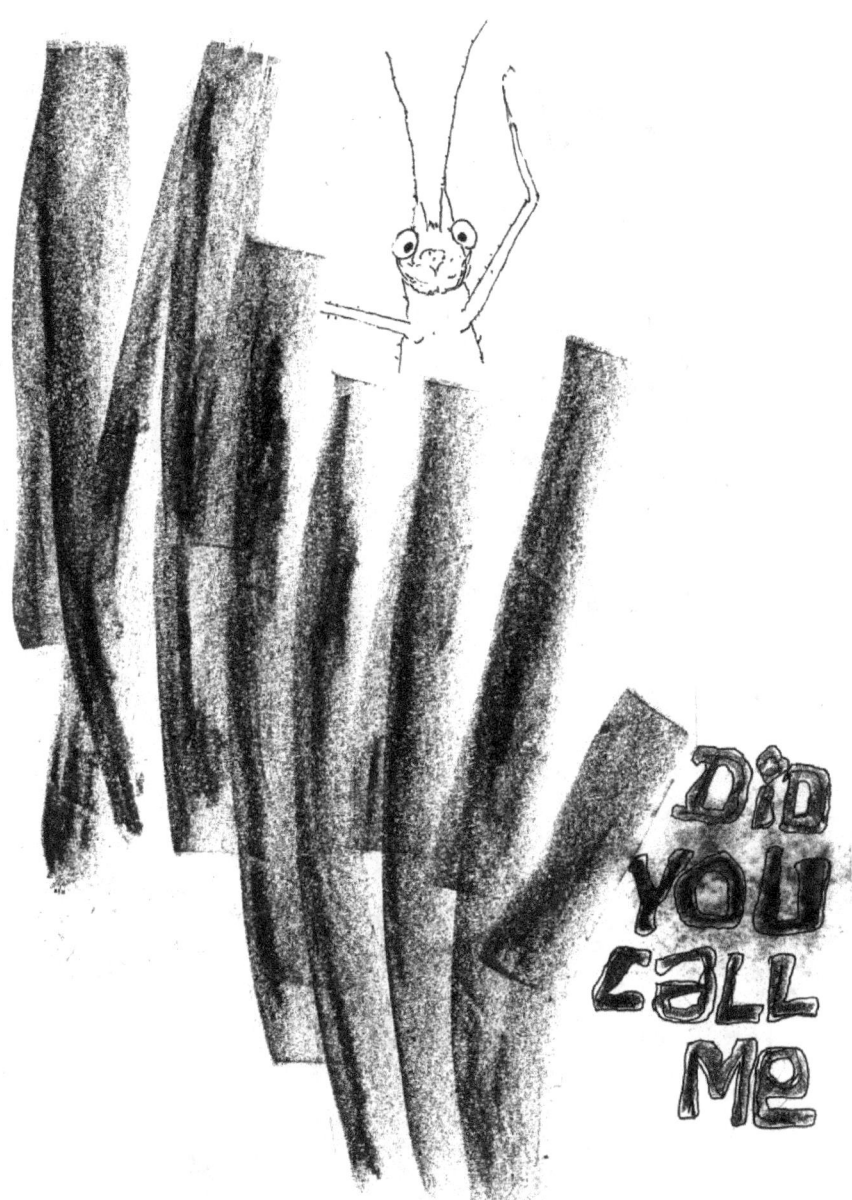

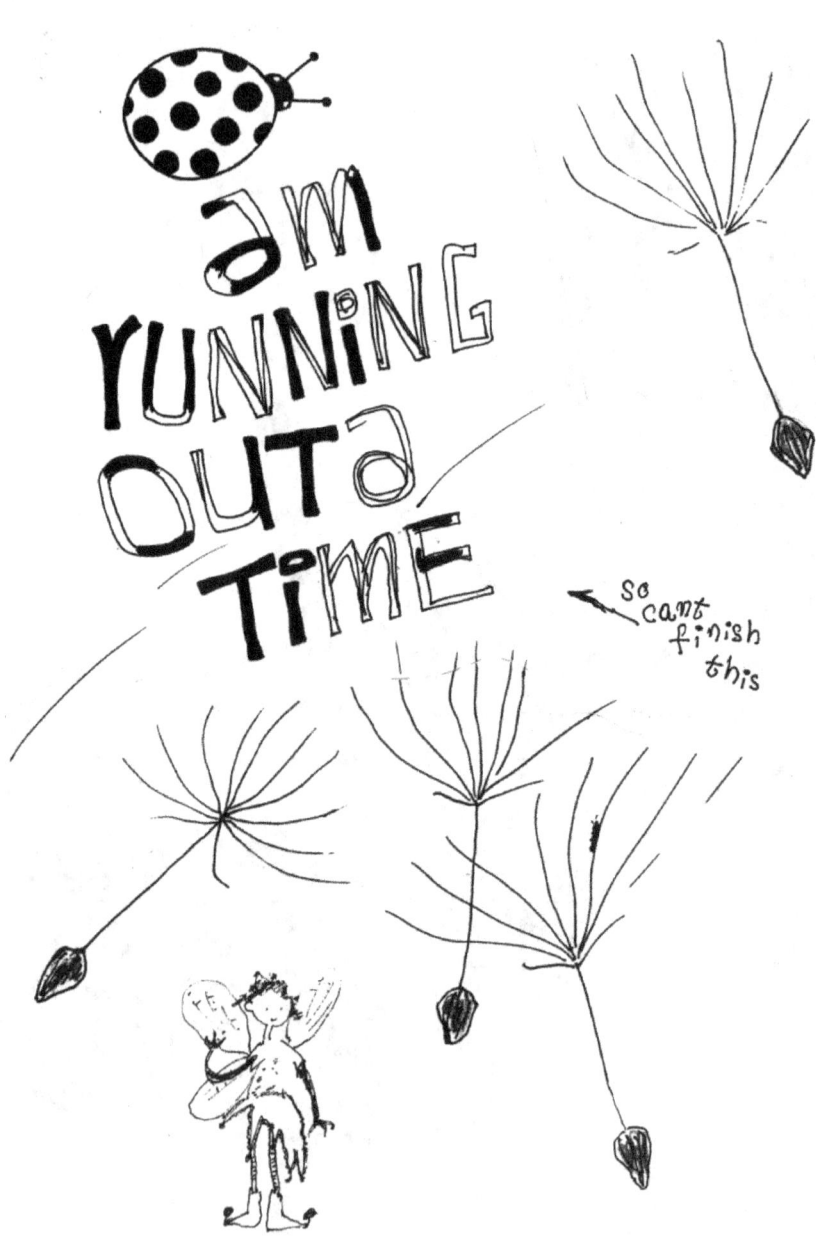

WHAT I WANTED WAS A SWORD NOT A KITCHEN KNIFE...

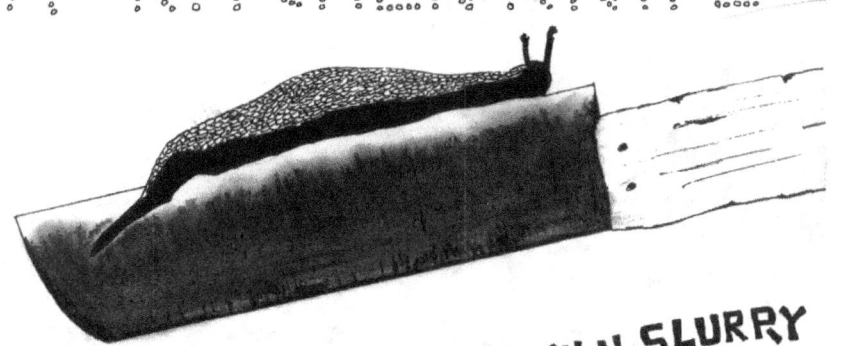

● a SLUG WHO IS SLOW N SLURRY SWALLOWS A SWORD

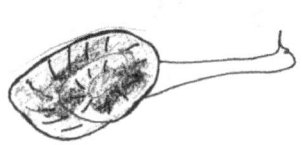
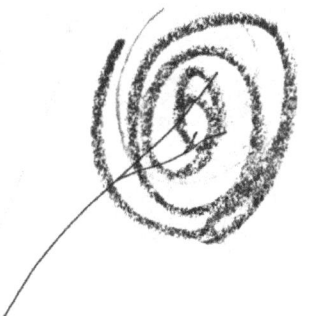

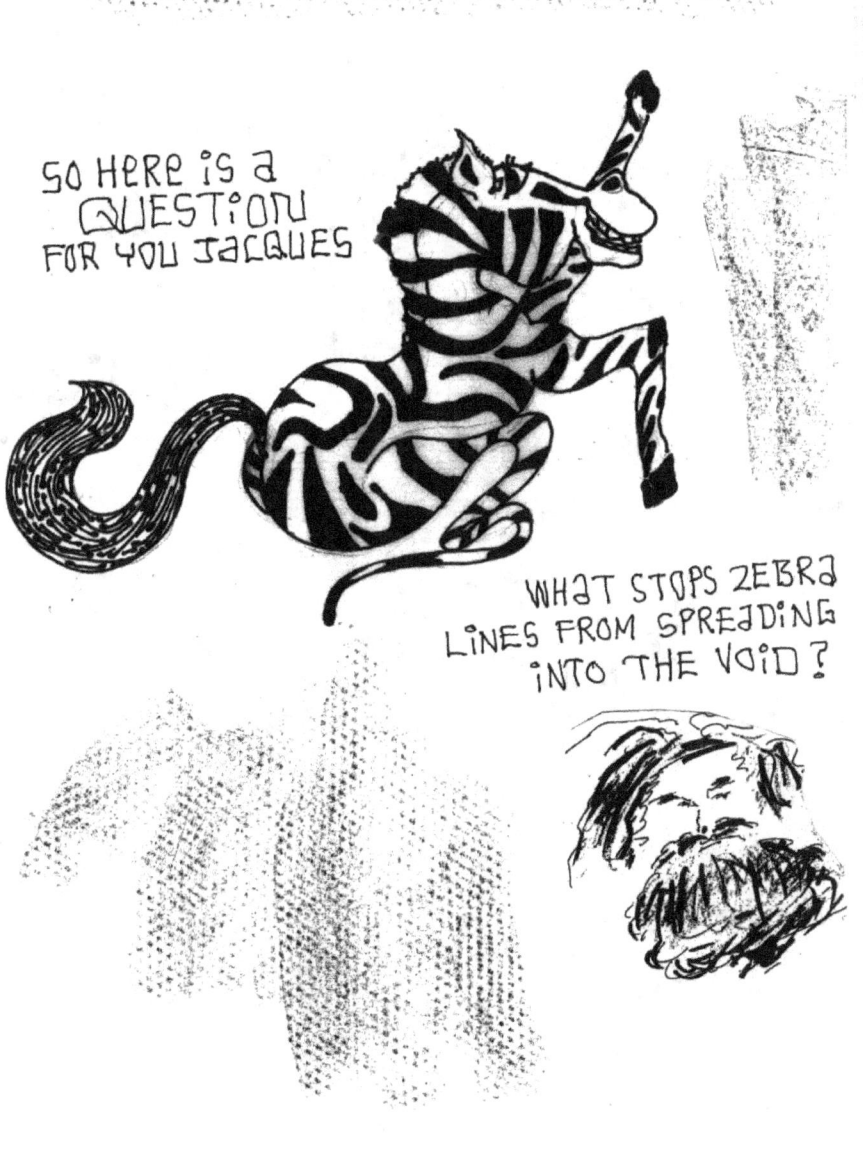

So here are the new bestselling titles

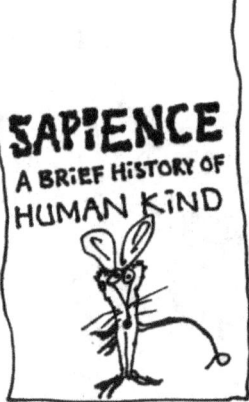

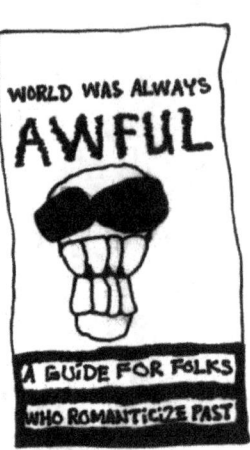

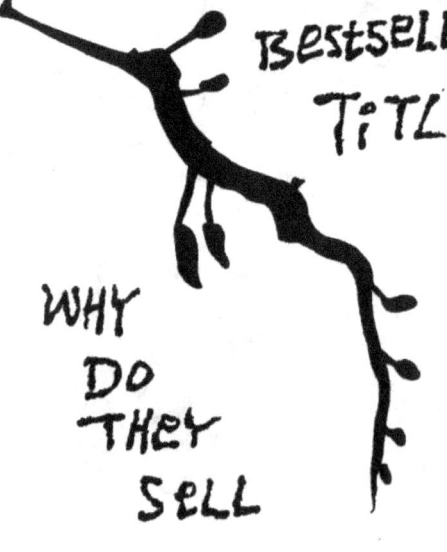

Why do they sell

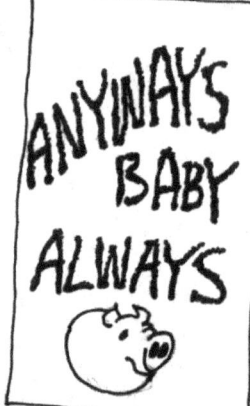

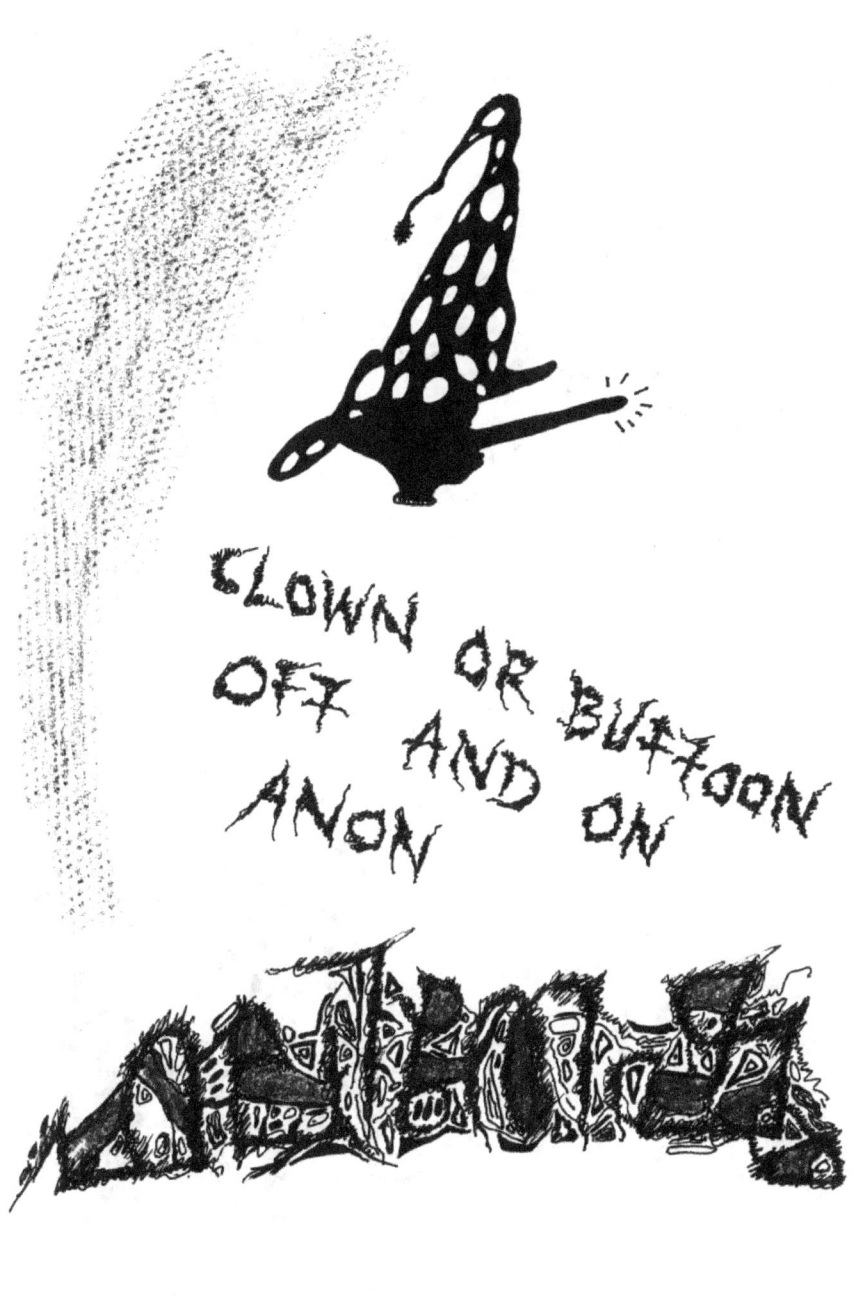

laugh at self
it is free
~~[scribbled out text]~~
LAUGH iT OFF

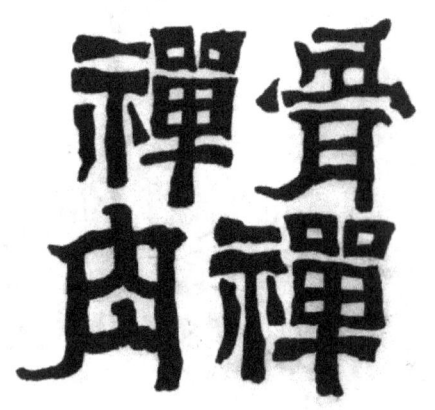

Hey, Mayhem, when are you happening?

Maybe by May

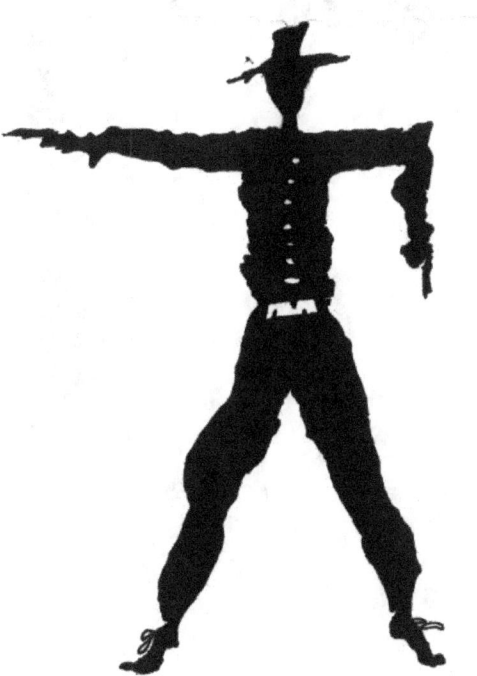

FANCYDRESS PARTY

grrrrr8!

ROLL ON HALLOWEEN!

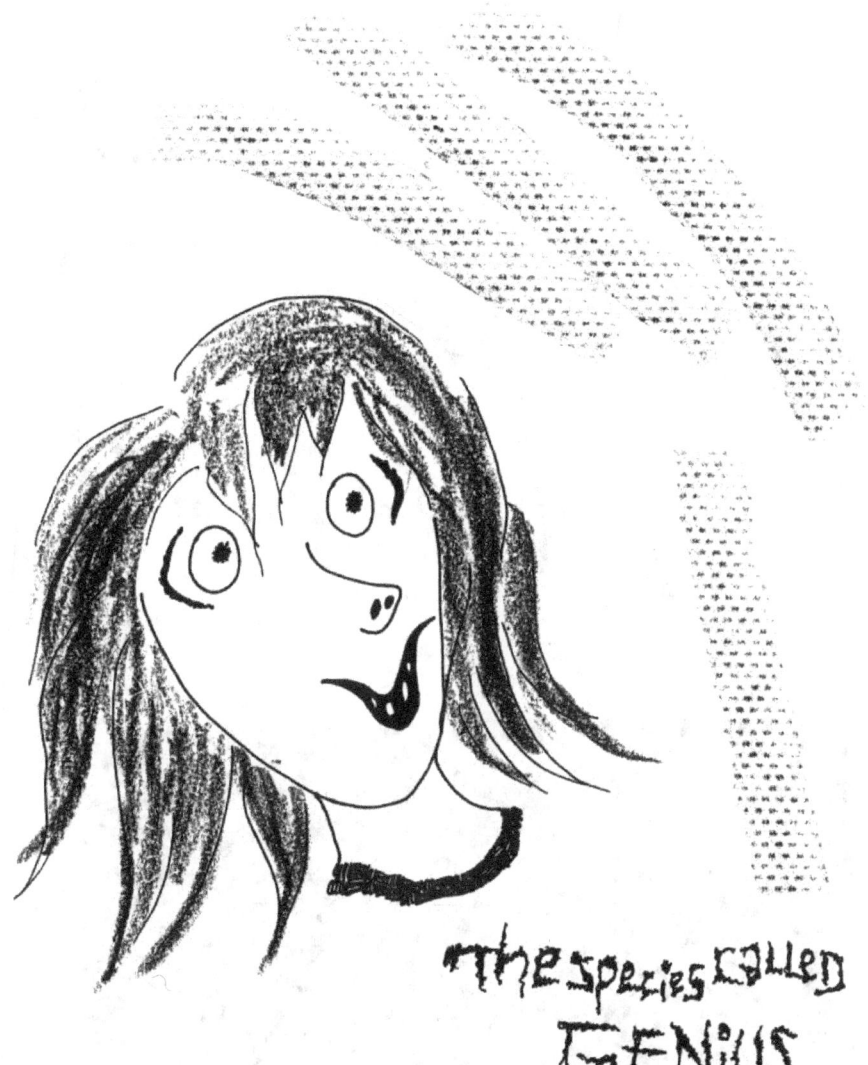

SHOULD I SHOOT MYSELF OR HAVE A SHOT OF TEQUILA — CAMUS

QUILL YOURSELF AMIGO

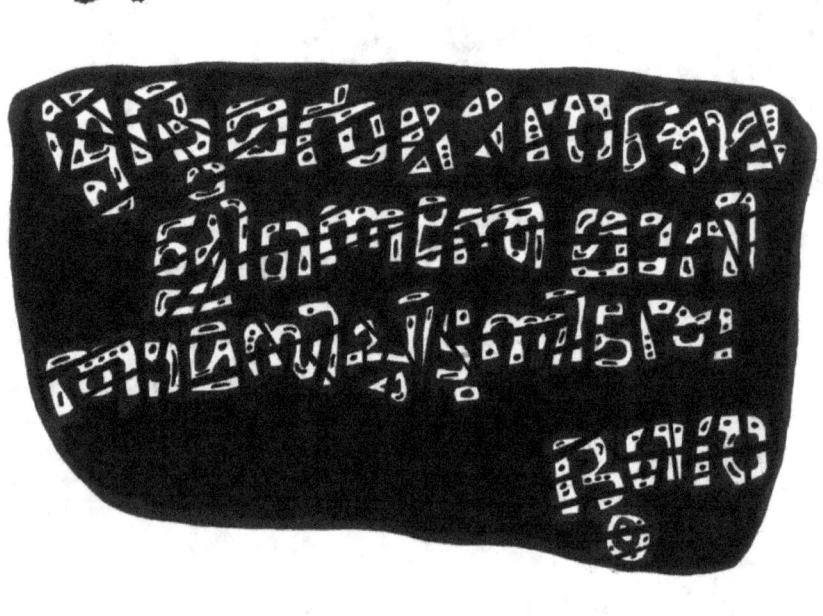

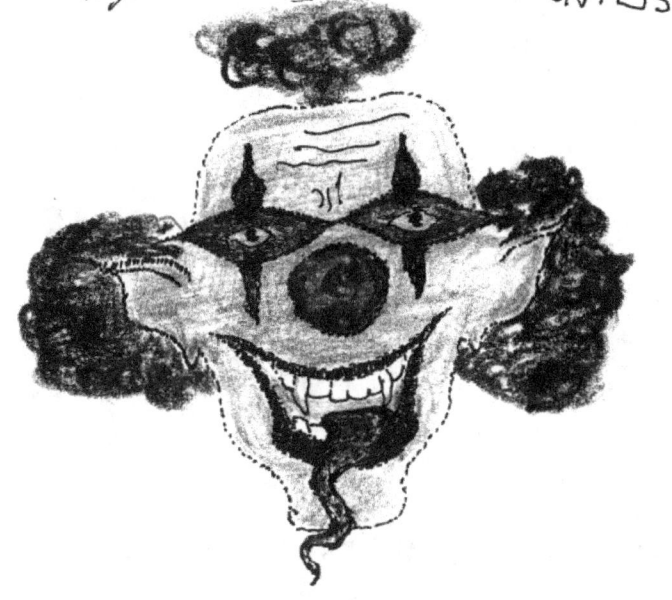

WHY CANT ONE BE A STAR ✱

WELCOME TO ALLEGORY

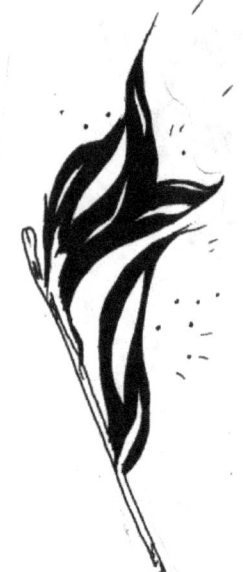

ONE THAT TWINKLES AND ALSO HAS FREEWILL

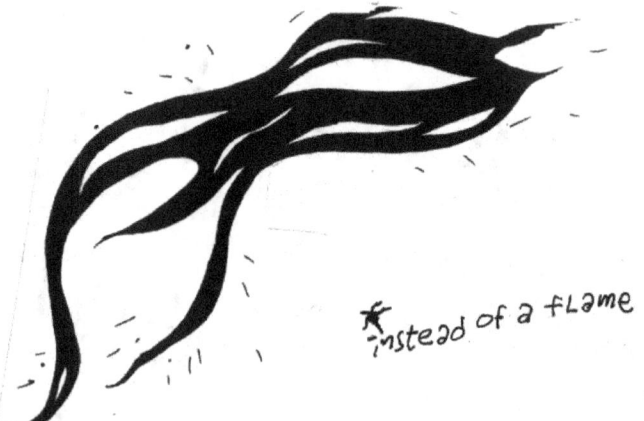

✱ instead of a flame

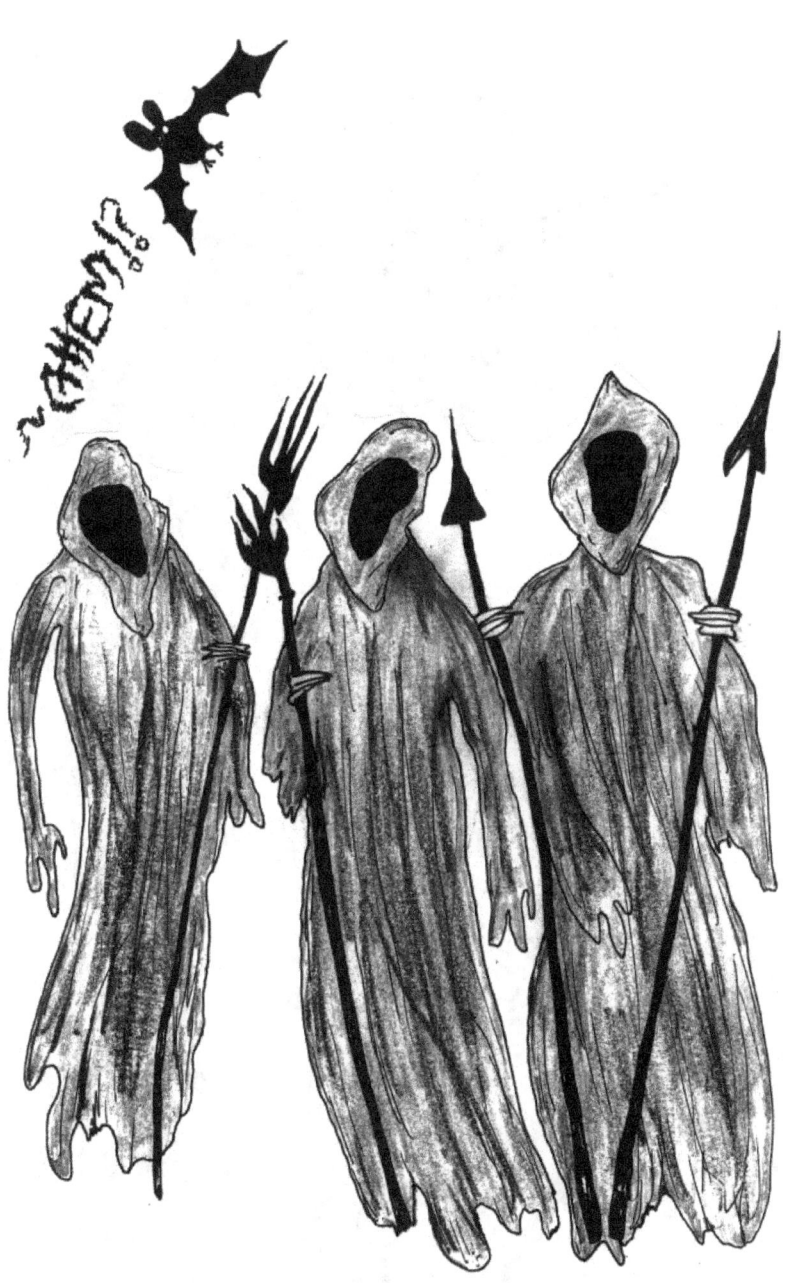

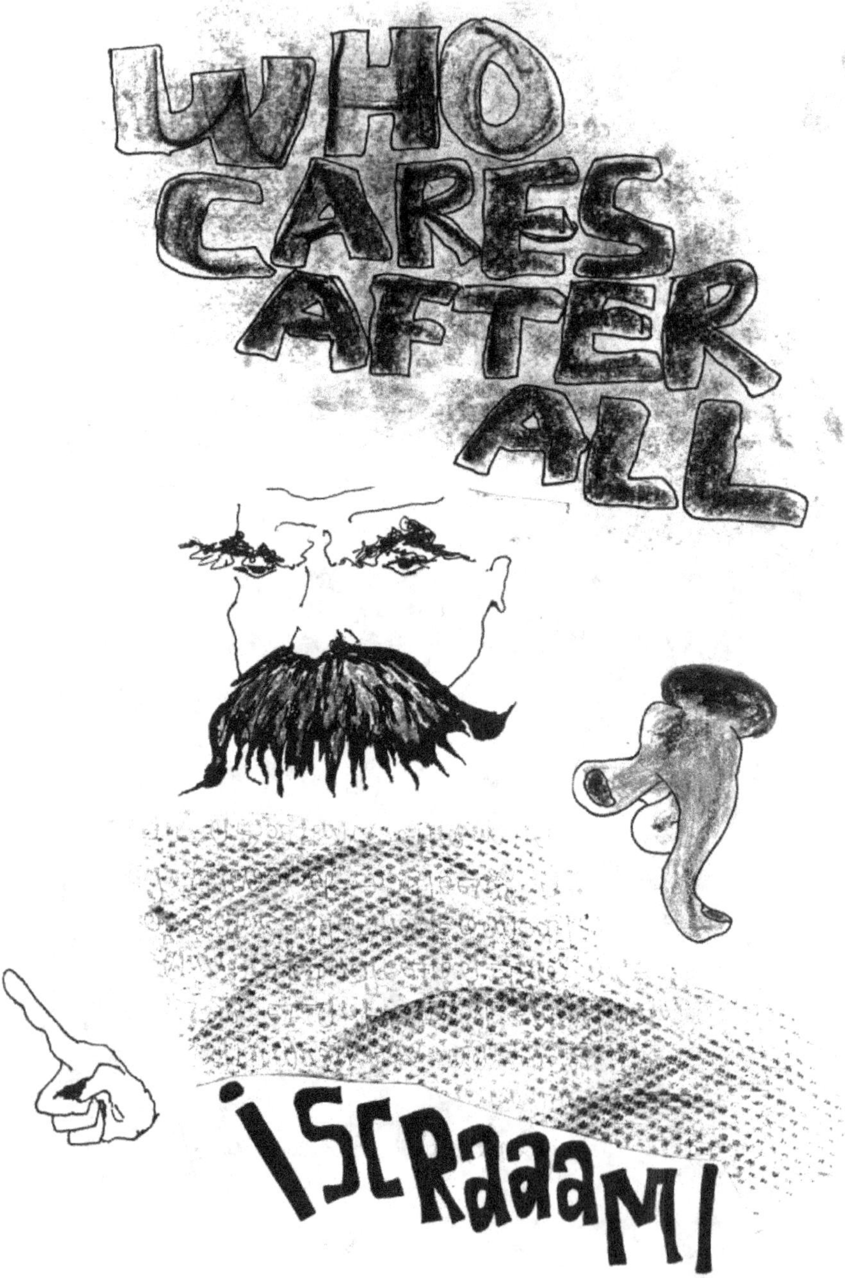

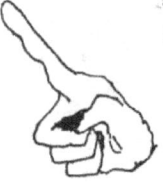

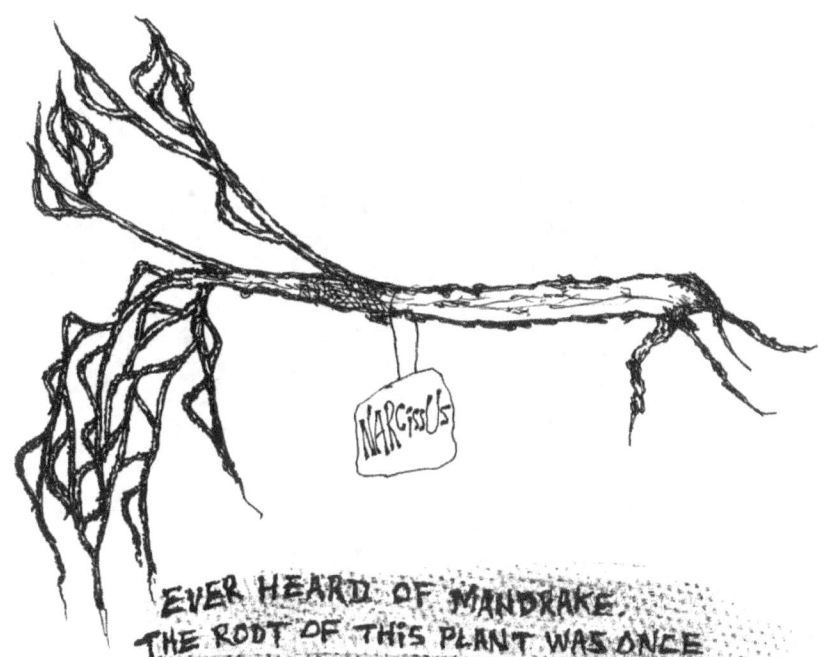

Ever heard of mandrake. The root of this plant was once thought to resemble the human form and to shriek when pulled up. It was supposed to be very unlucky to do it.

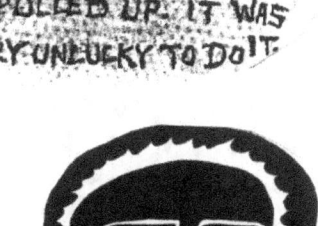

MORE FOLKLORE GALORE

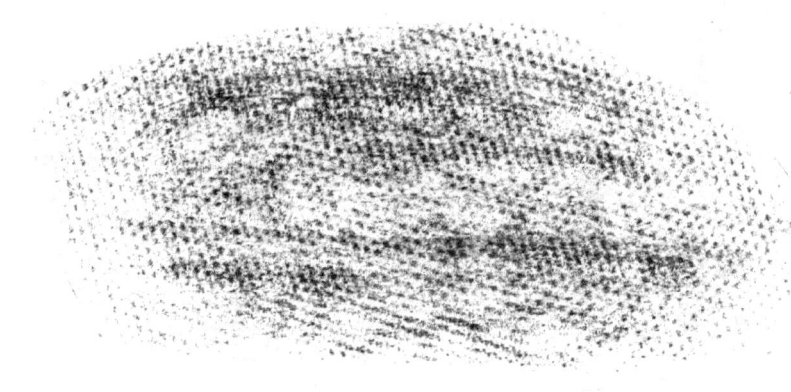

LETHARGY OR LASSITUDE

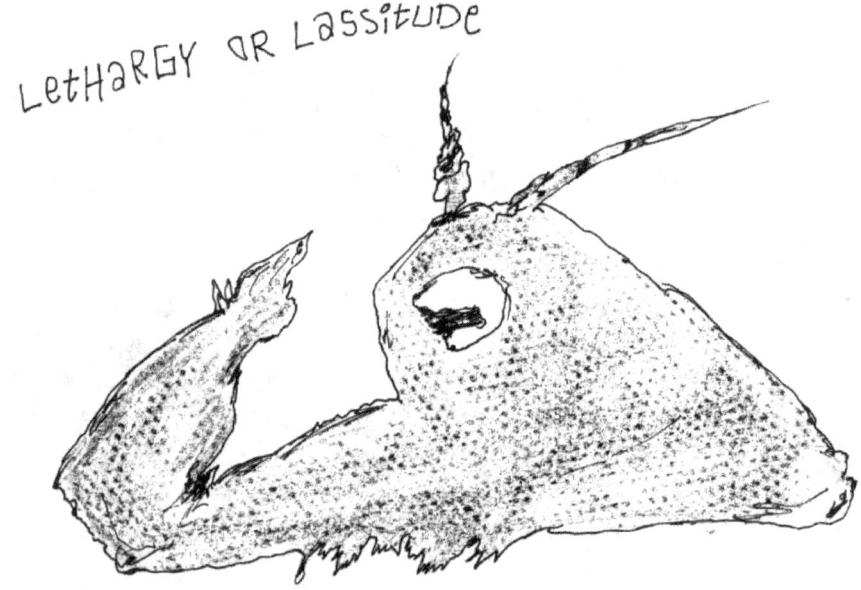

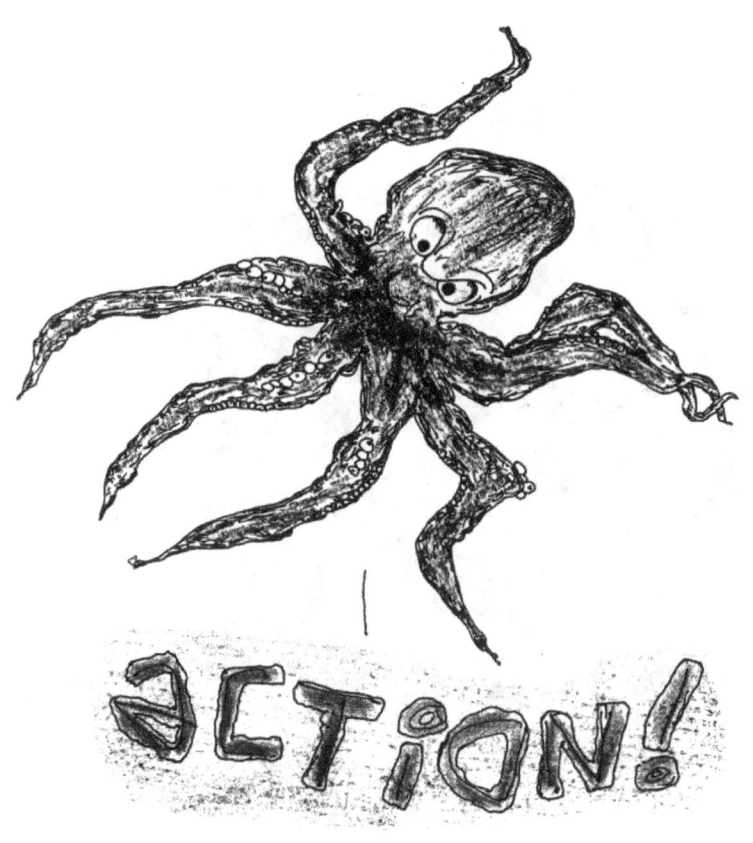

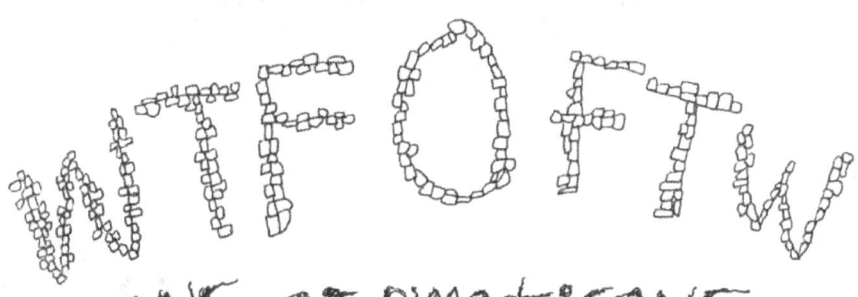

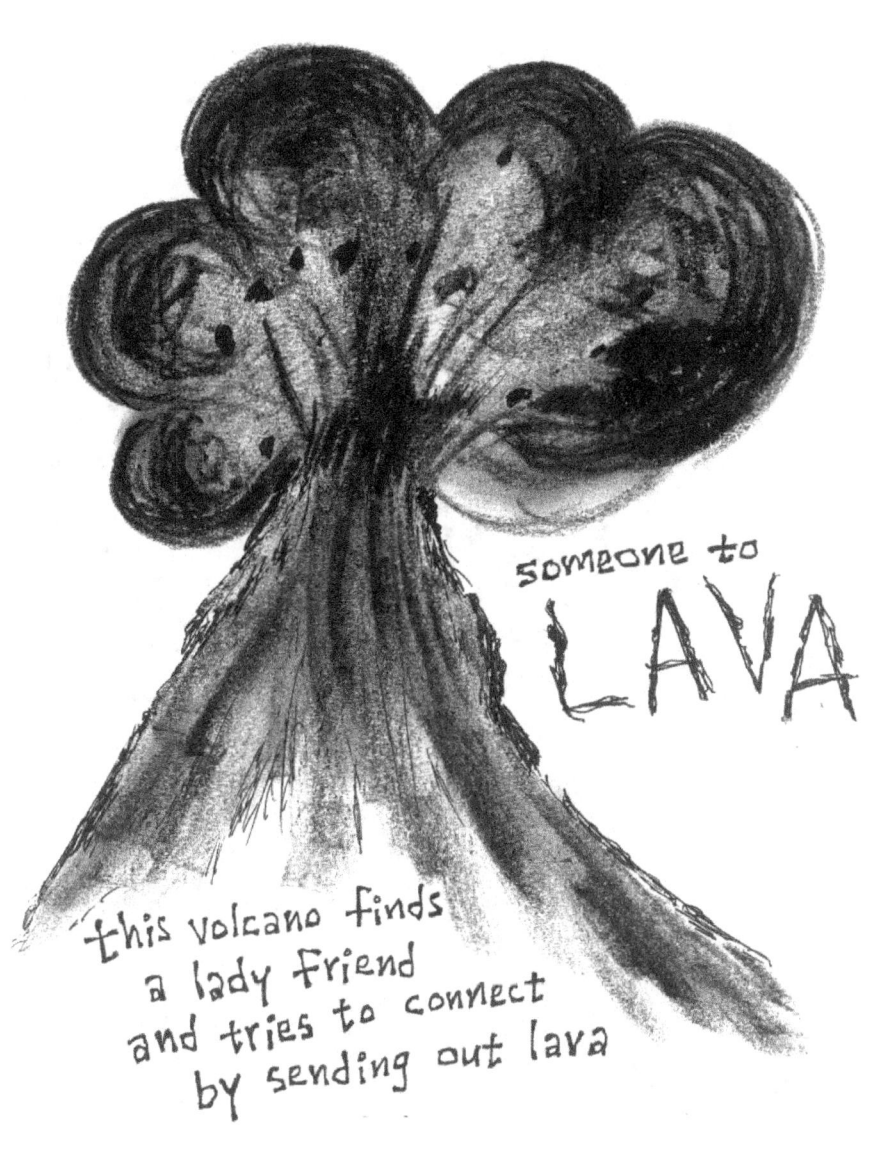

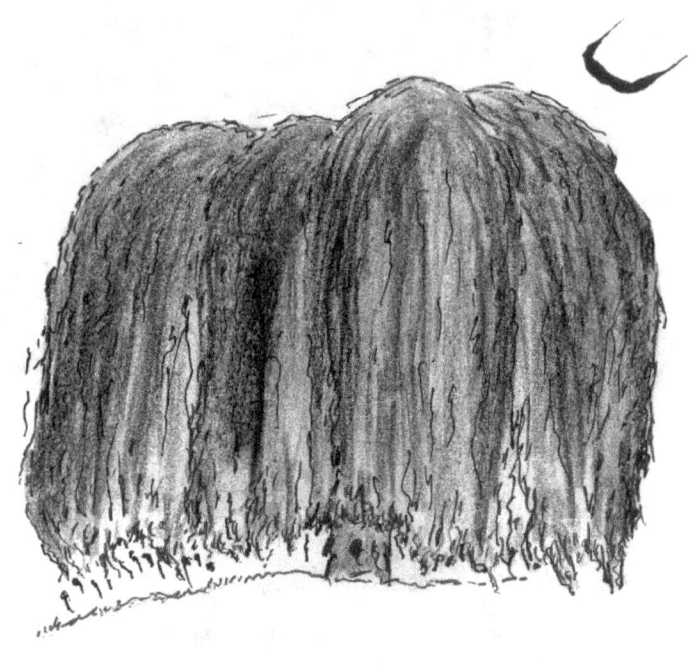

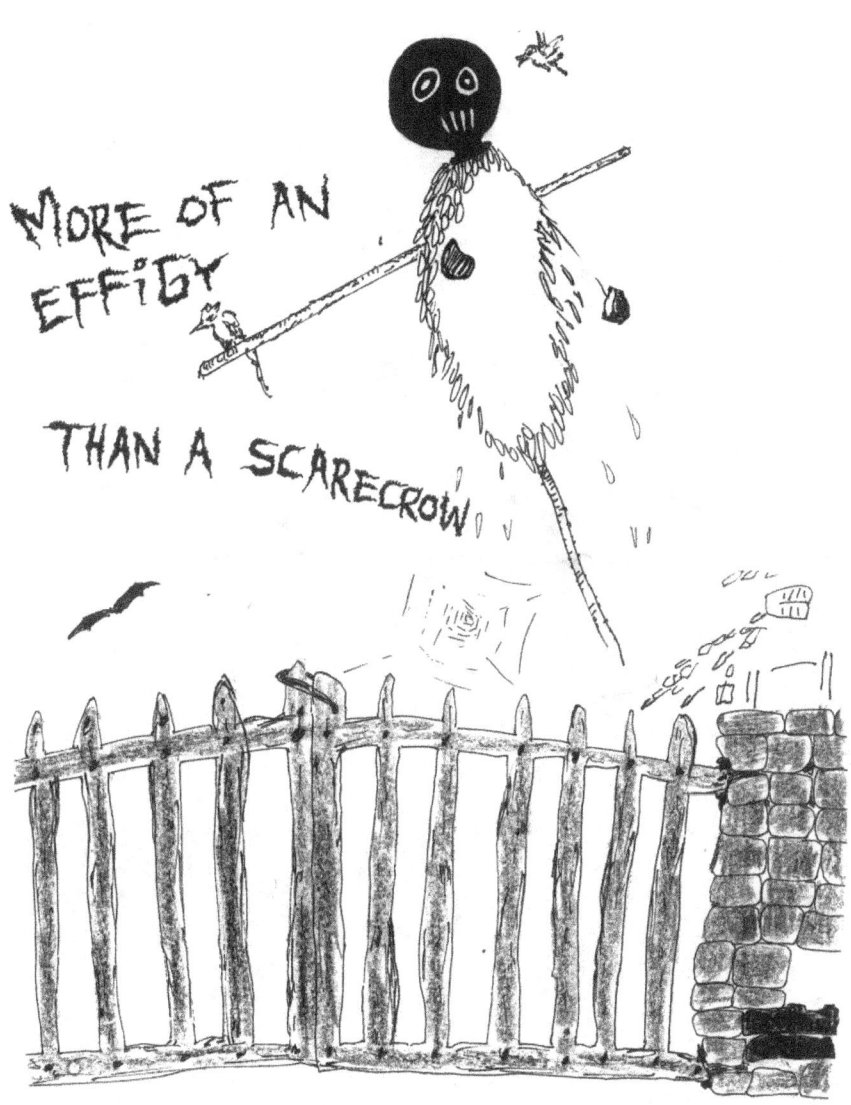

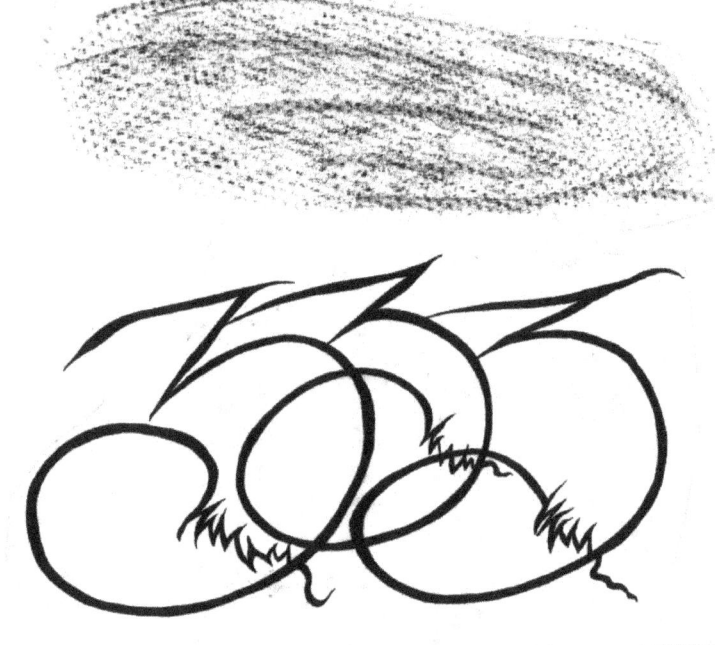

BETWEEN THE DOPPELGANGER AND THE ALTEREGO

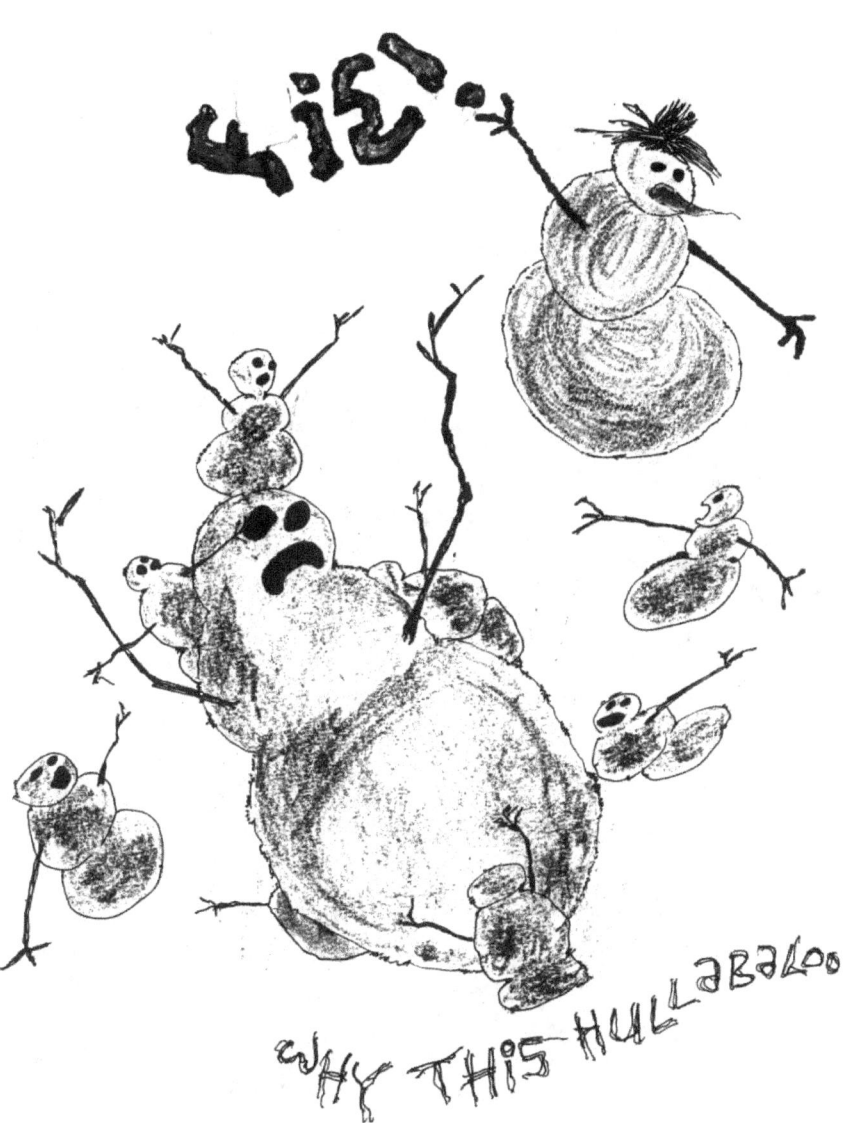

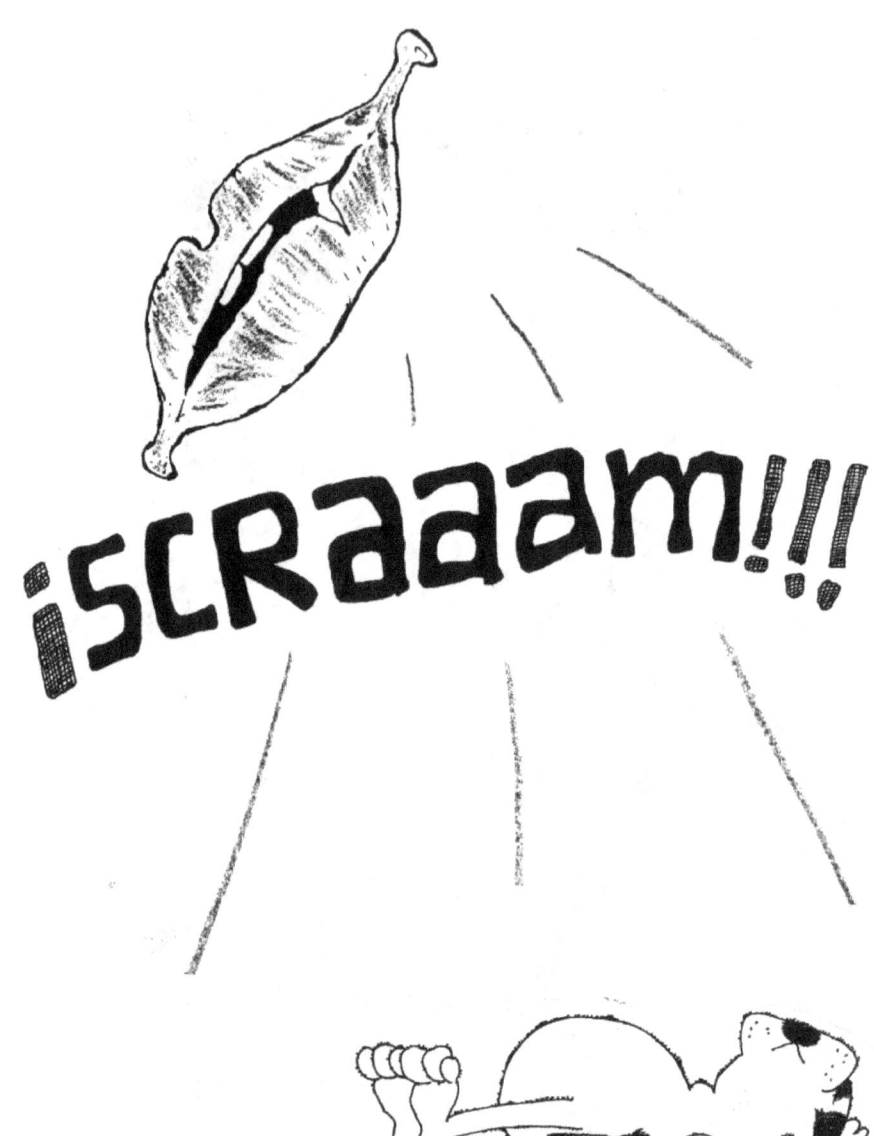

NOT MY SHOW

NOT MY CIRCUS, GUYS.
NOR THE CLOWNS.
NEVER THE CHEERS.

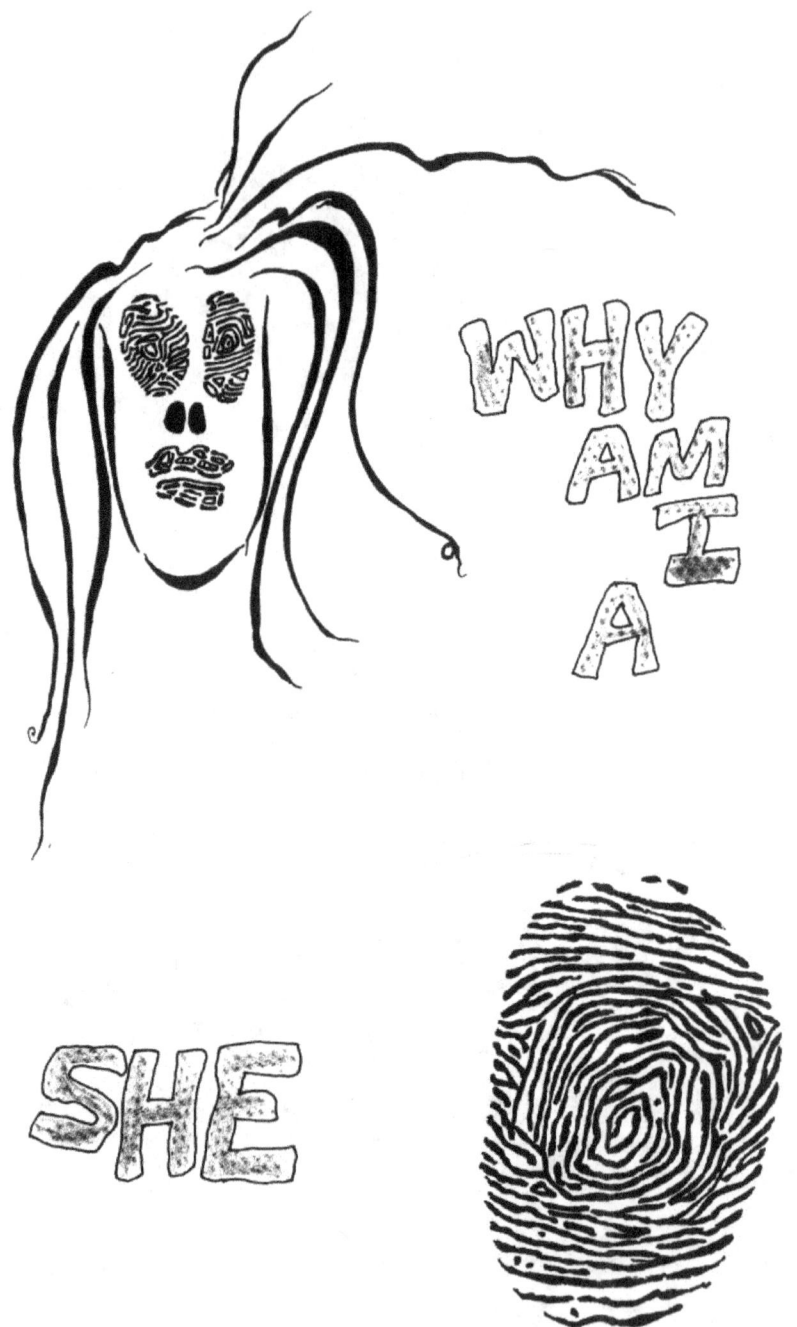

HISTORY OF THE FEMALE

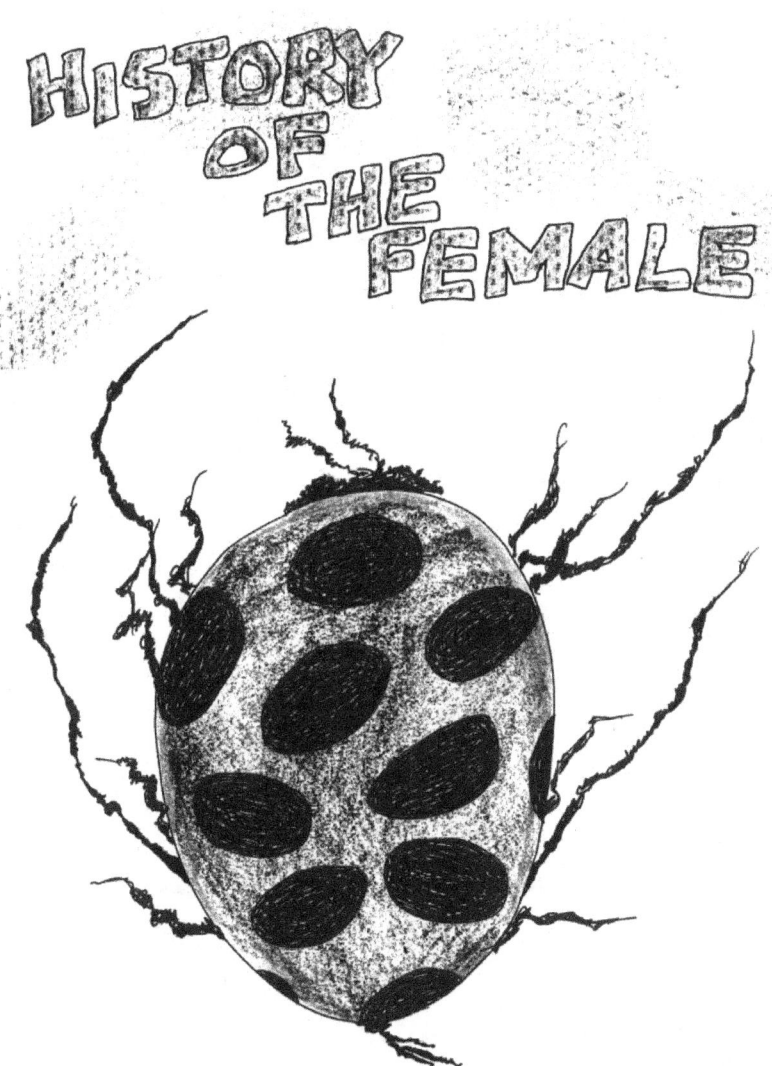

FROM LADYBIRD BOOKS

I BLINK THEREFORE I AM NOW THINK WHAT IF I STINK

ABSTRACT IBUGESIC OBSCURE

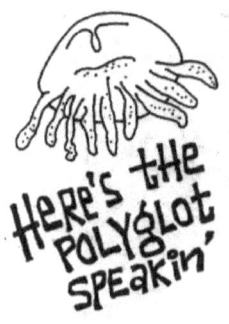

Here's the POLYGLOT speakin'

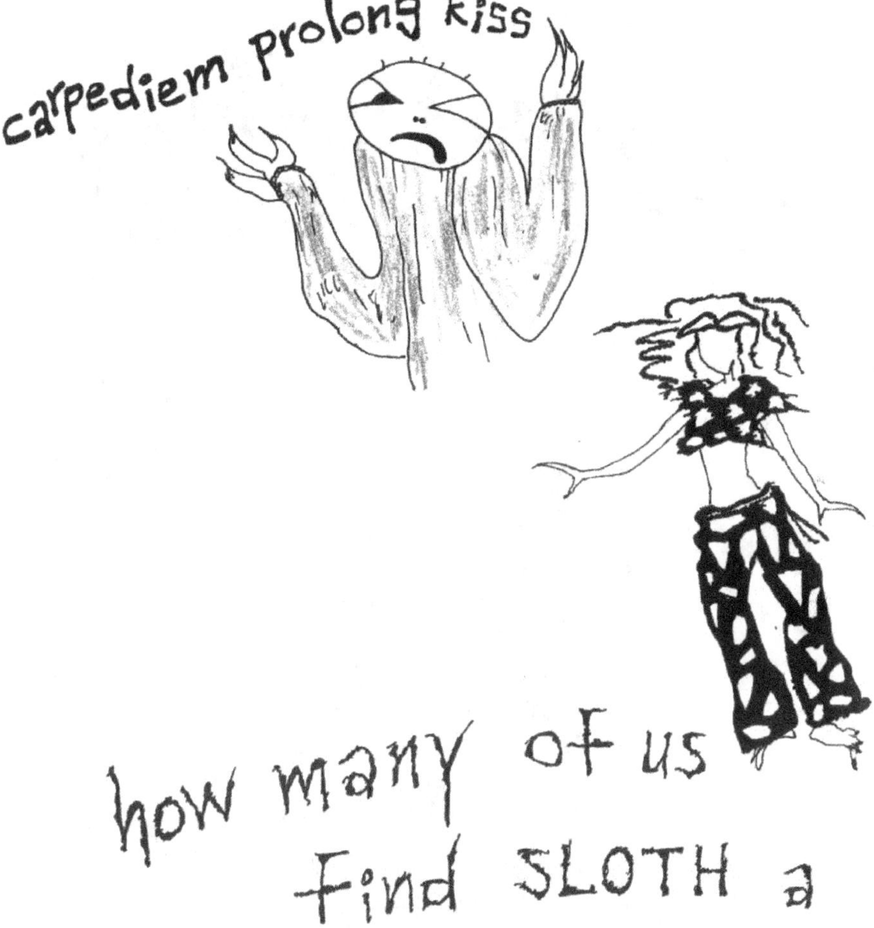

carpediem prolong kiss

how many of us
Find SLOTH a
Favorite

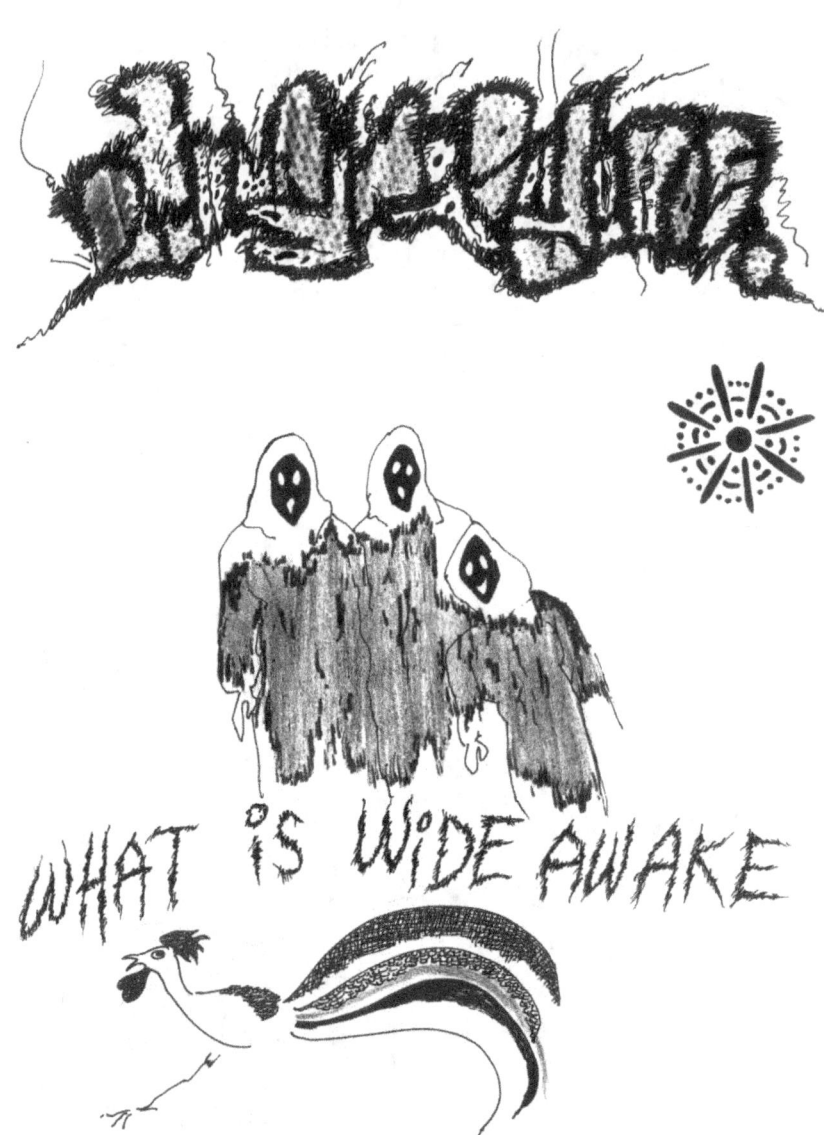

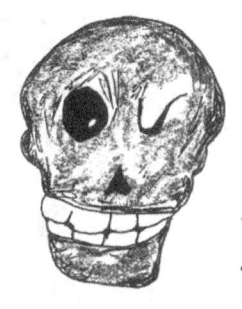

You at Least are
Free to Have
a MORNING HARDON
WHEREAS OtHERS are Not

WANK DUDE WANK

**ALERT
BIG BRO GETTING DOWN
TO BRASS TACKS**

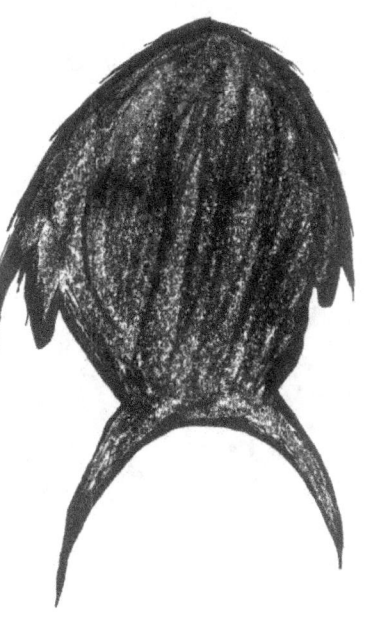

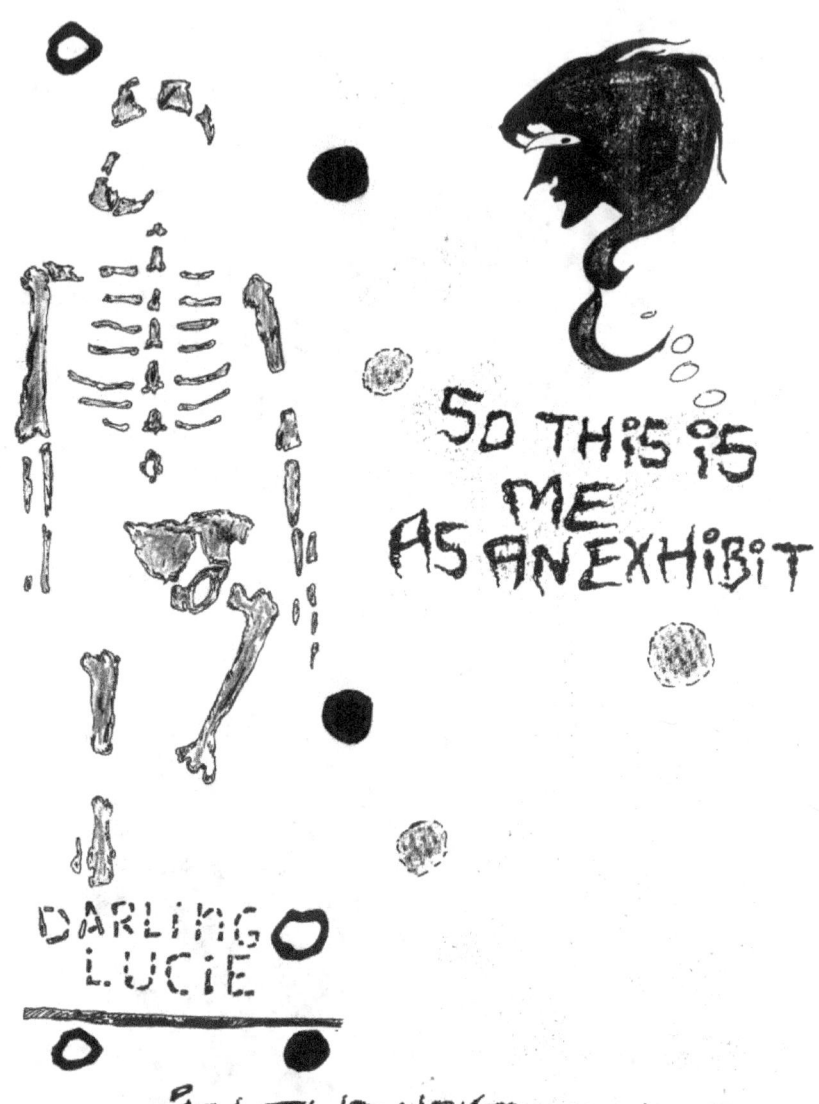

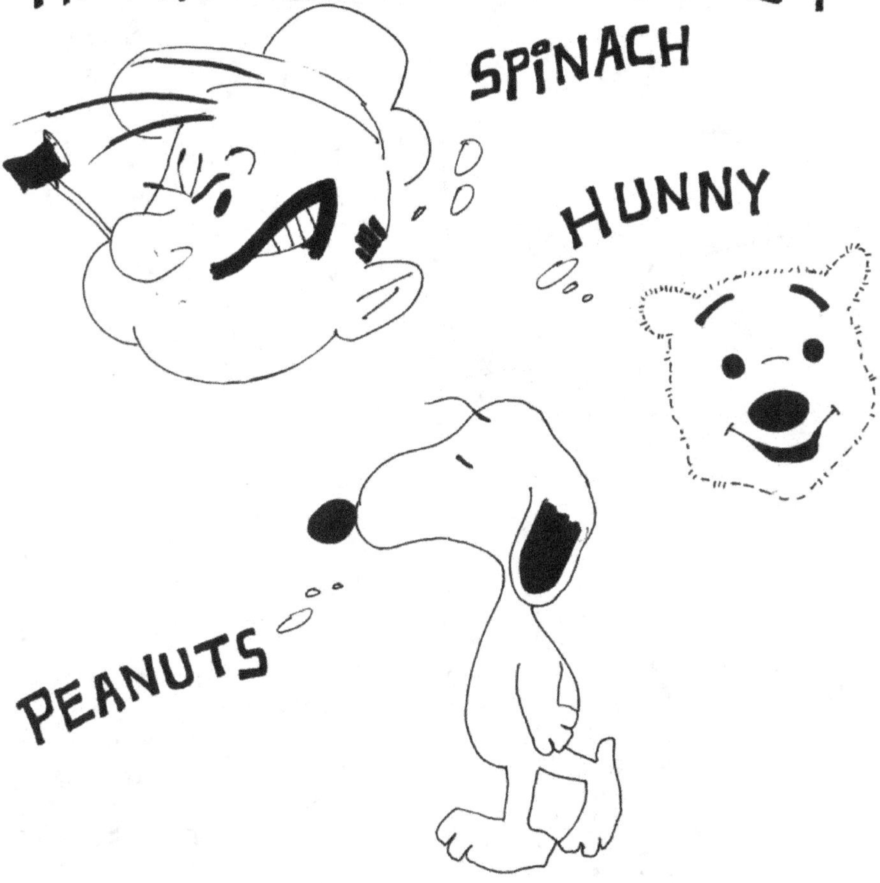

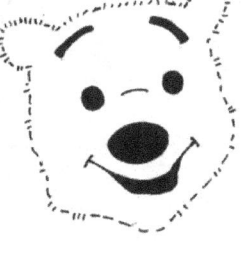

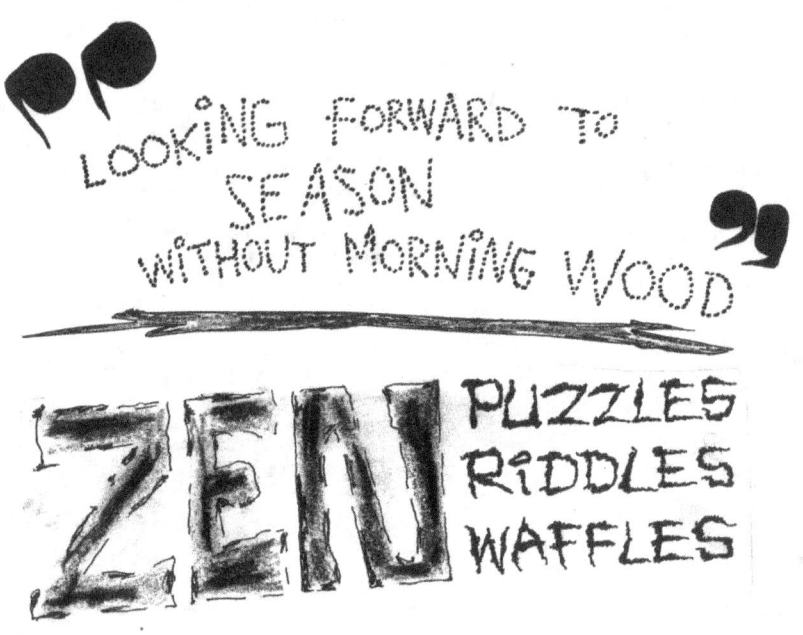
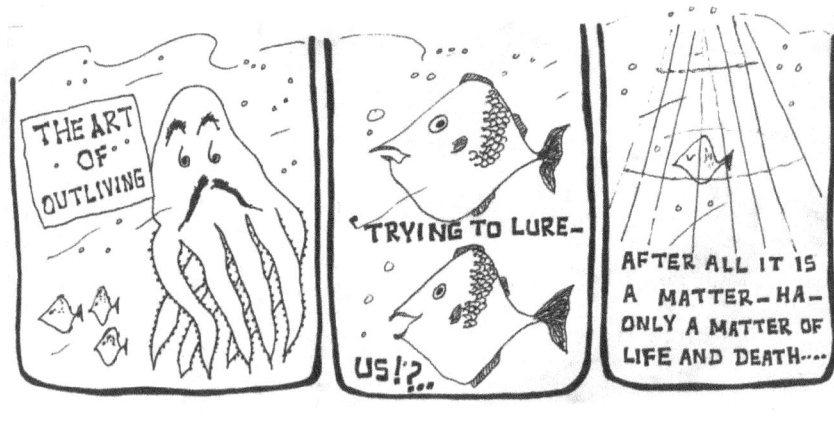

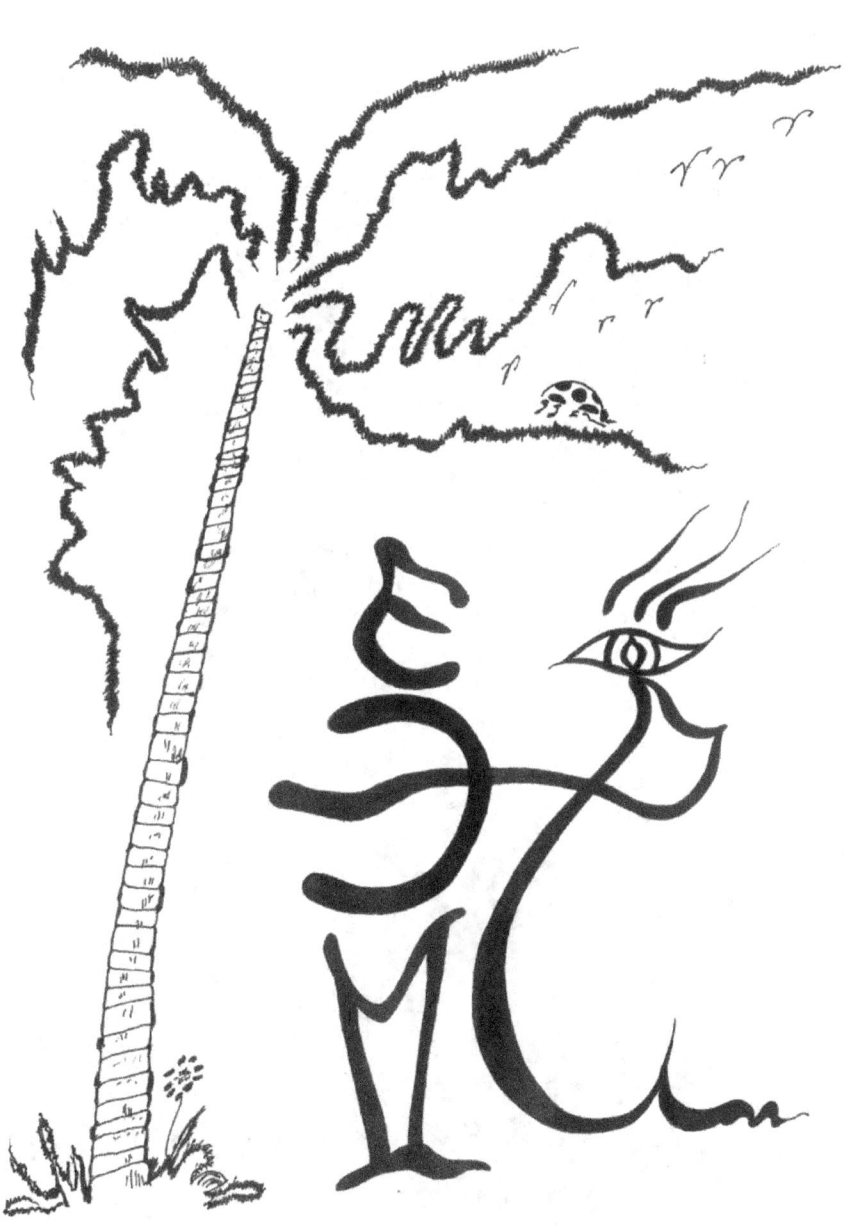

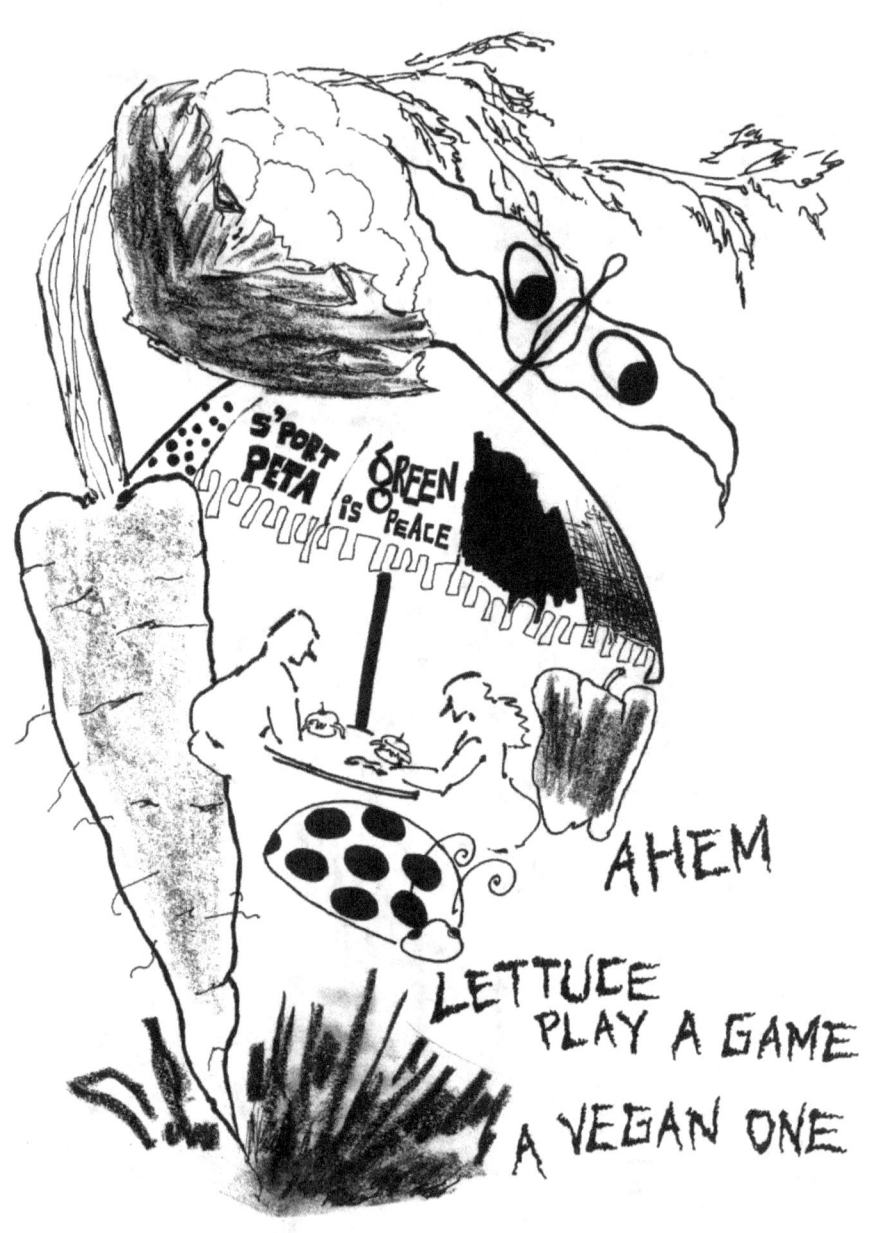

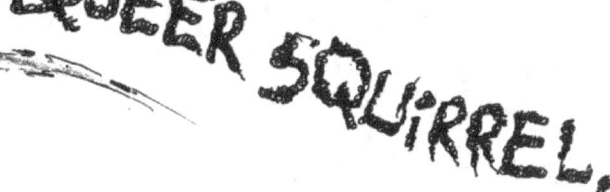

HELLO CROW, QUEER SQUIRREL, LINGUIST!

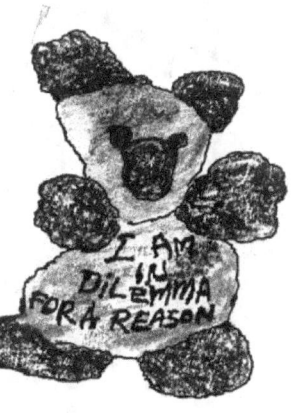

I AM IN DILEMMA FOR A REASON

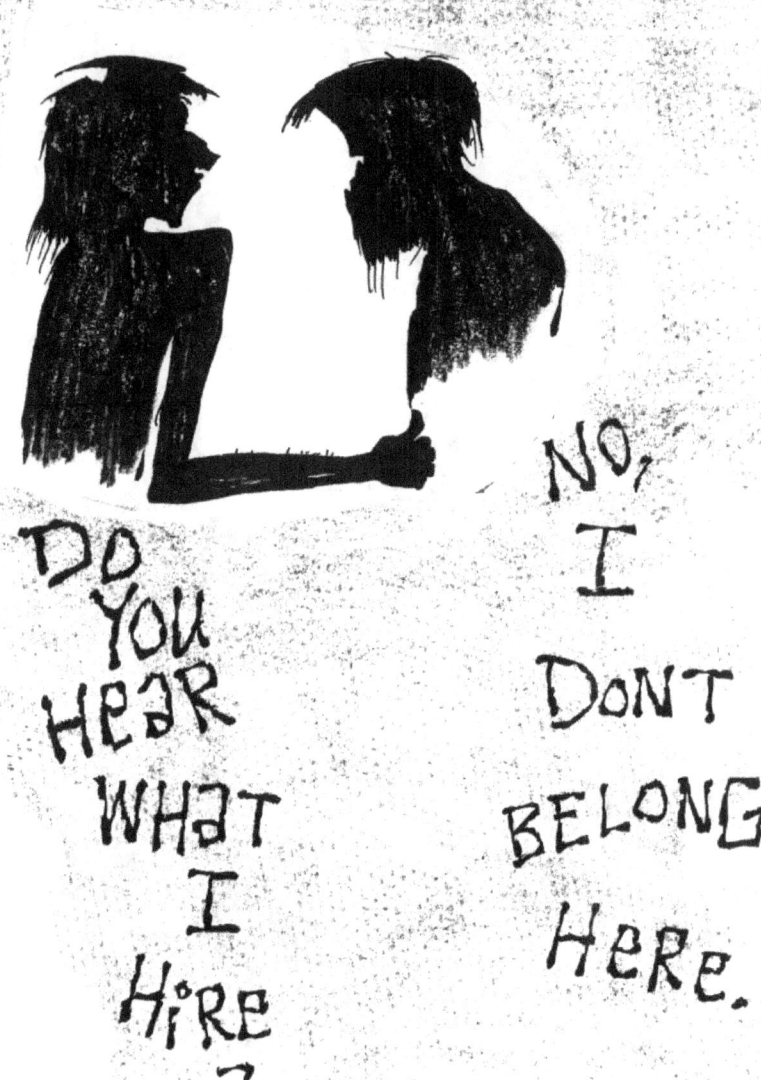

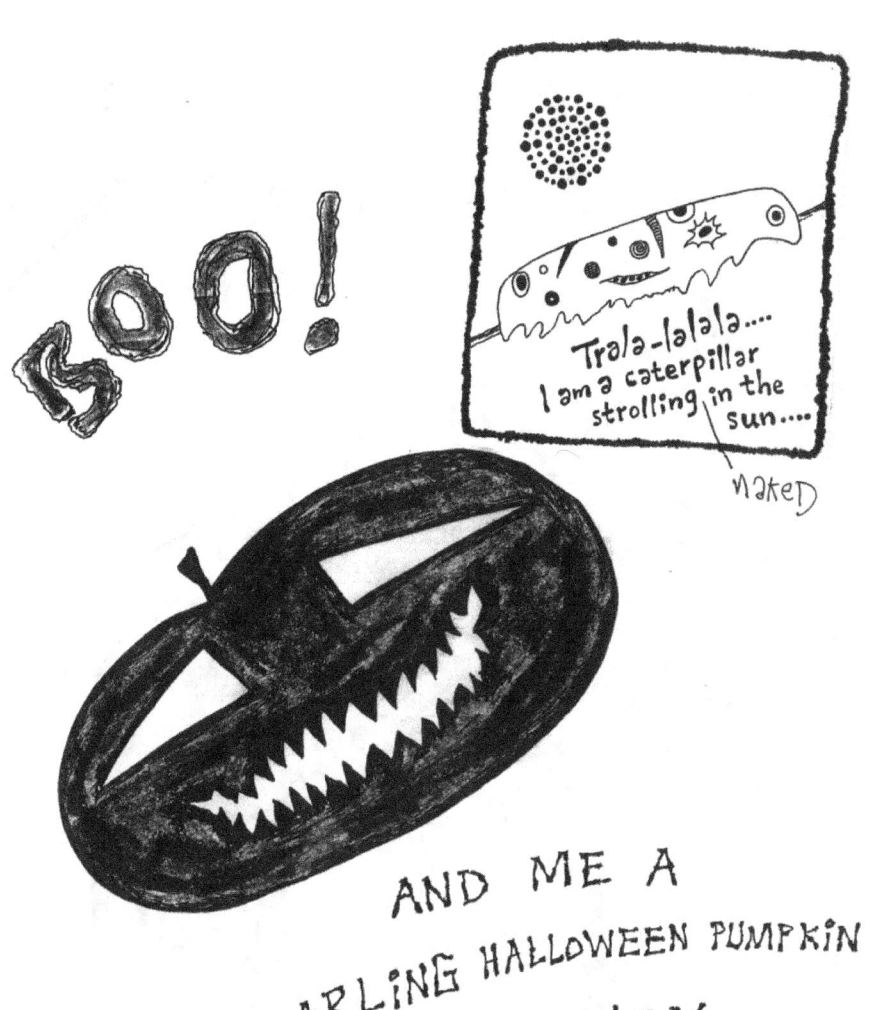

WHAT IS WABI SABI

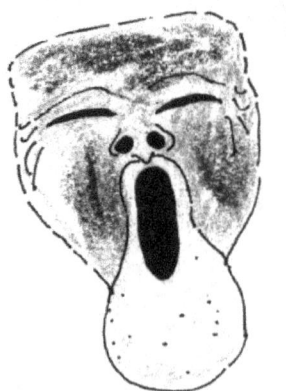

YOU KNOW ONE WHEN YOU YAWN

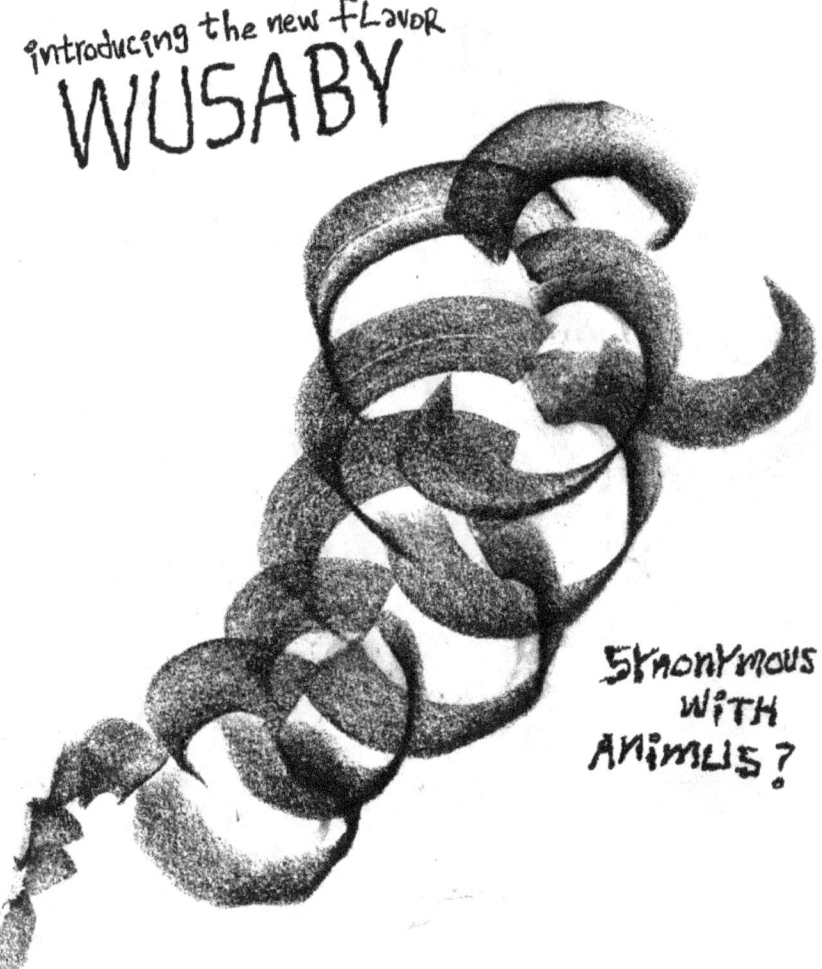

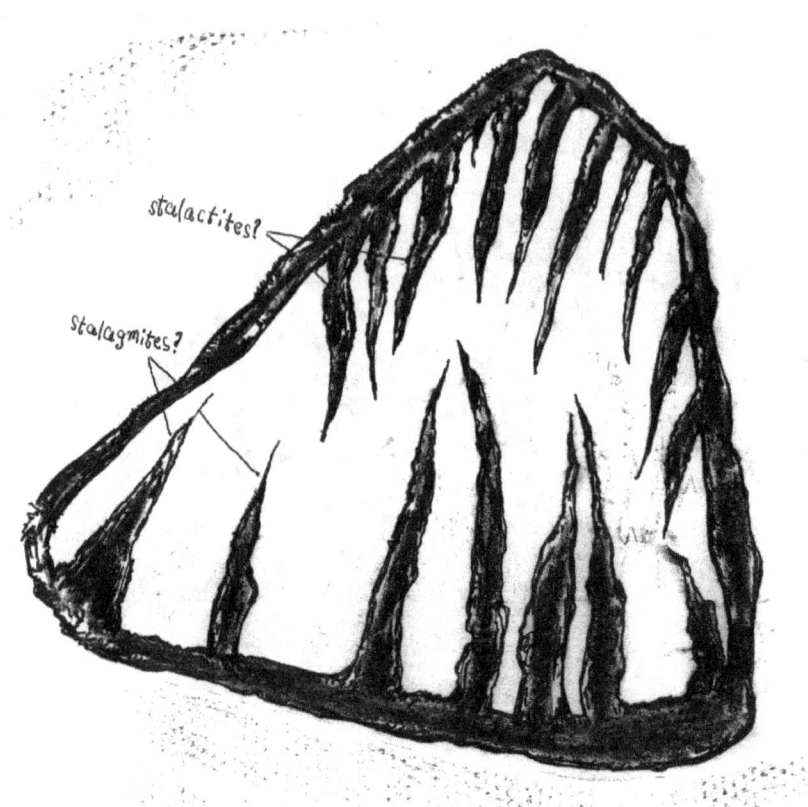

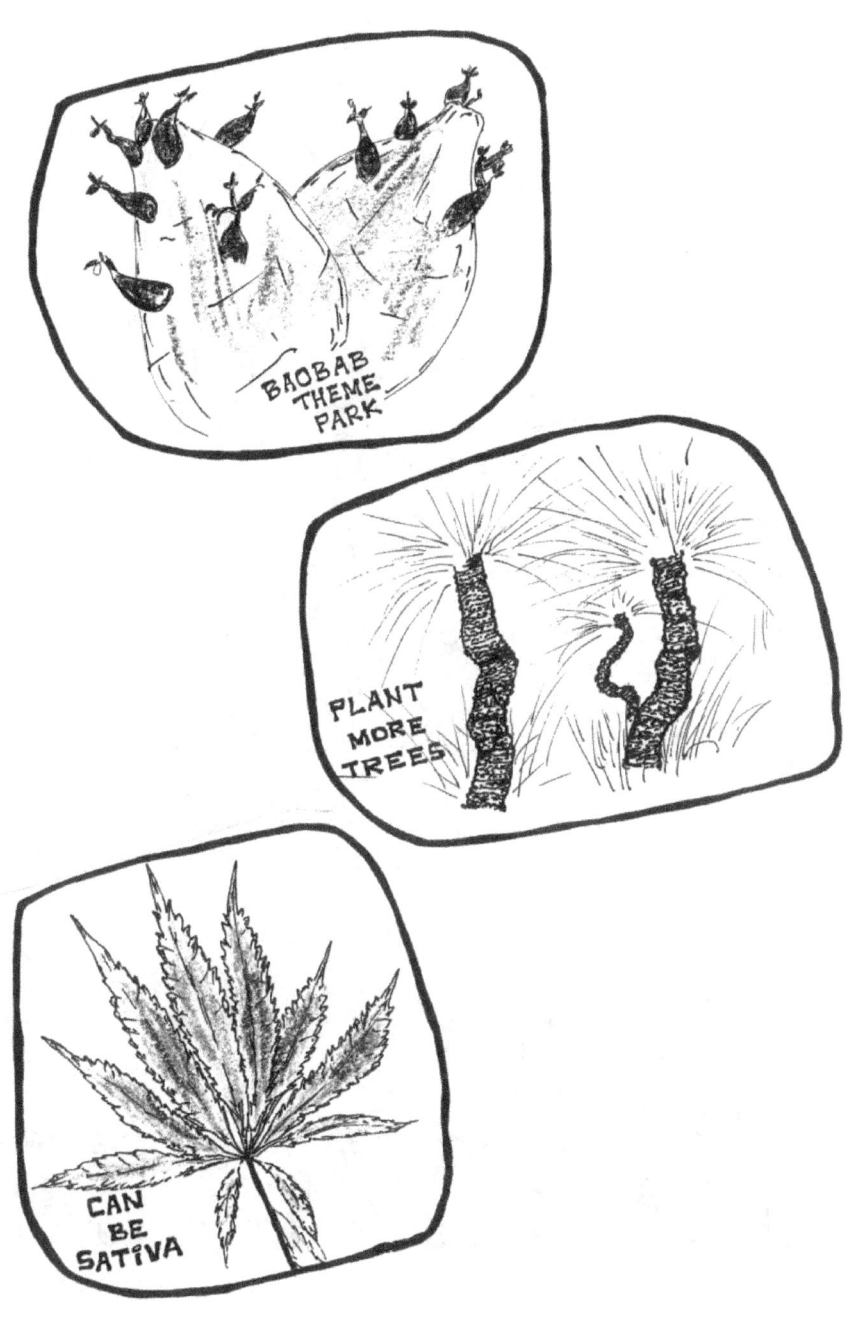

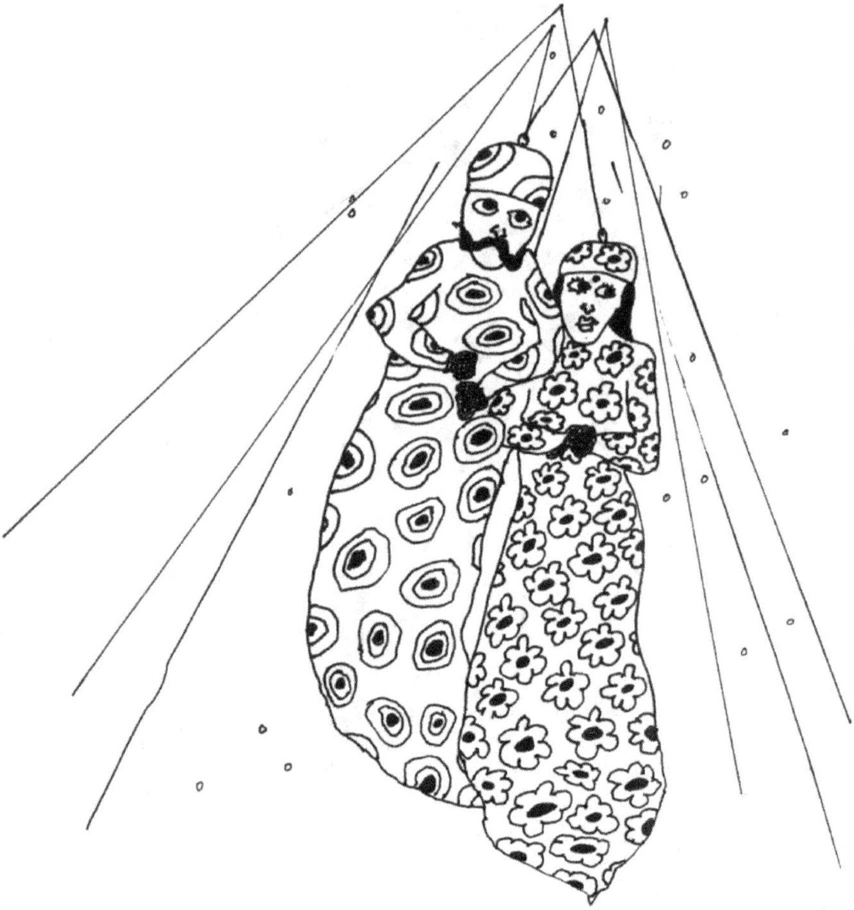

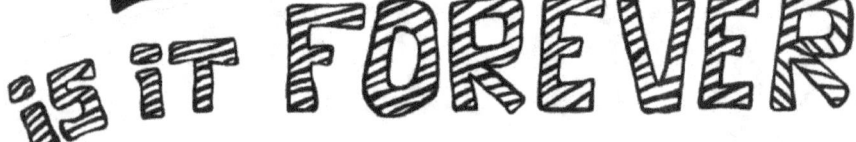

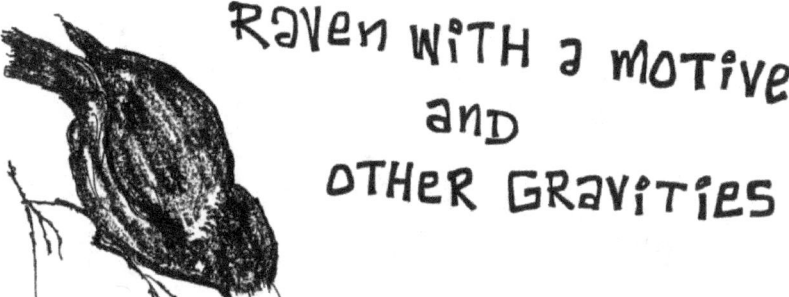

Raven with a Motive and Other Gravities

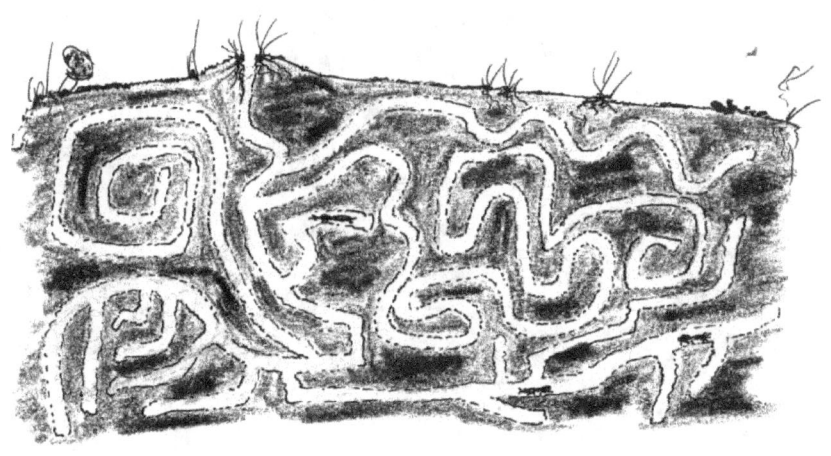

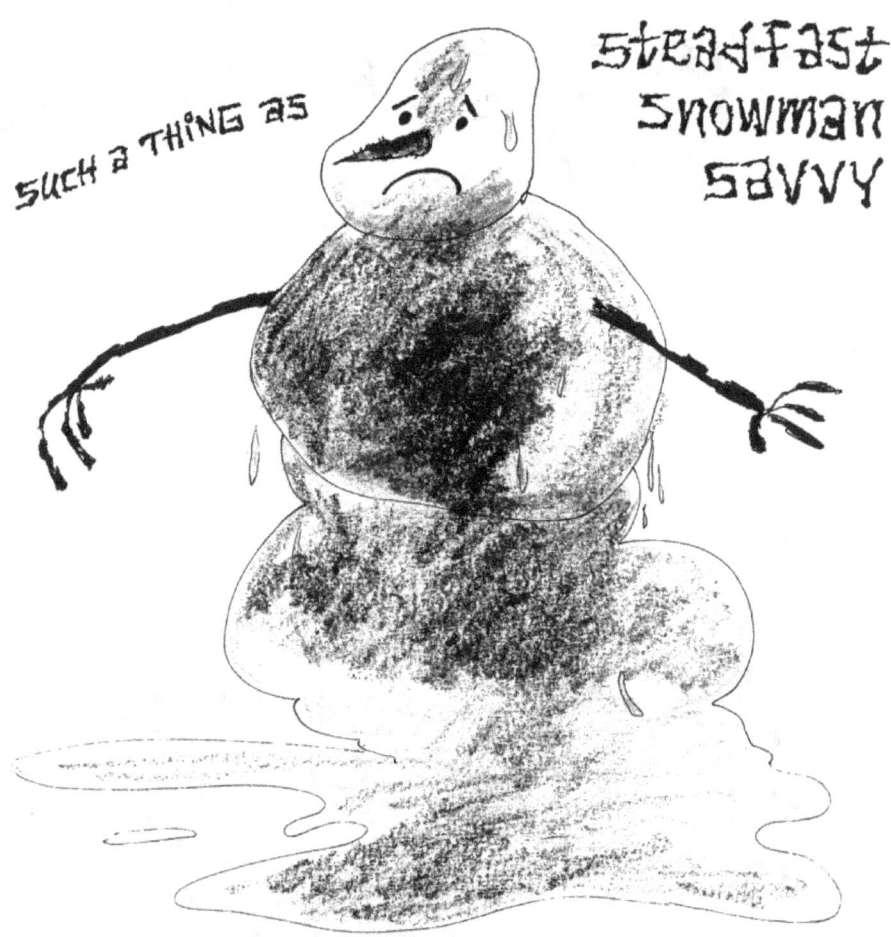

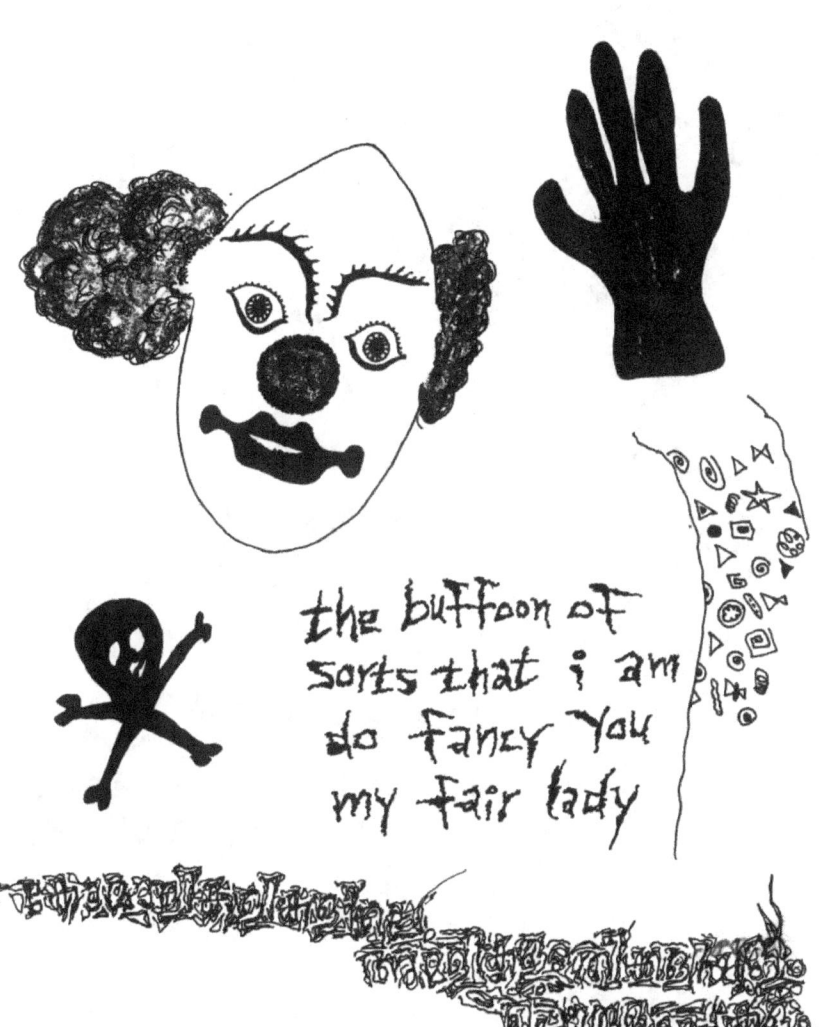

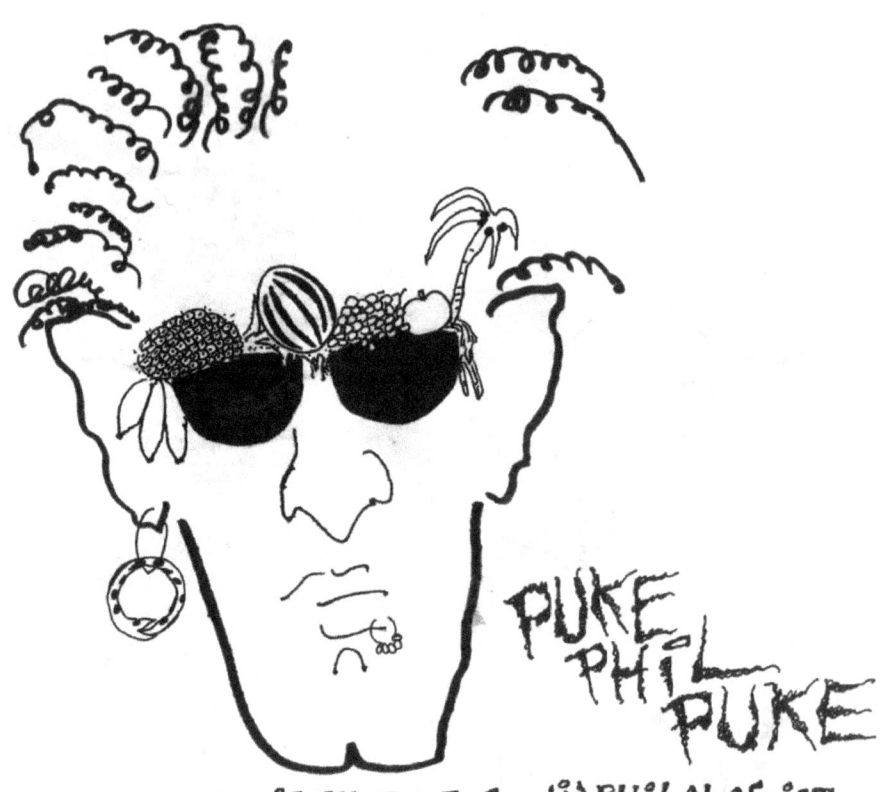

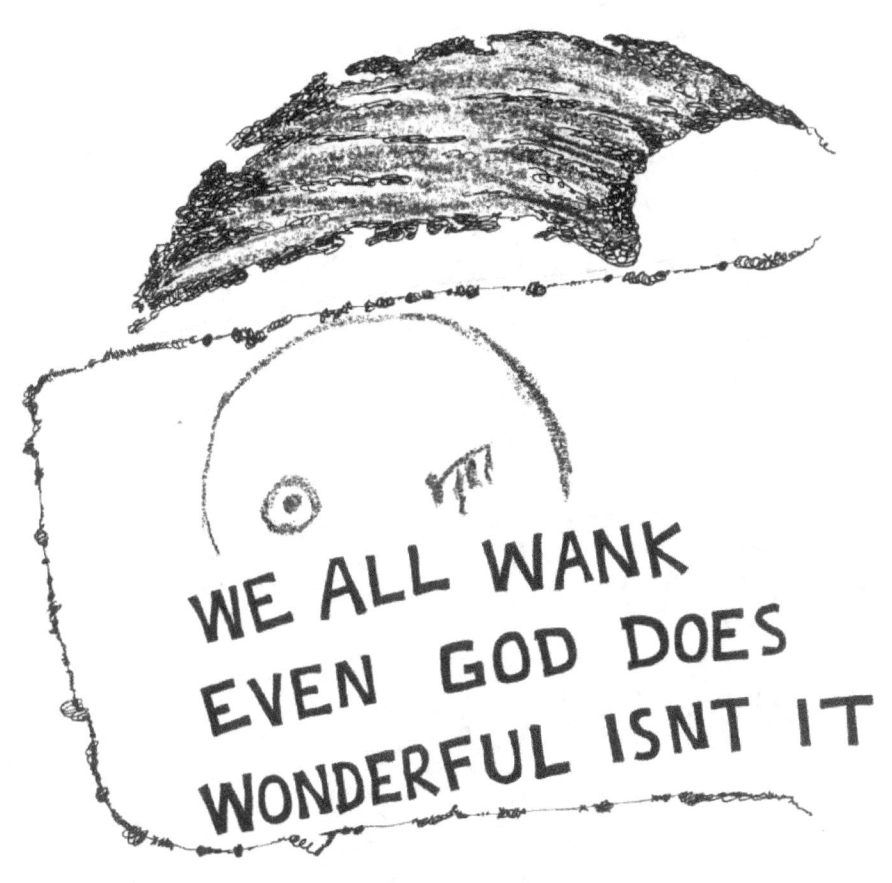

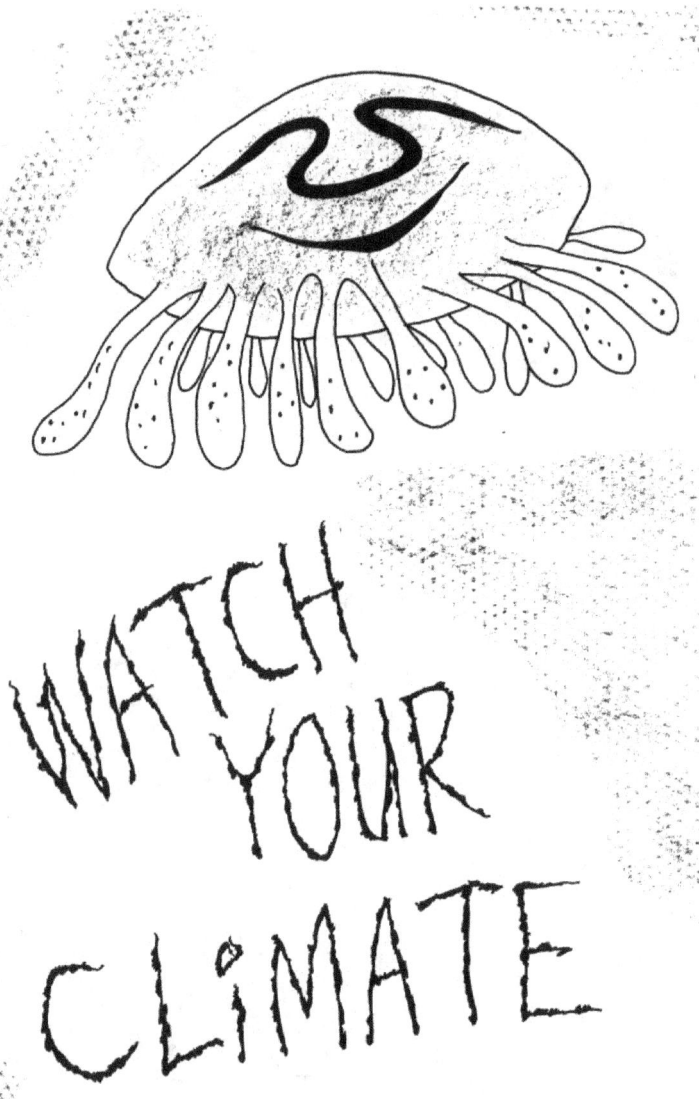

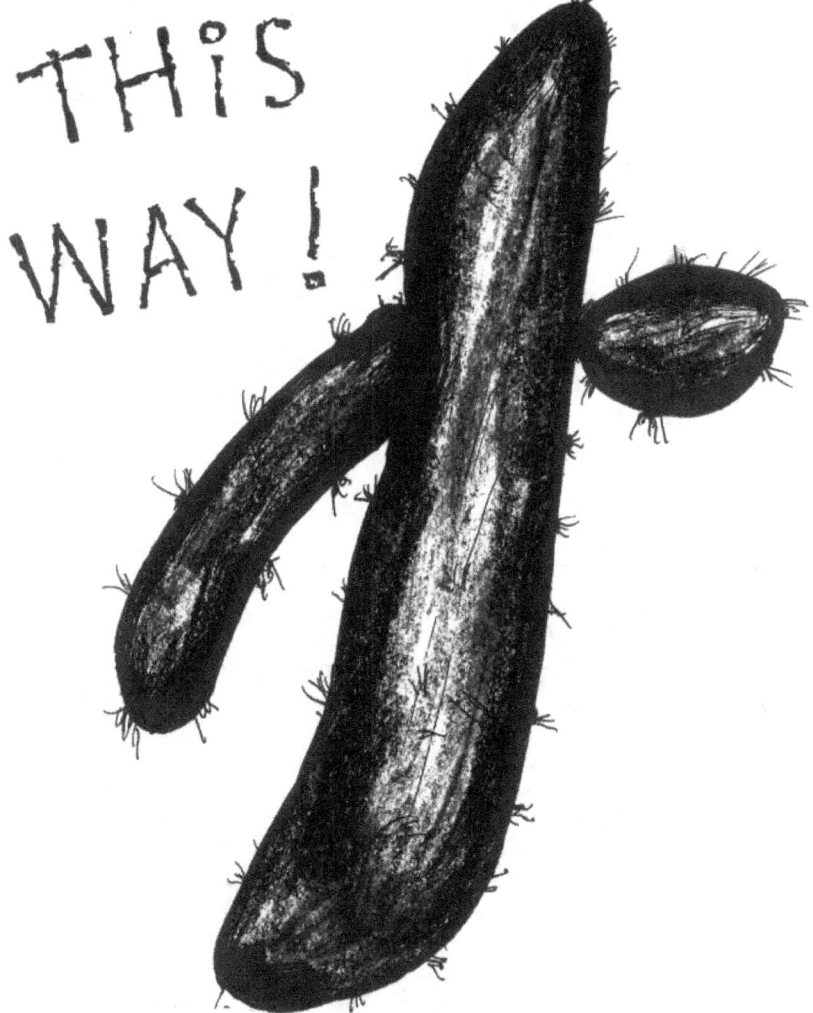

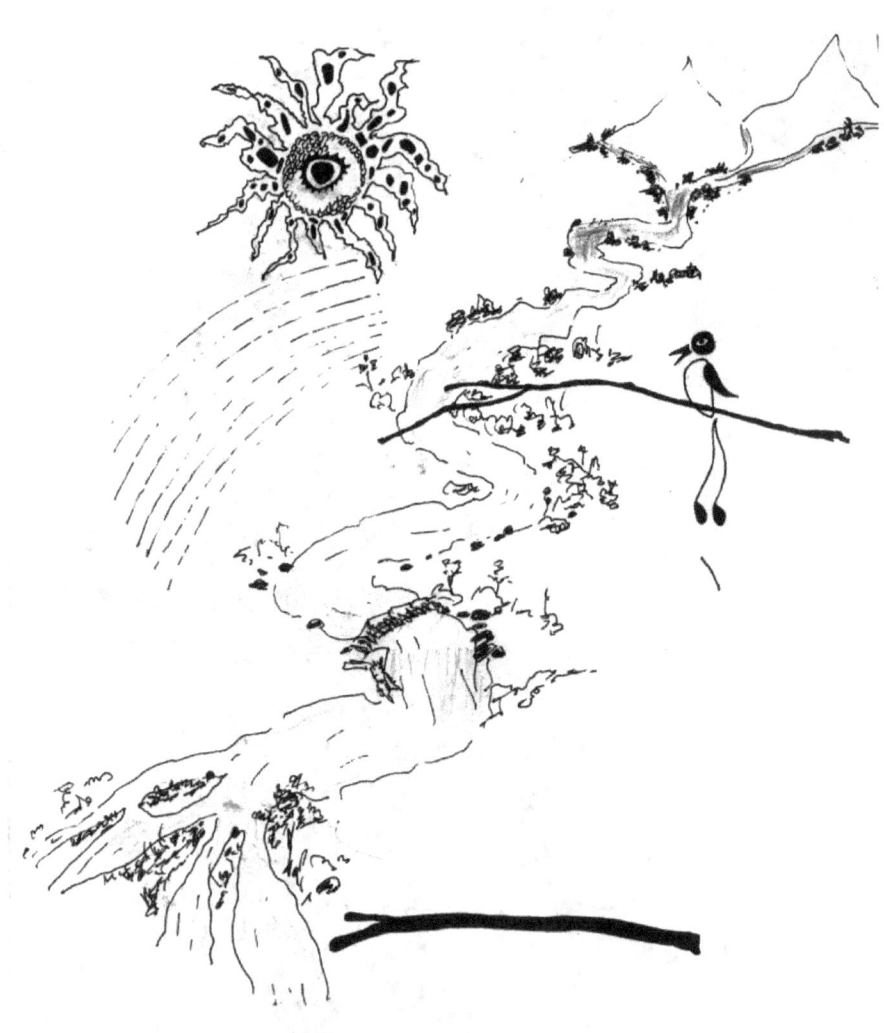

REALITY IS A MYTH

WHEN YOUR VOCAB COUNTS

Use 'GALORE' and 'PLETHORA' in a sentence and differentiate between 'eventually' and 'consequently' simultaneously

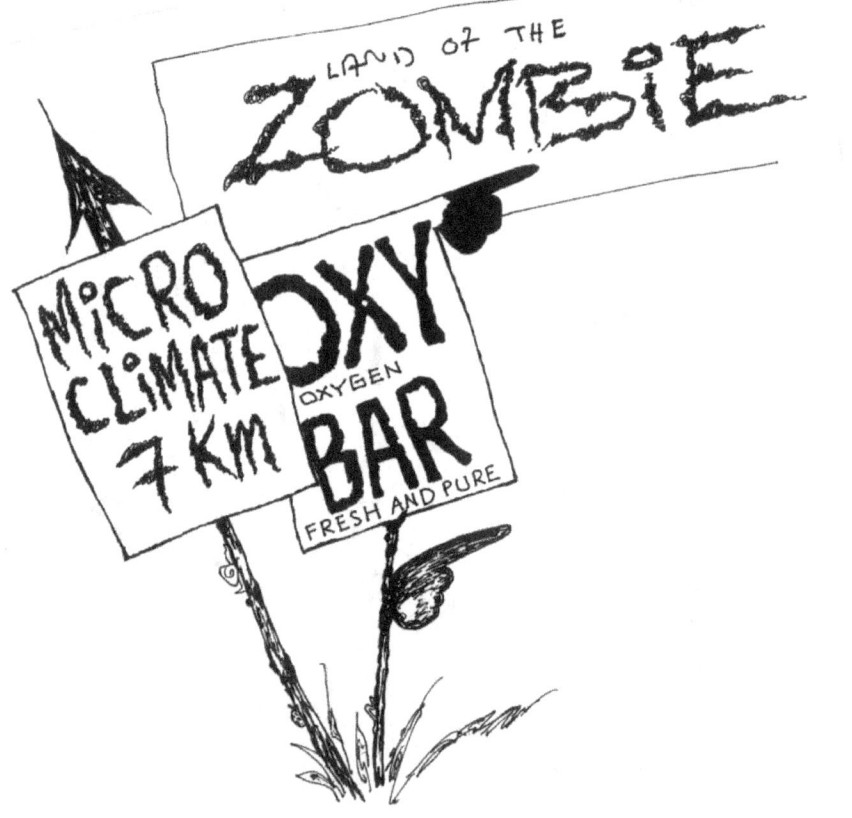

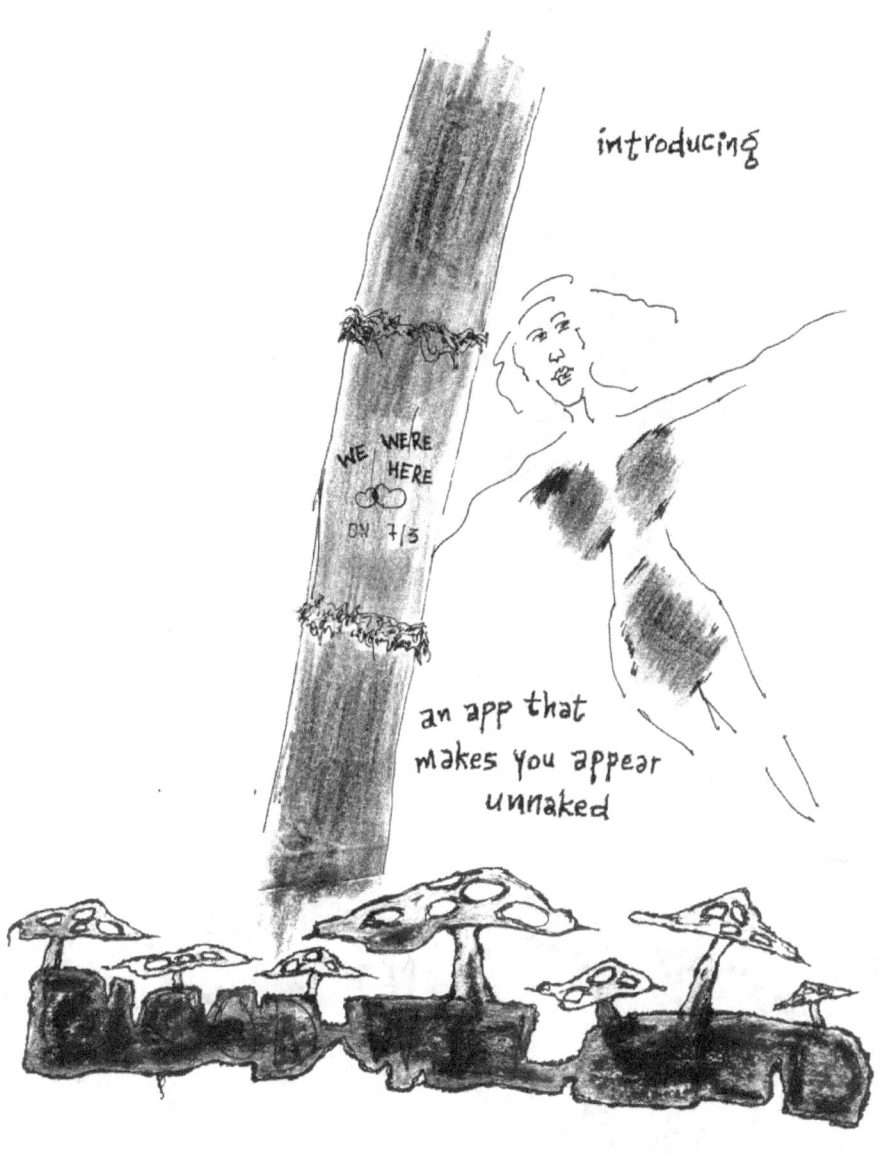

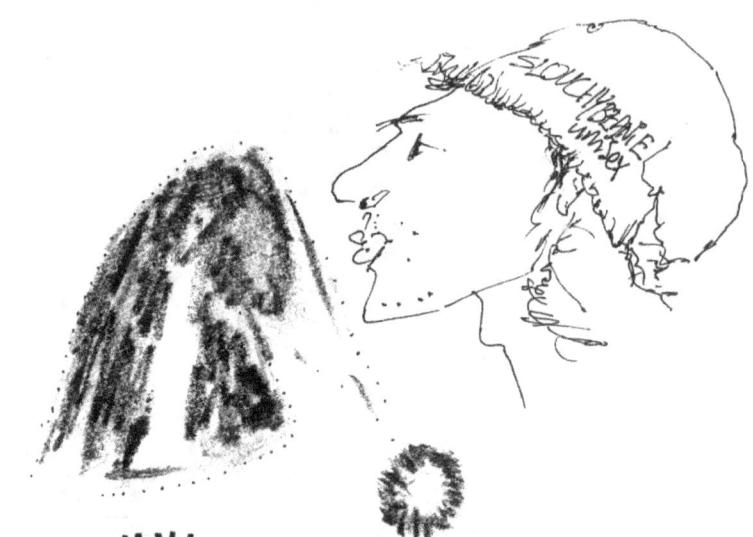

WHO/WHAT IS AN APOCALYPSO?

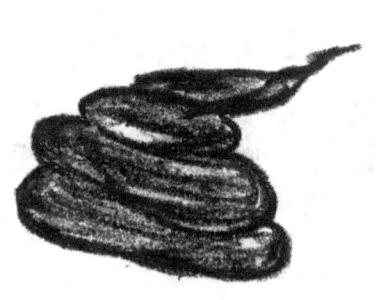

We at least are free to have a morning hardon

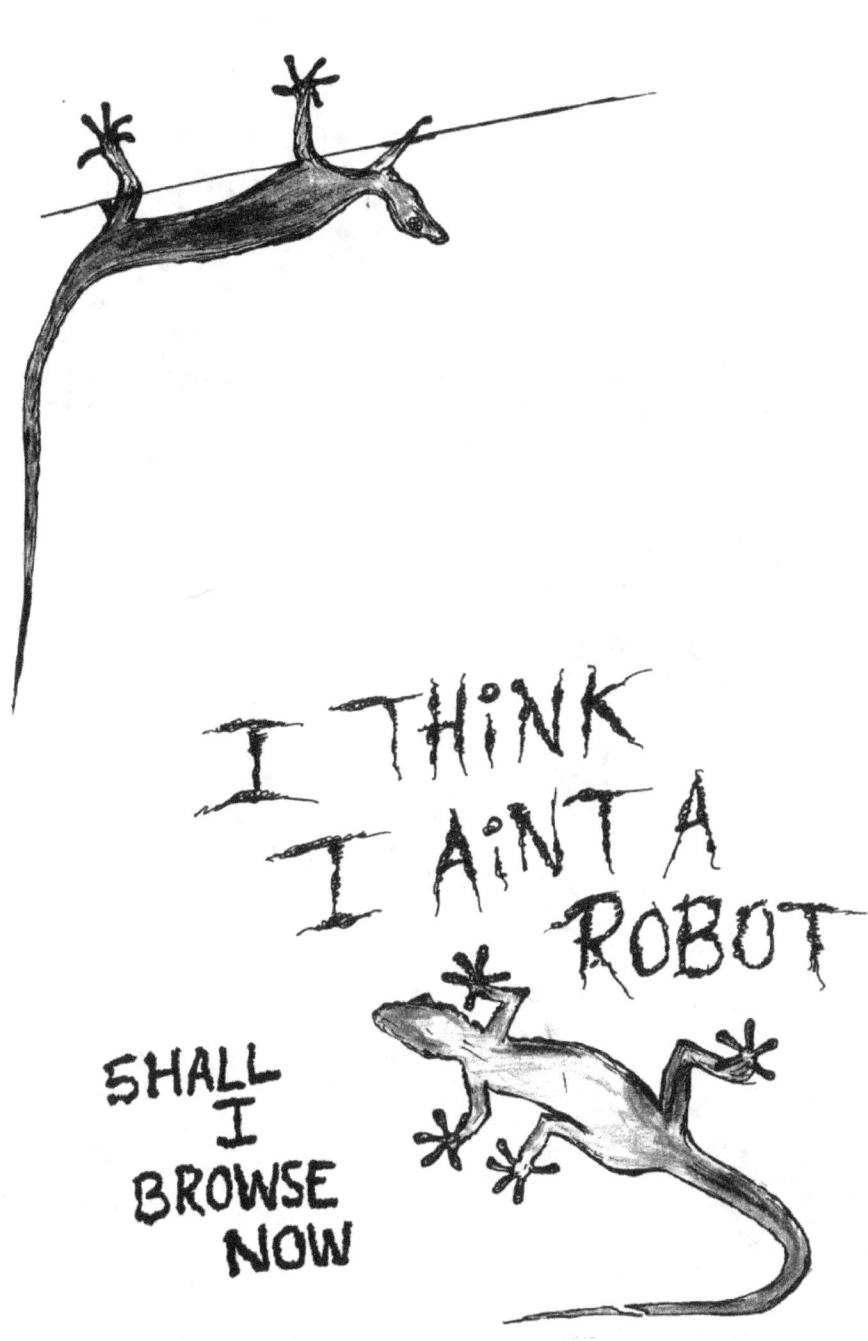

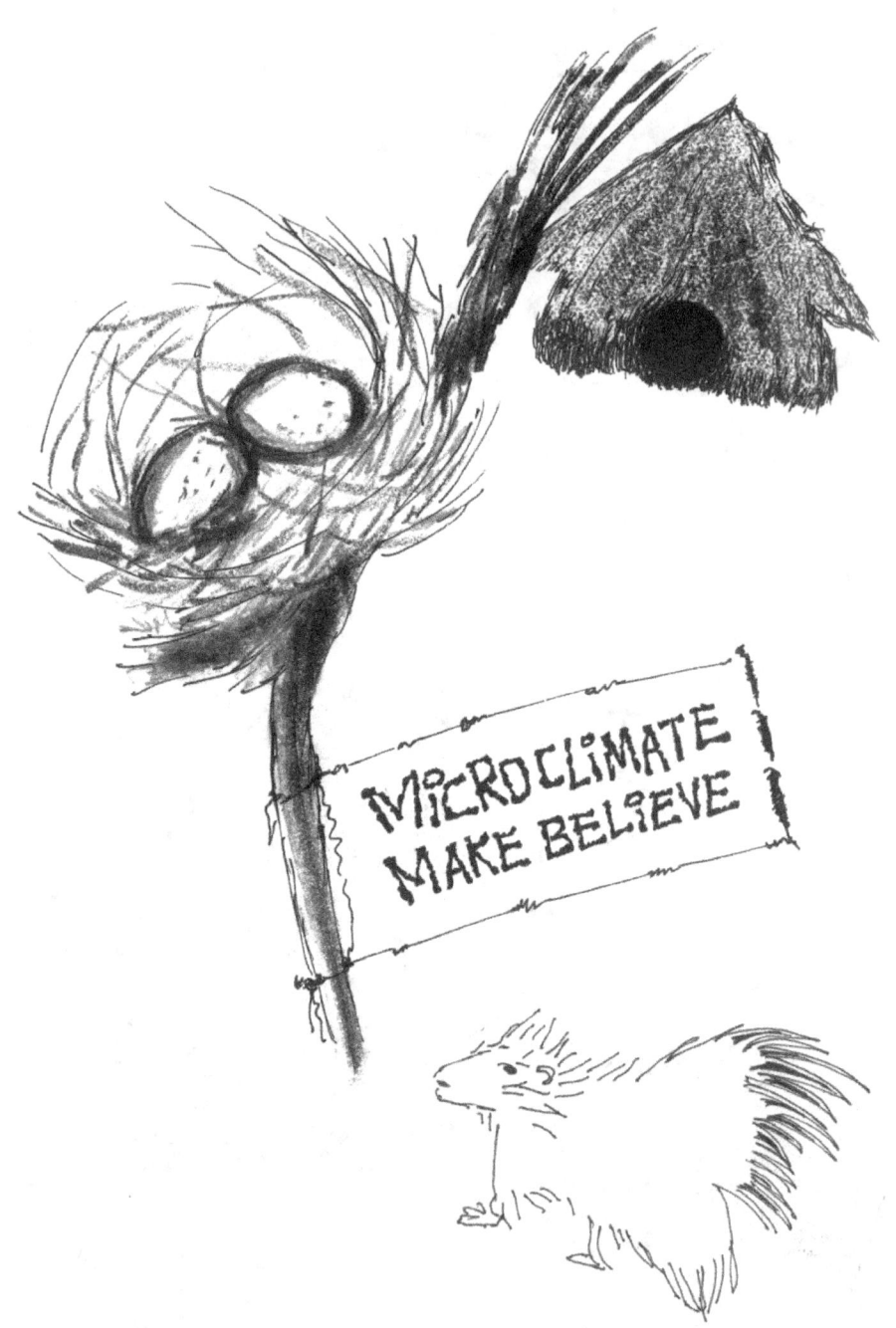

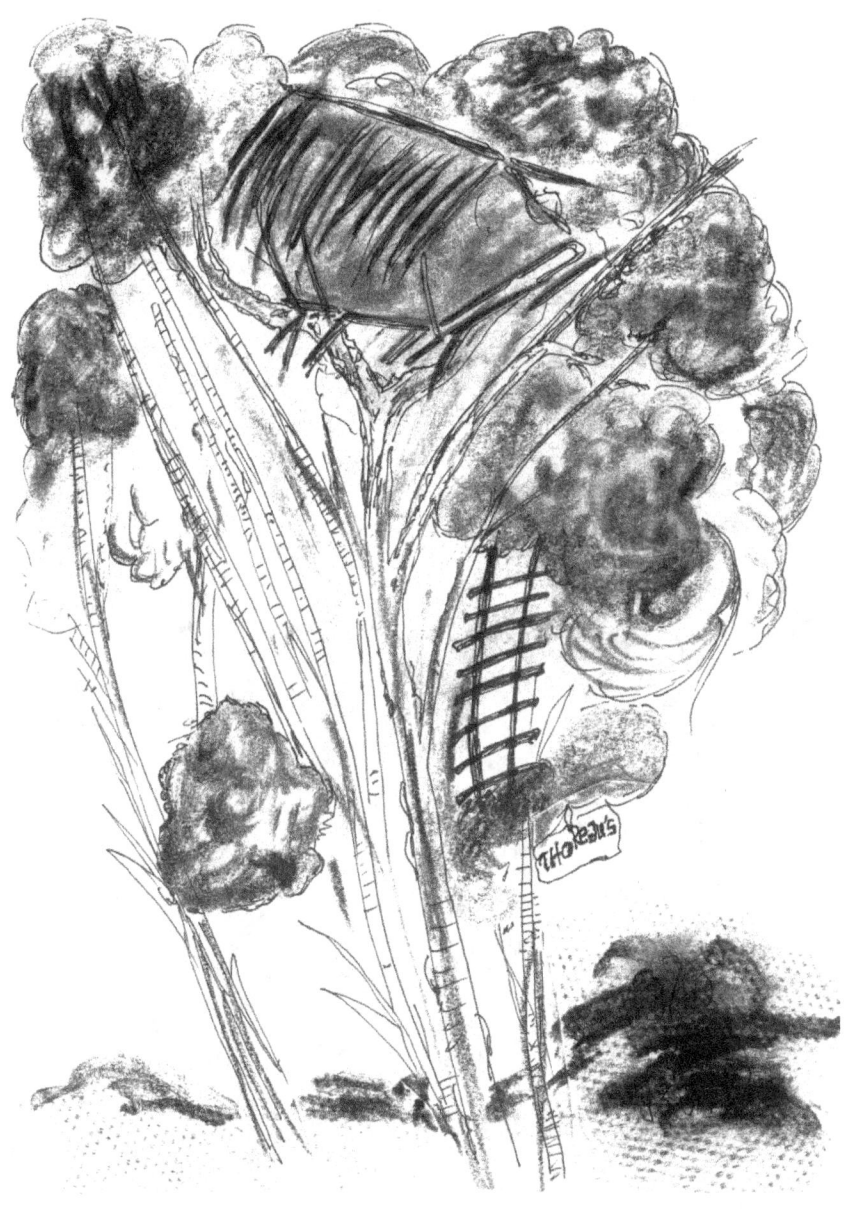

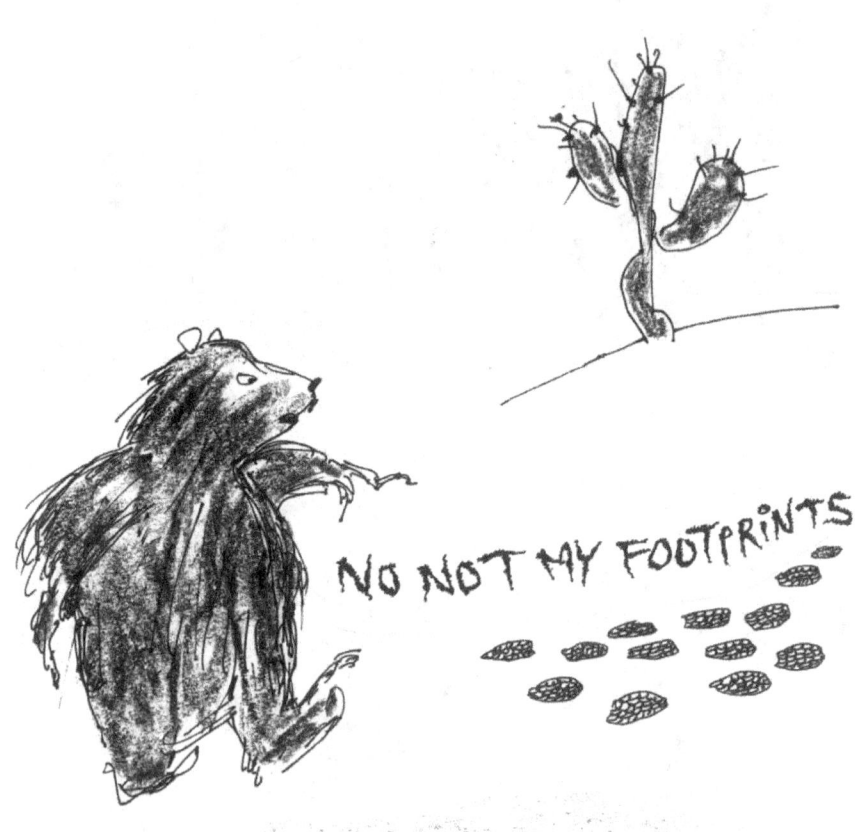

BREW A NEW HEBREW

WHEN YOUR LANG
AND SLANG GET
STALE

TOGETHER

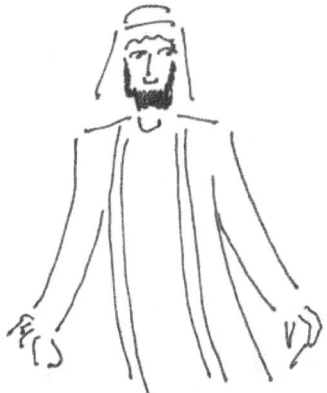

EUPHEME

so i coin this euphemism
for the word euphemism
which sounds stale
and offensive already

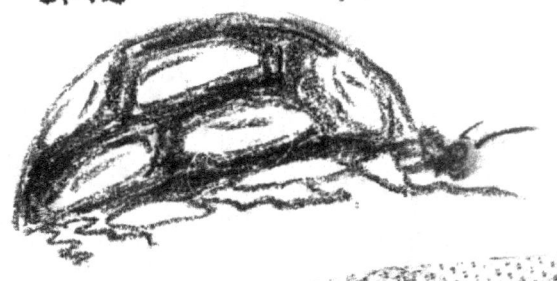

NOW LET US TALK ABOUT...
YEAH, SOMETHING ELSE!

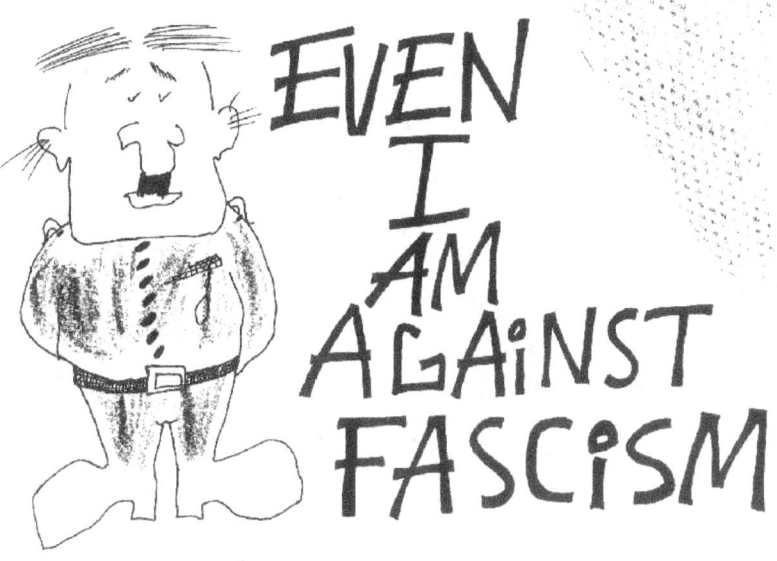

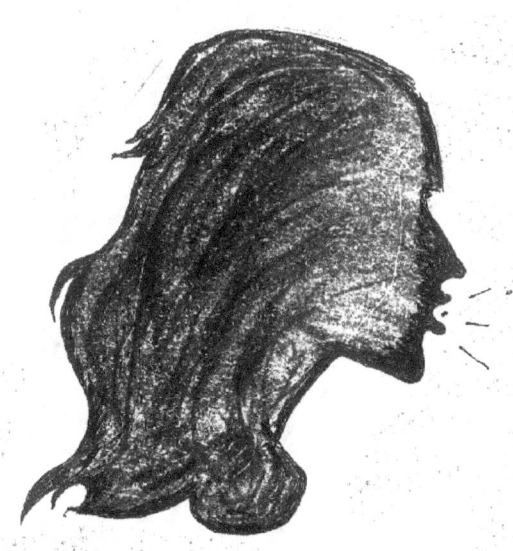

WHEN AI ~~WRITES~~ EDITS SOLILOQUIES

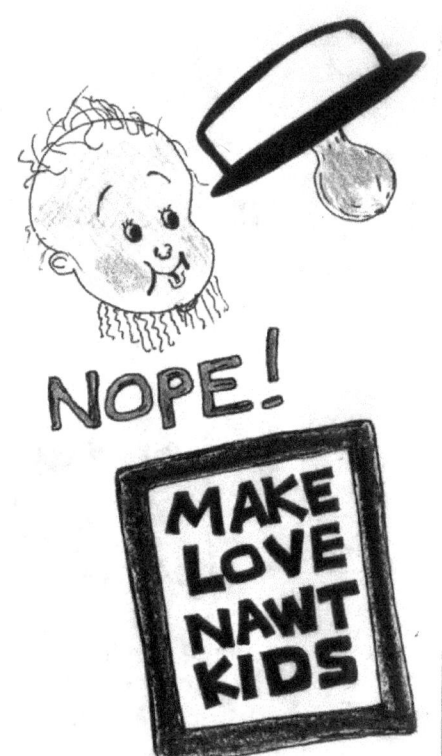

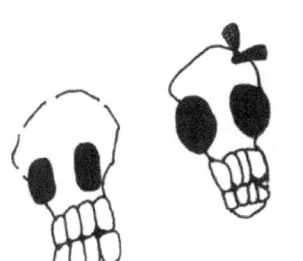

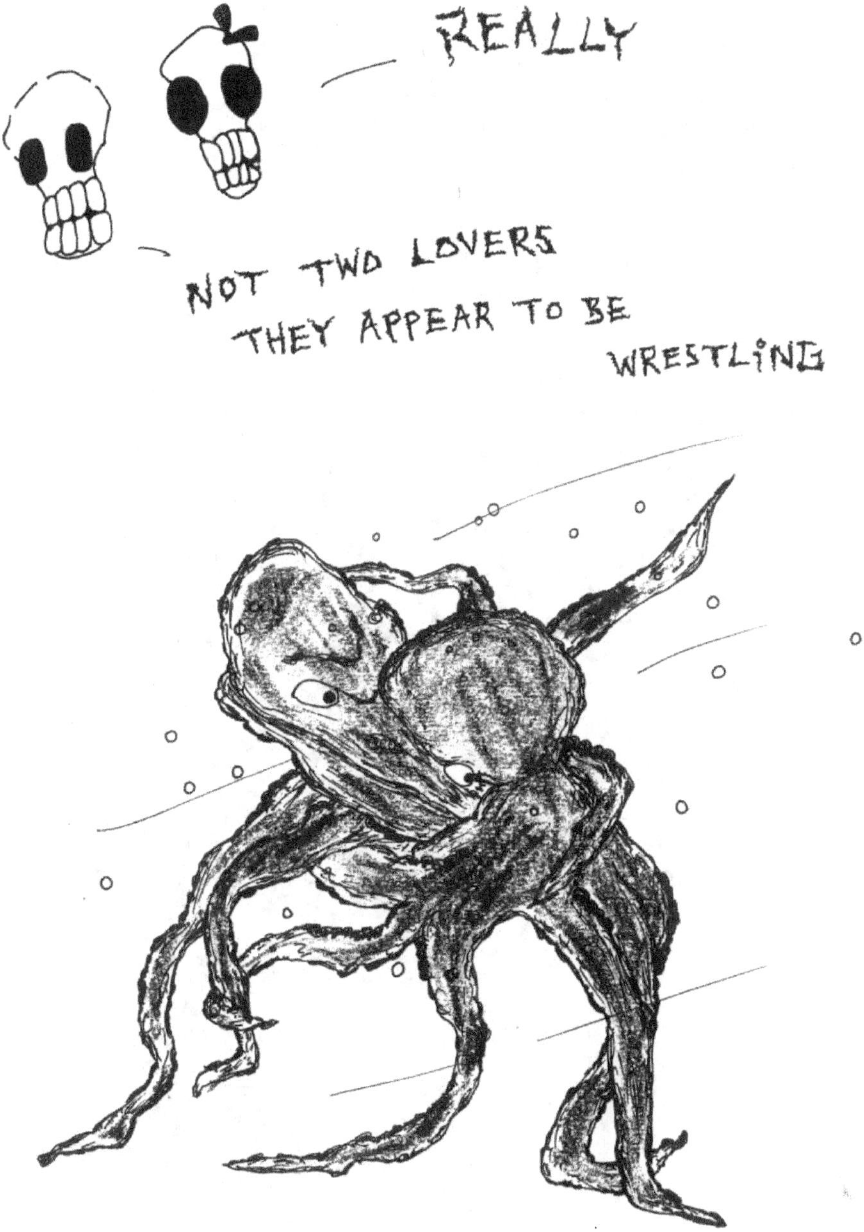

REALLY

NOT TWO LOVERS
THEY APPEAR TO BE
WRESTLING

Ever heard of
a four line
verse form called
Tequila

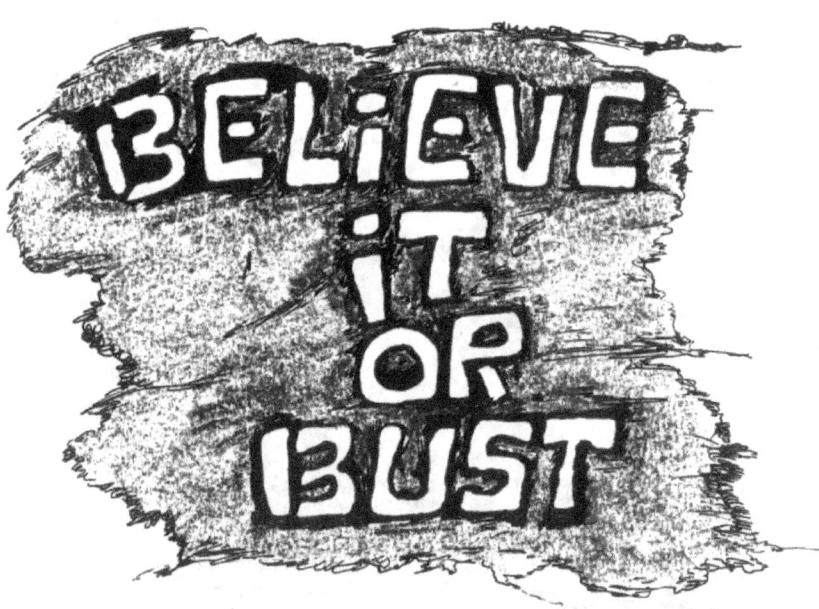

Believe it or bust

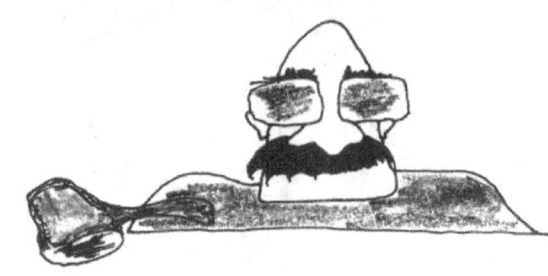

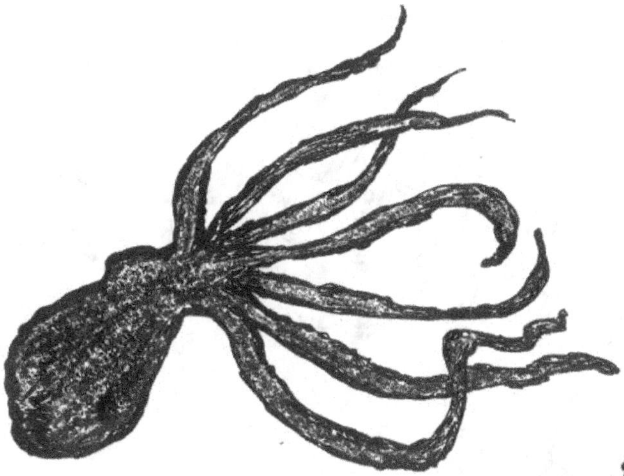

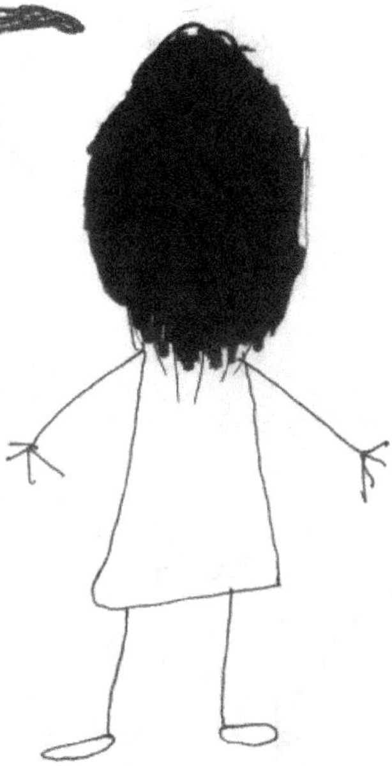

IT IS
A WORLD
OF MAKEBELIEF

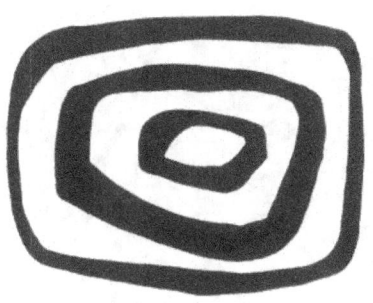

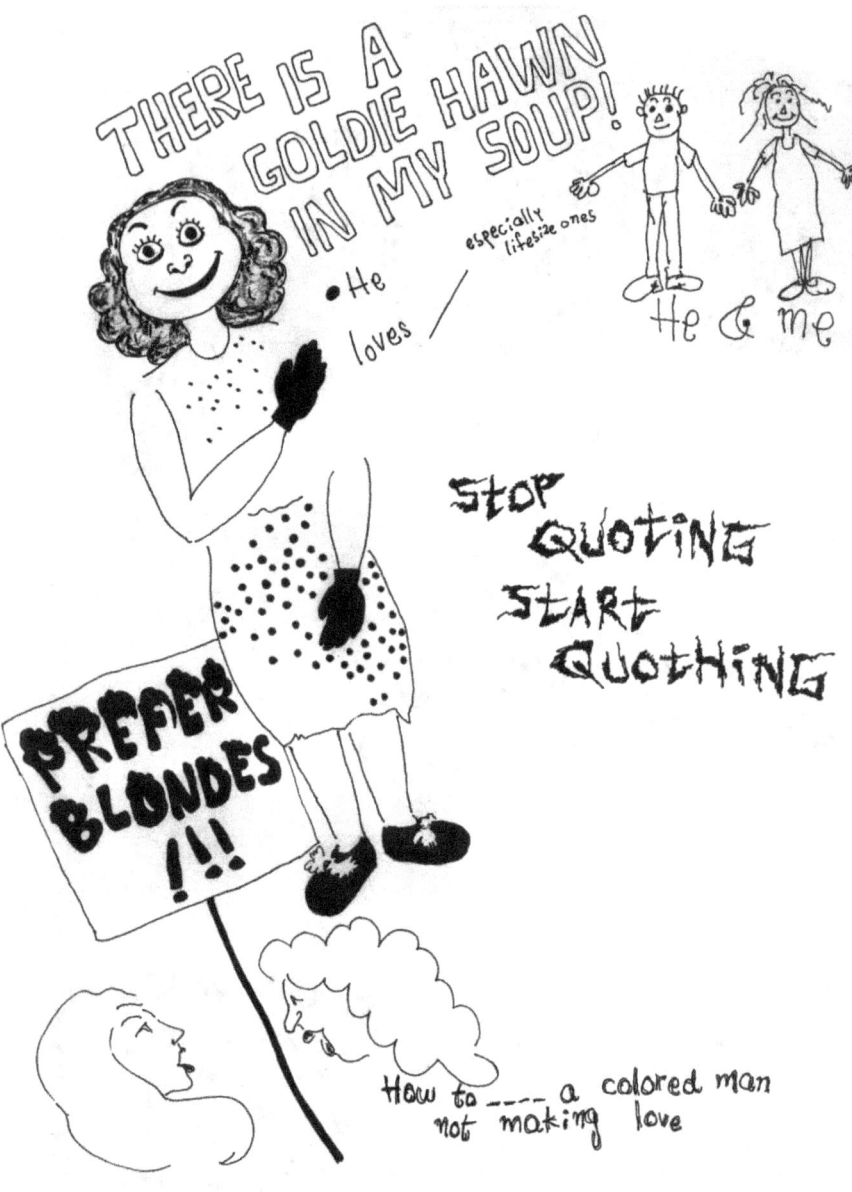

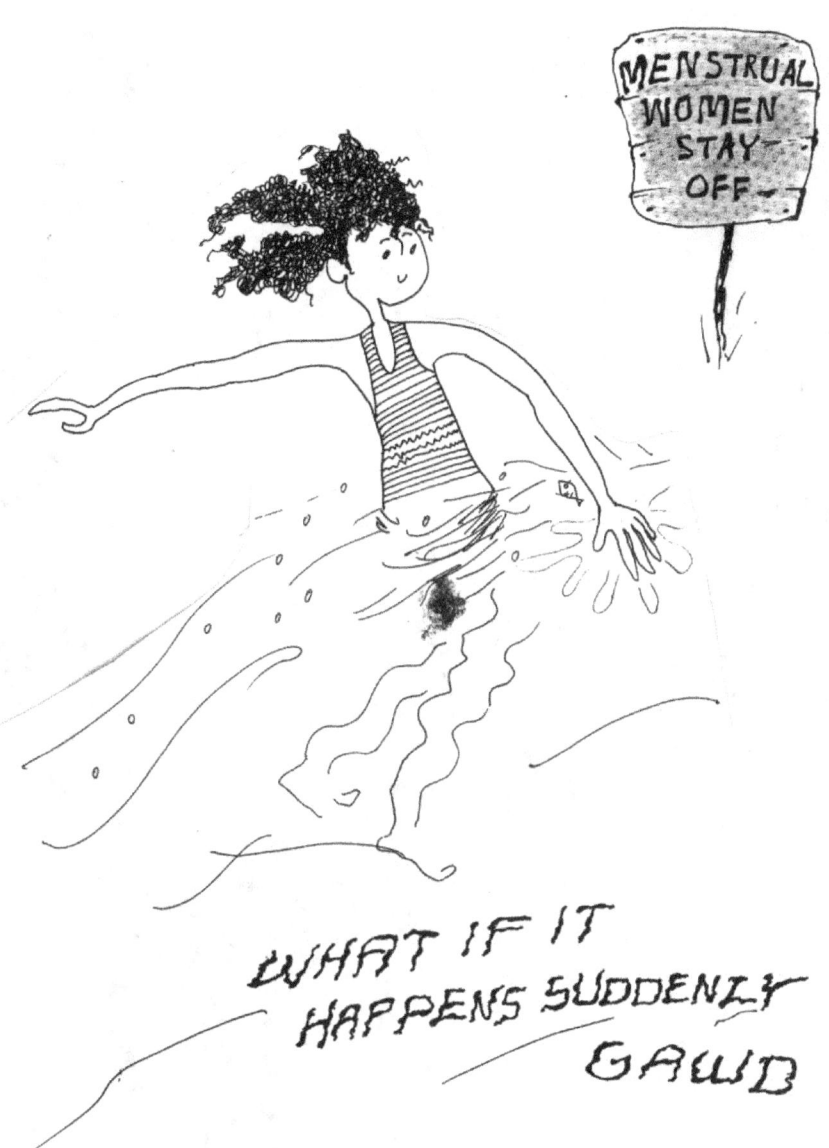

GAWD: ARE THERE SHARKS IN THAT LAKE?

DOES A PLEASURE THRESHOLD EXIST

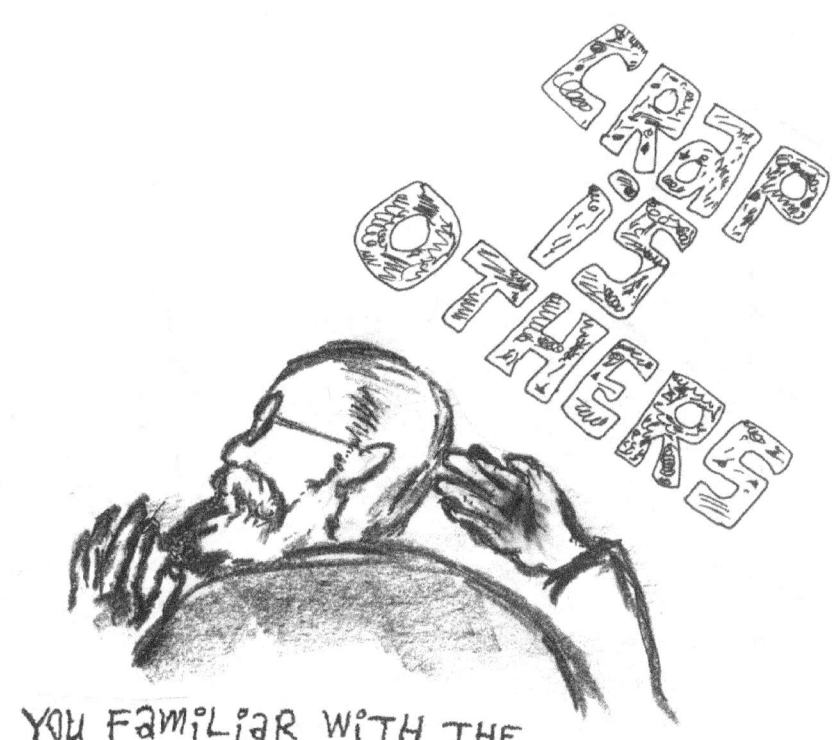

YOU FaMiLiaR WiTH THE
BLUFF YOUR WAY™ series?

BLUFF YOUR WAY iN
★ COGNAC
★ FUCKING
★ SLANG
★ SODOMY
★ NiHiLiSM
★ BUFFOONERY
★ COCKTAILS
........★ BLUFFiNG

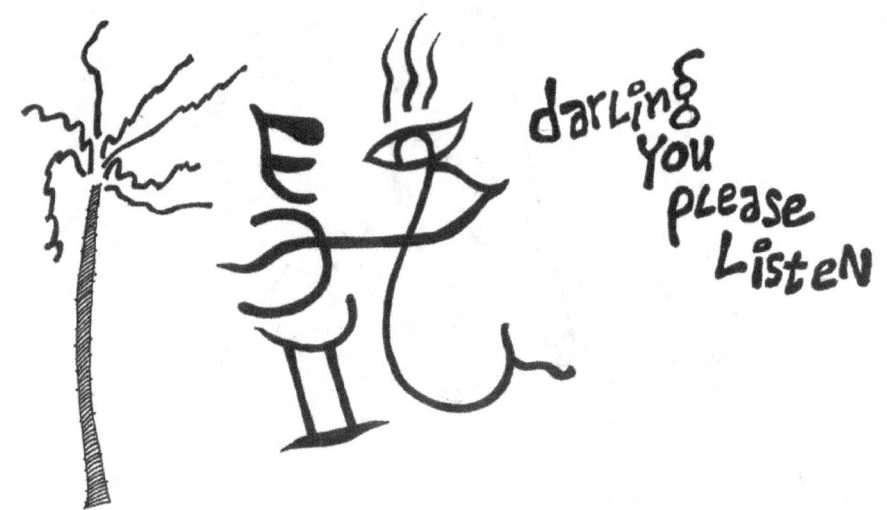

tHERE iS a vampiRE wannaBE in EVRYBUDDY....

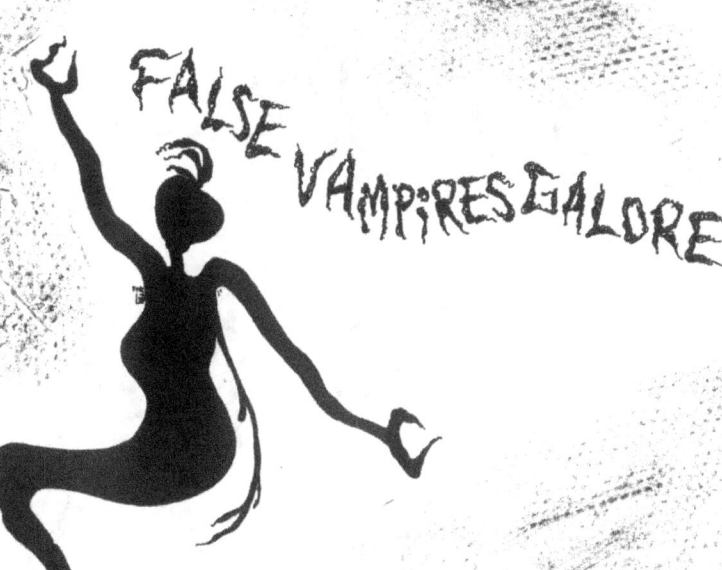

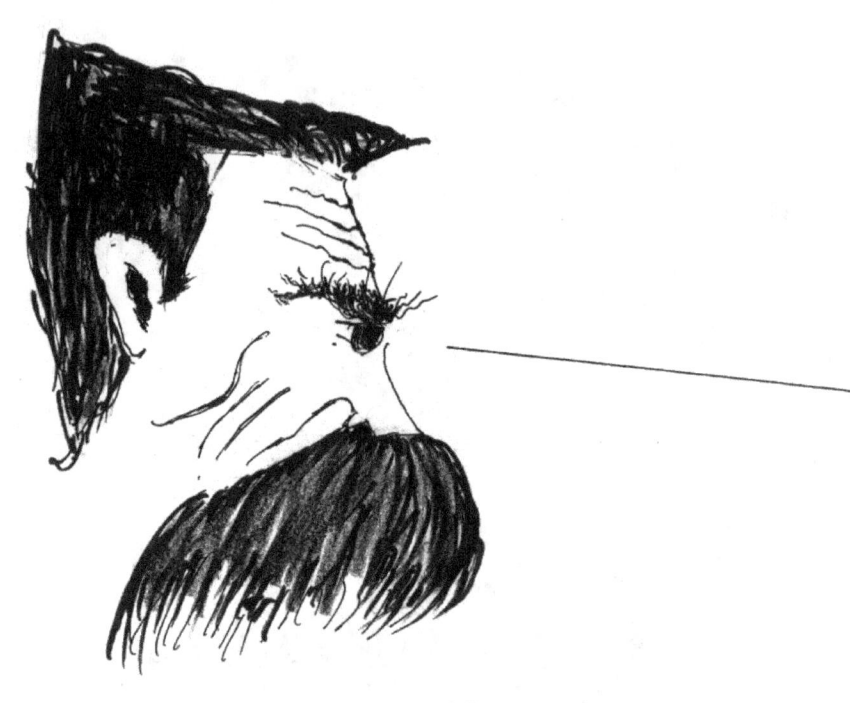

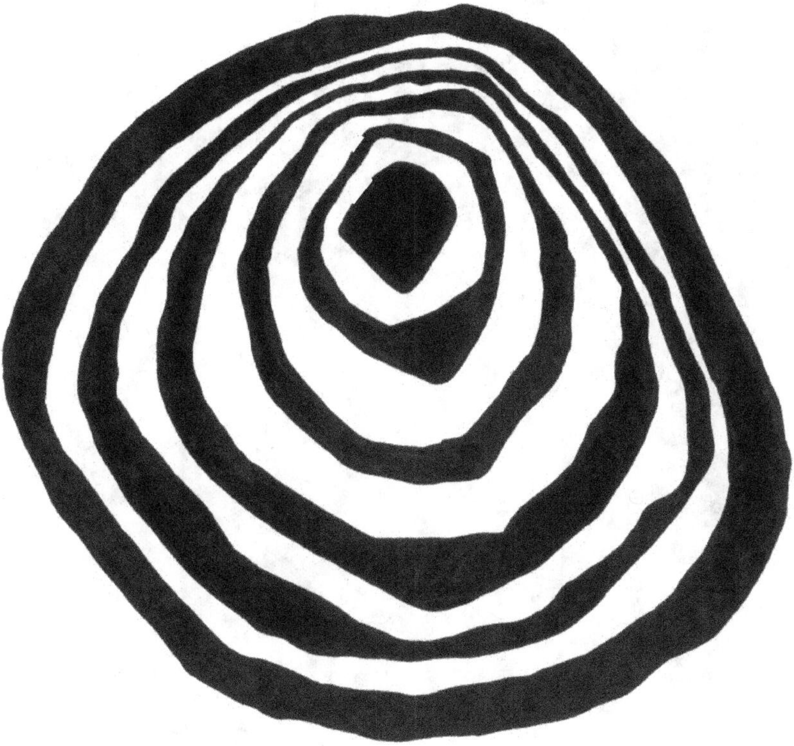

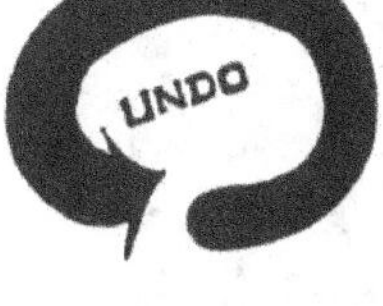

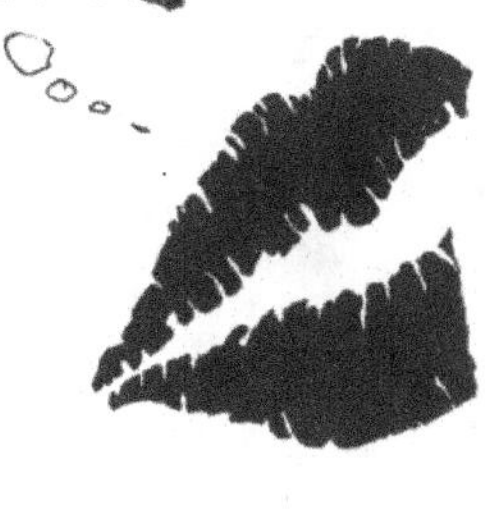

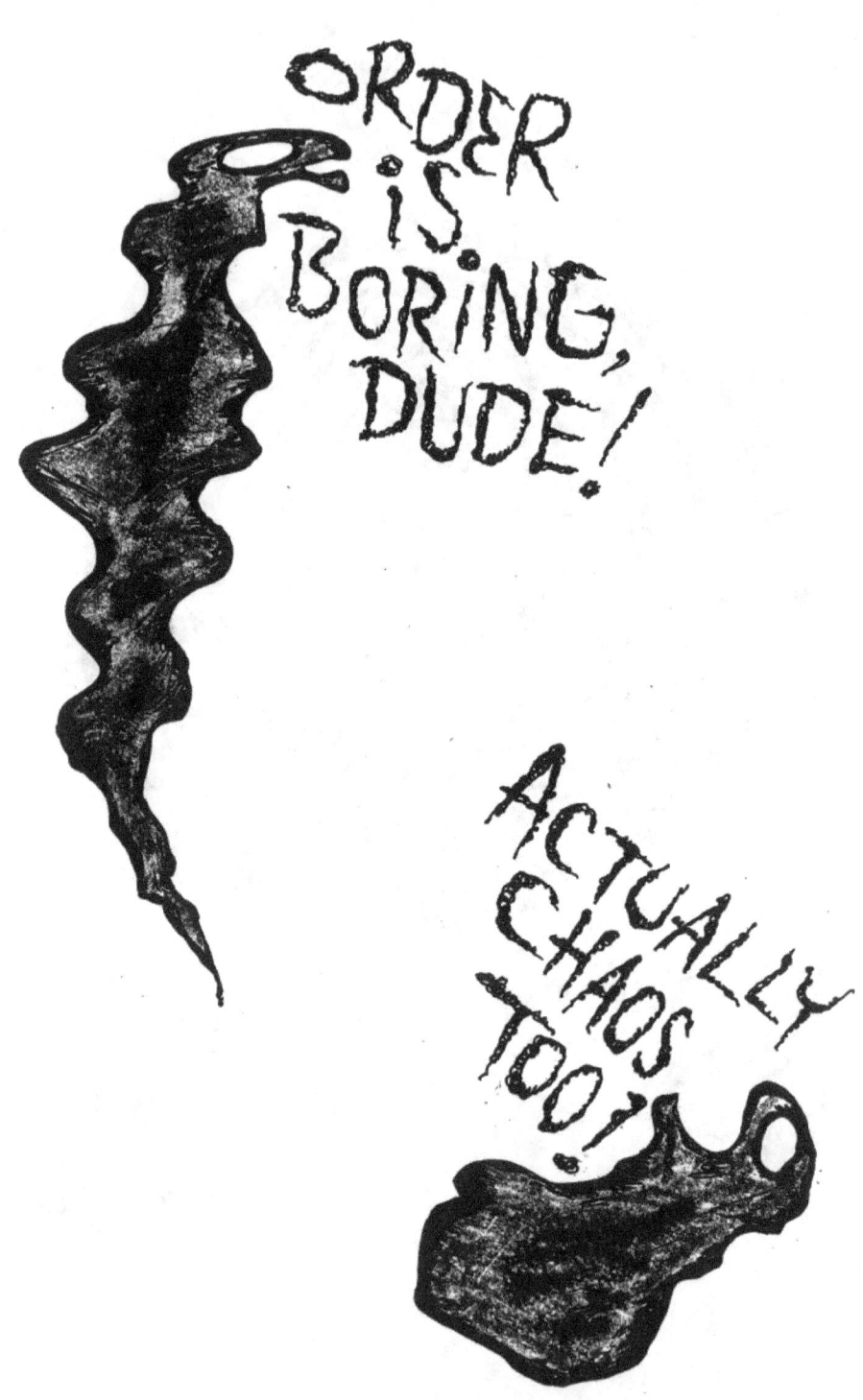

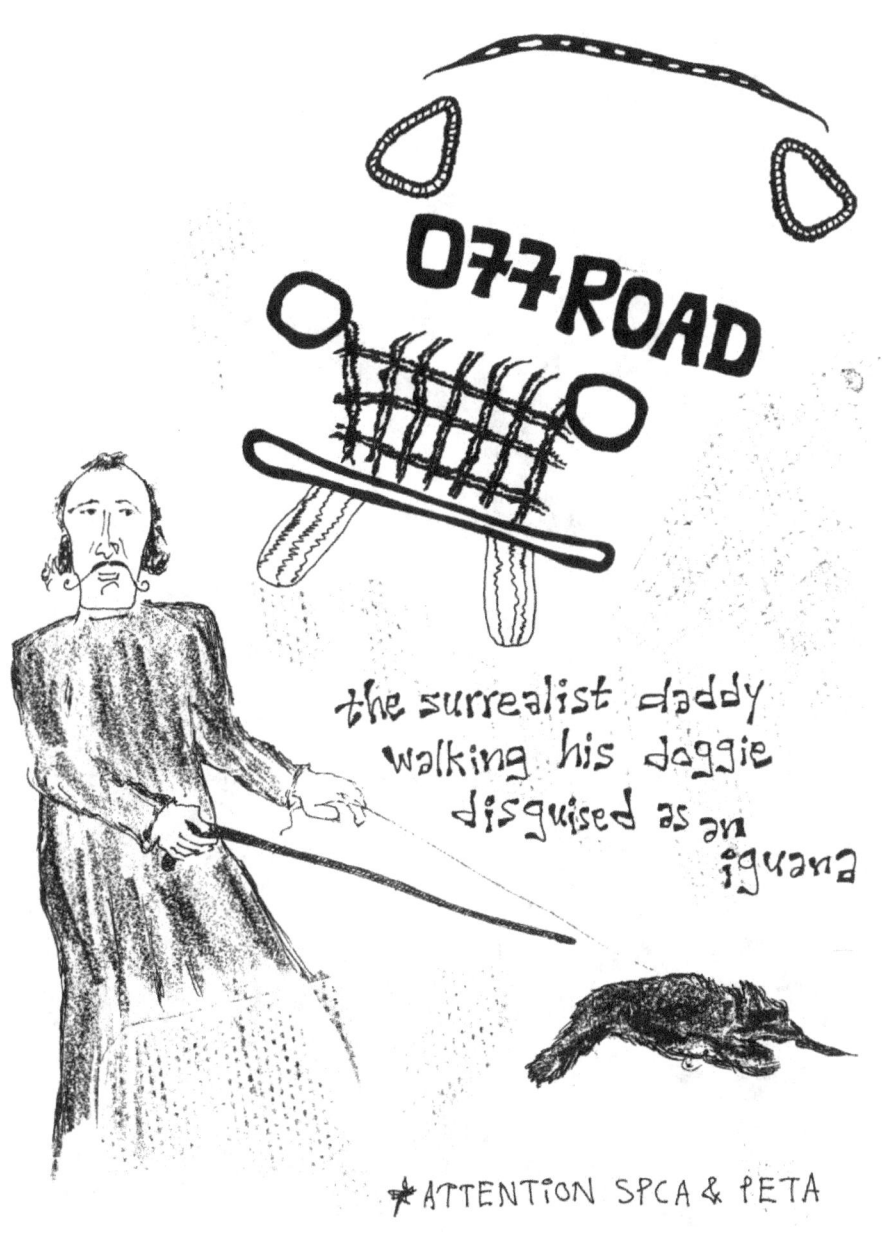

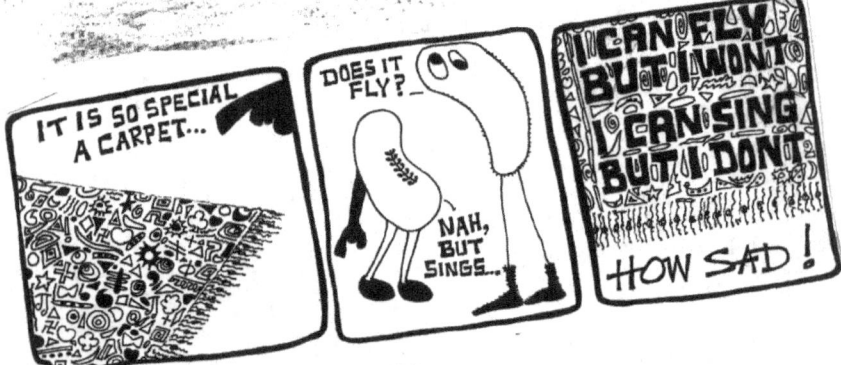

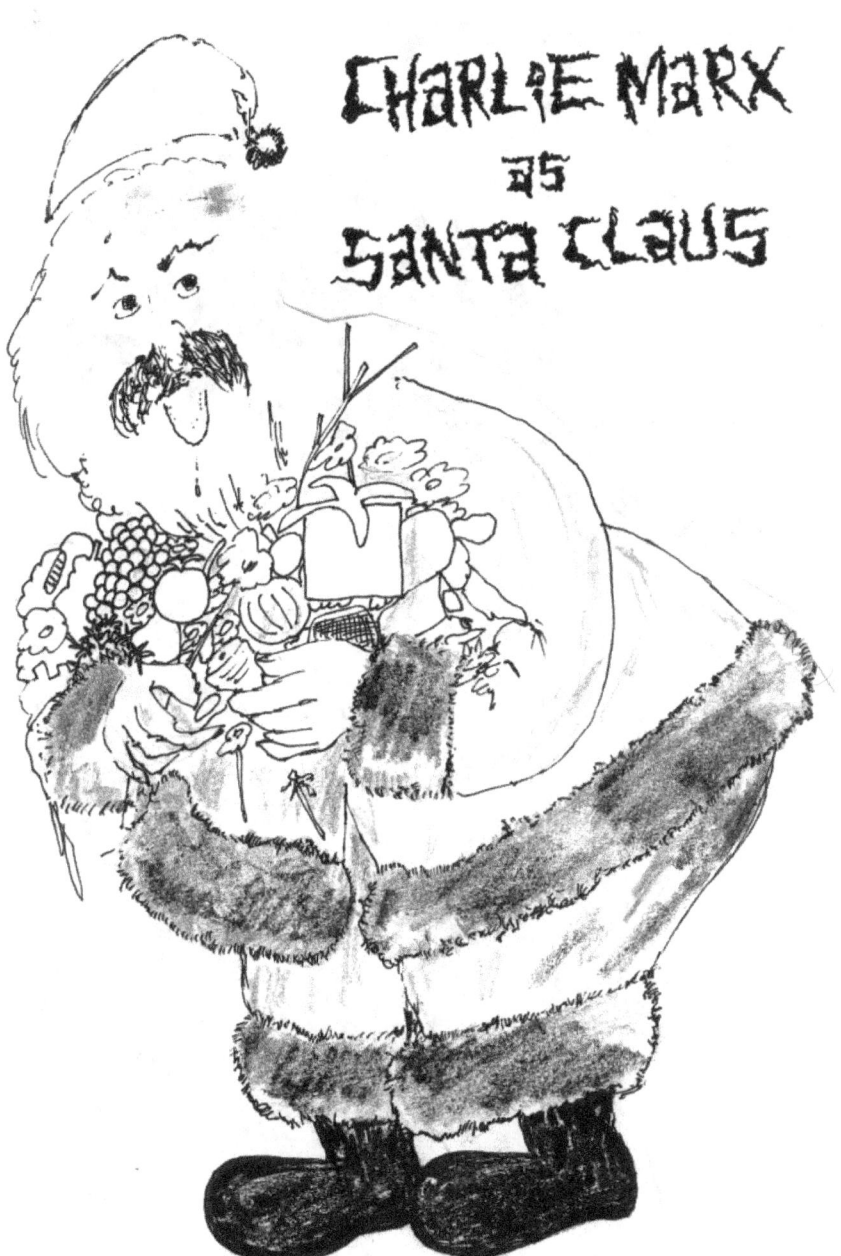

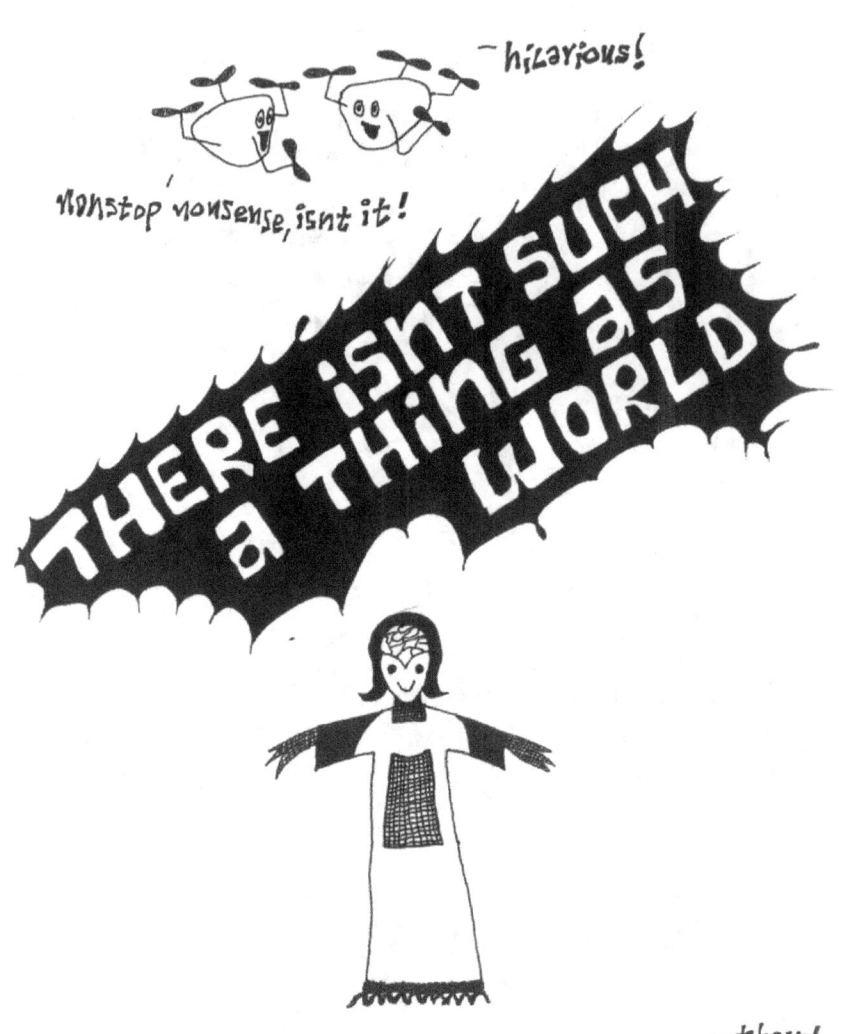

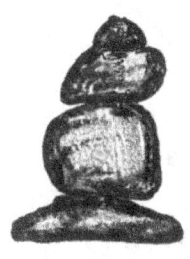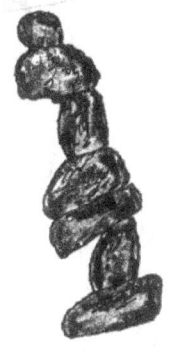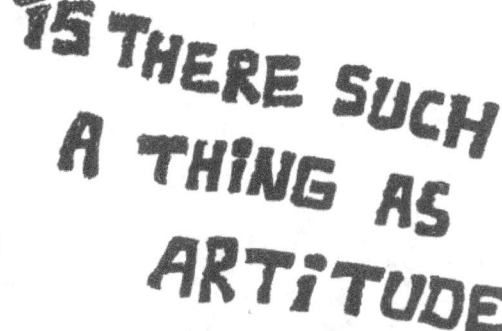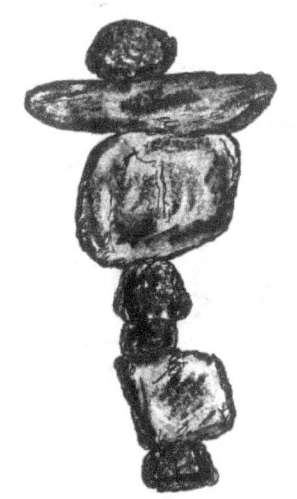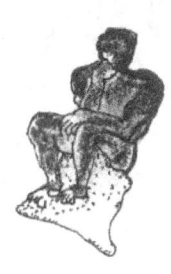

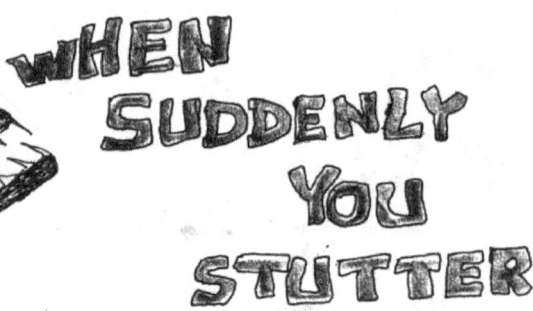

WHEN SUDDENLY YOU STUTTER

5 5 Six was scared
b b because
5 5 5 seven eight nine

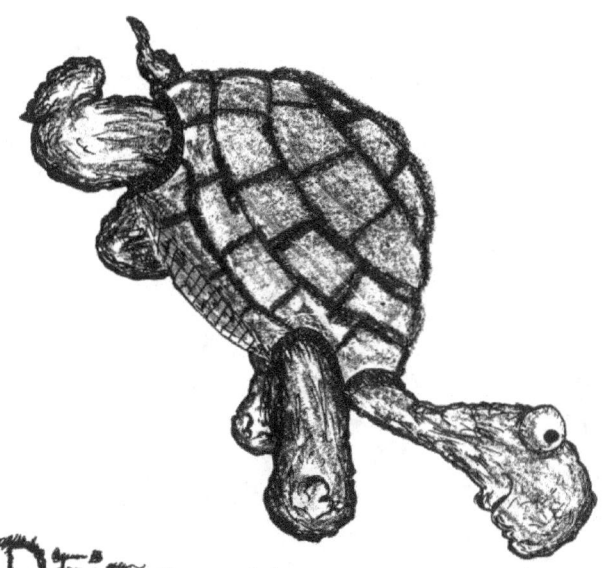

DEIGO THE TORTOISE*
WHOSE HIGH SEX DRIVE
SAVED THAT SPECIES

* ESIO TROT?

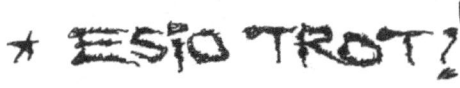

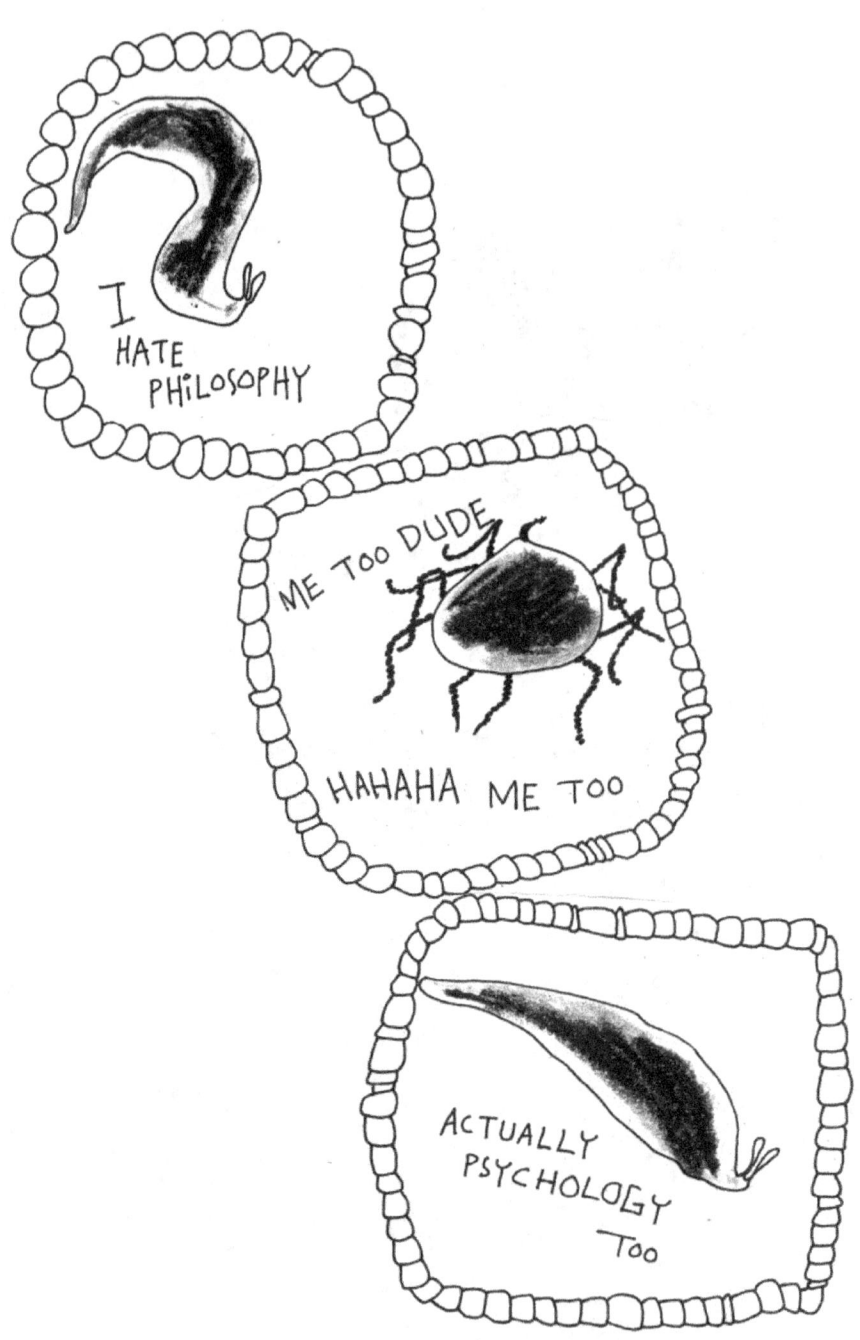

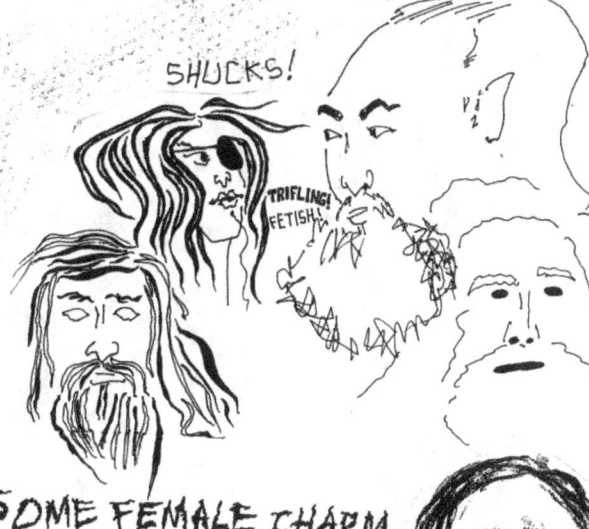

will
someone
steal
halloween *

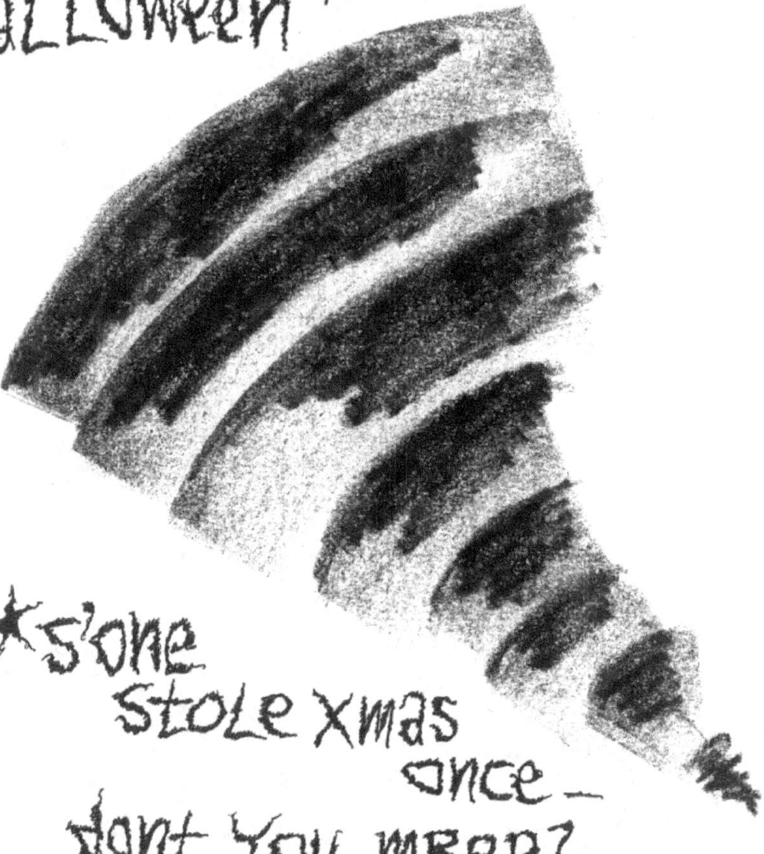

*s'one
    stole xmas
           once—
   dont you mber?

HOW WE SURVIVED COMMUNISM / LAUGHING

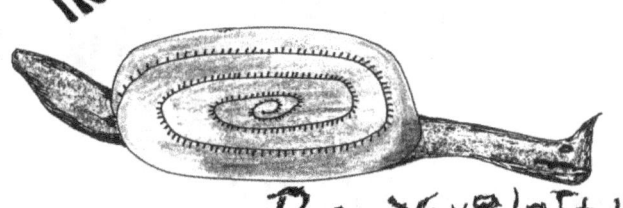

Raise your left hand
all who hasta
poetic licence and
the right occupied

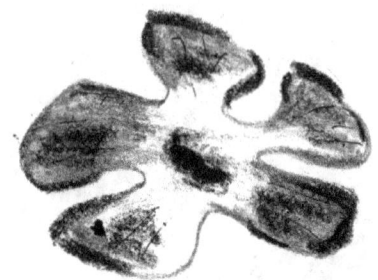

BLOOD

WiLL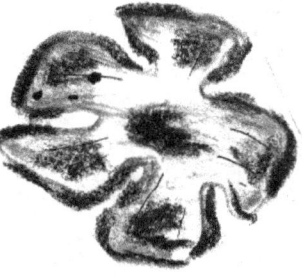

SHED

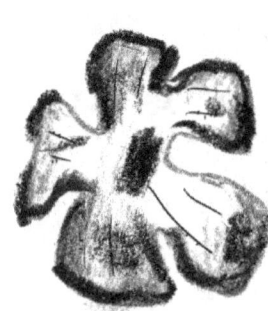

※ Replace WiLL with WOULD, WOULD YOU PLEASE!

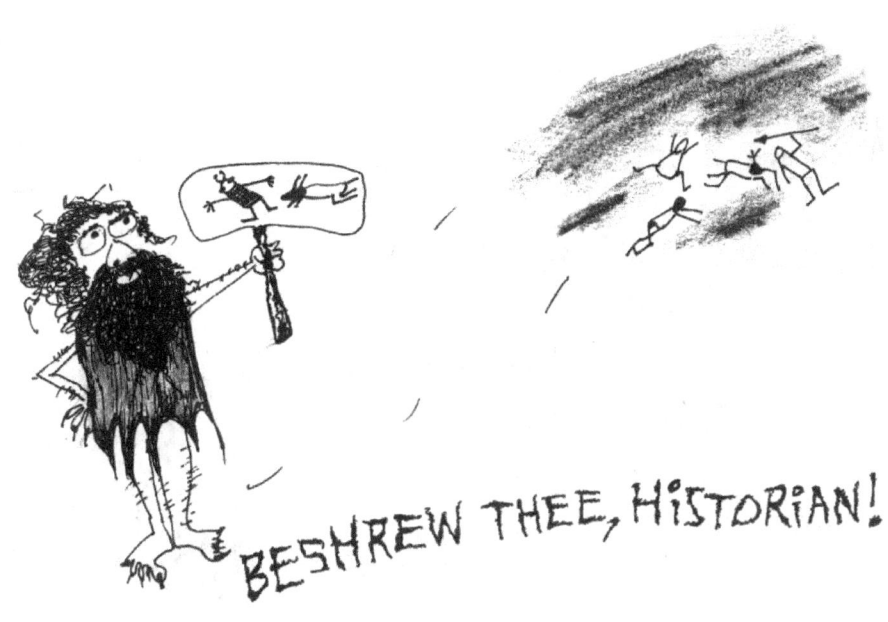

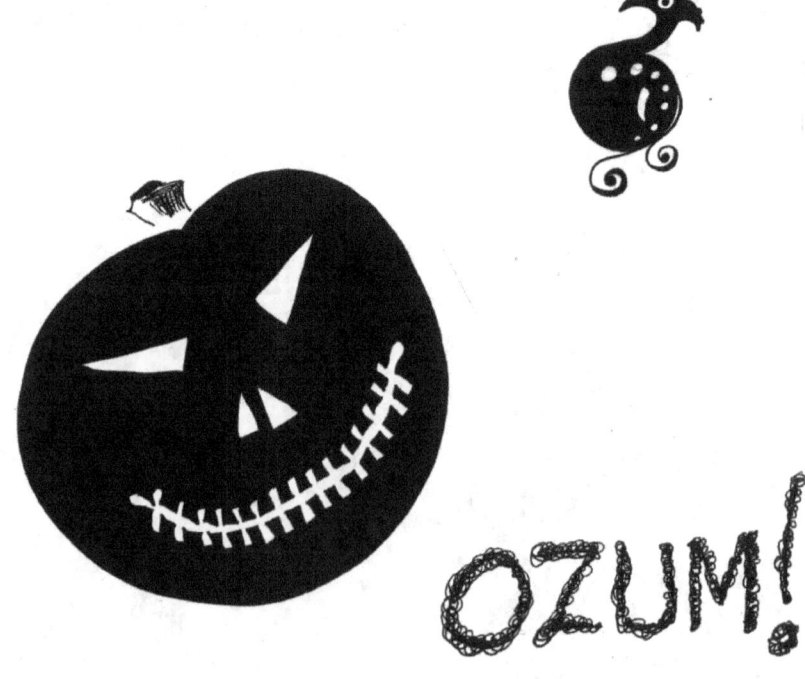

```
a
ab
abr
abra
abrac
abraca
abracad
abracada
abracadab
abracadabr
abracadabra
bracadabra
racadabra
acadabra
cadabra
adabra
dabra
abra
bra
ra
a
```

One shouldn't pronounce it

It only is meant to be depicted like this

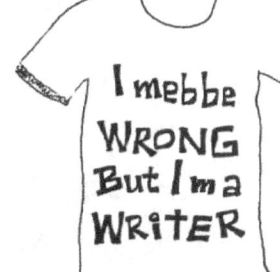

I mebbe WRONG But I'm a WRITER

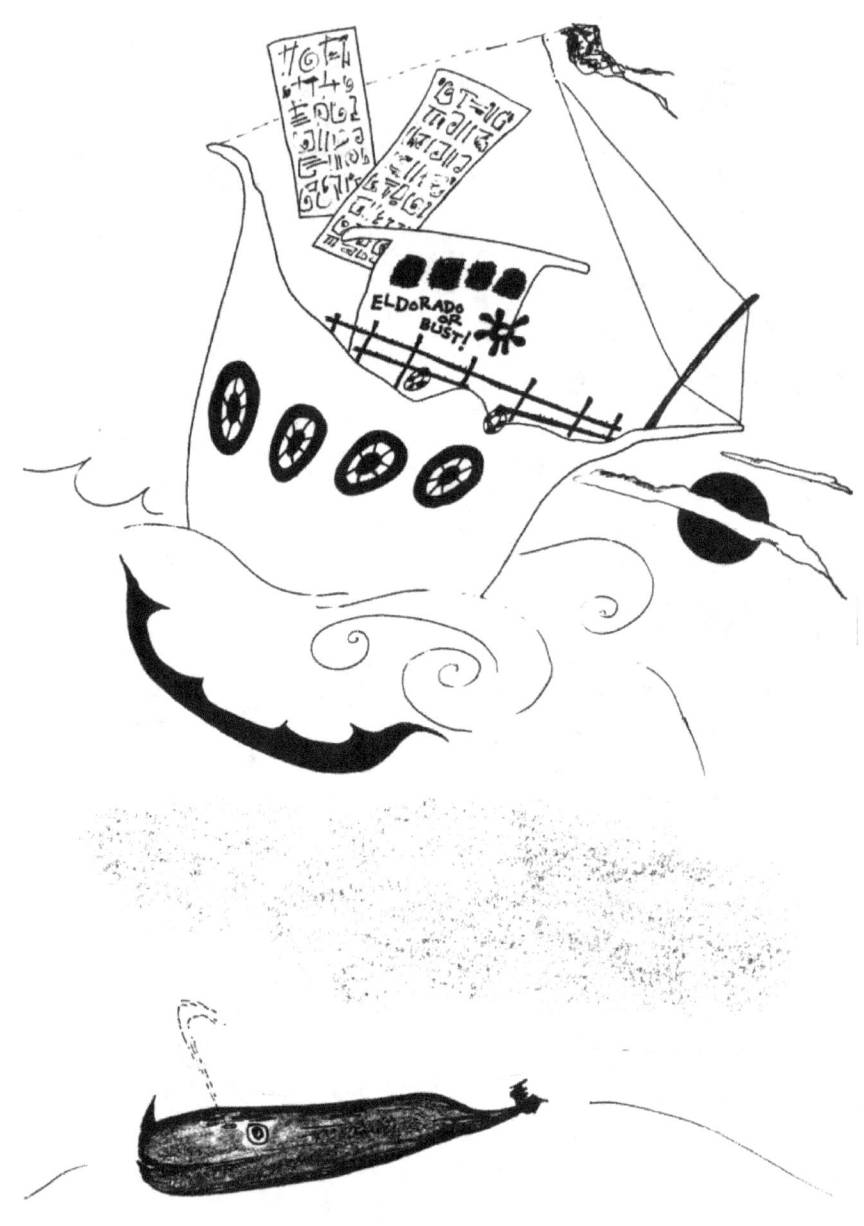

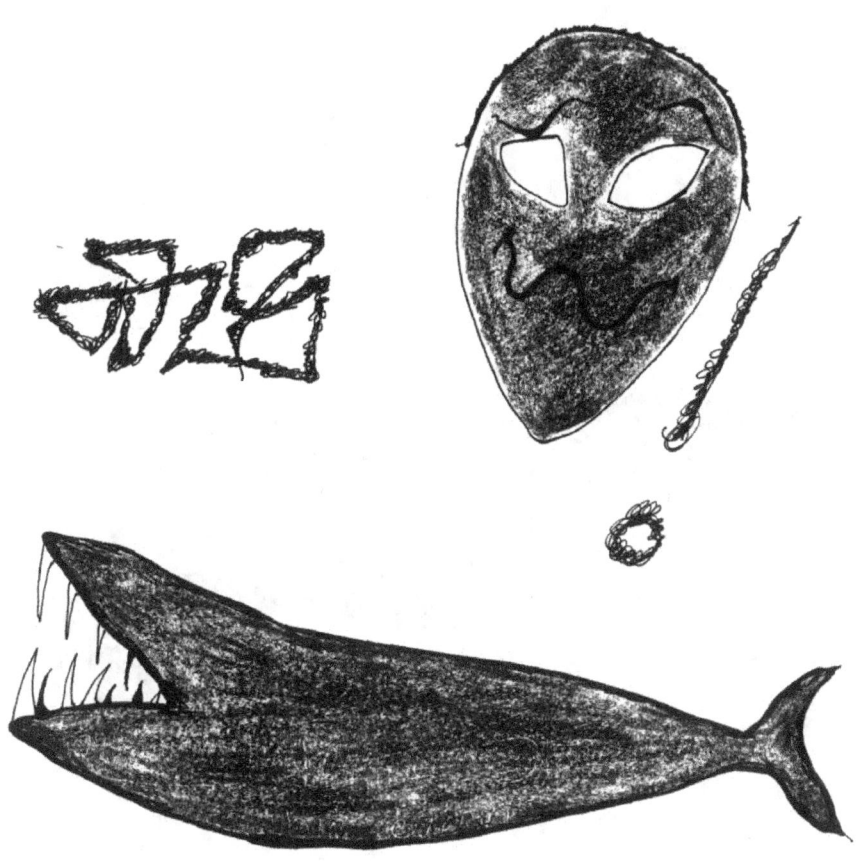

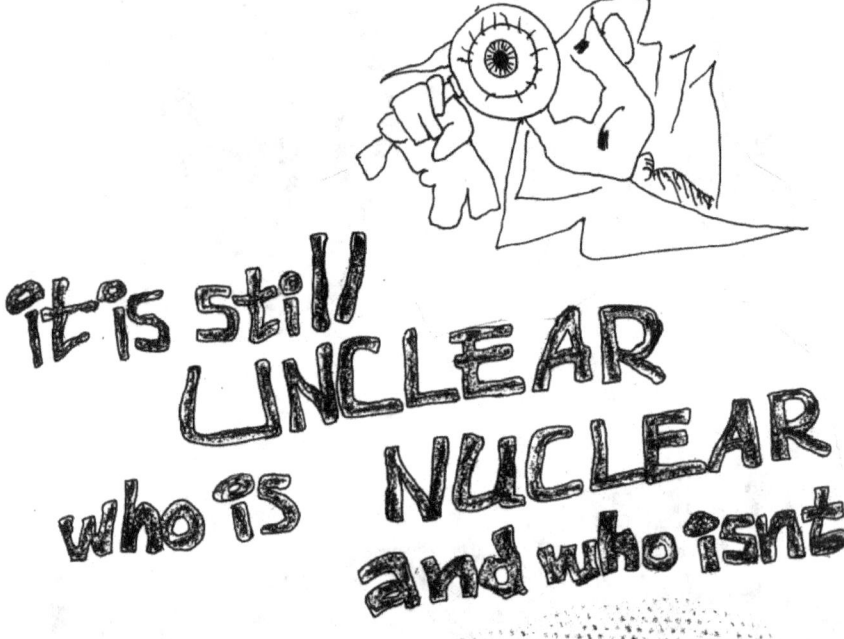

it is still UNCLEAR who is NUCLEAR and who isnt

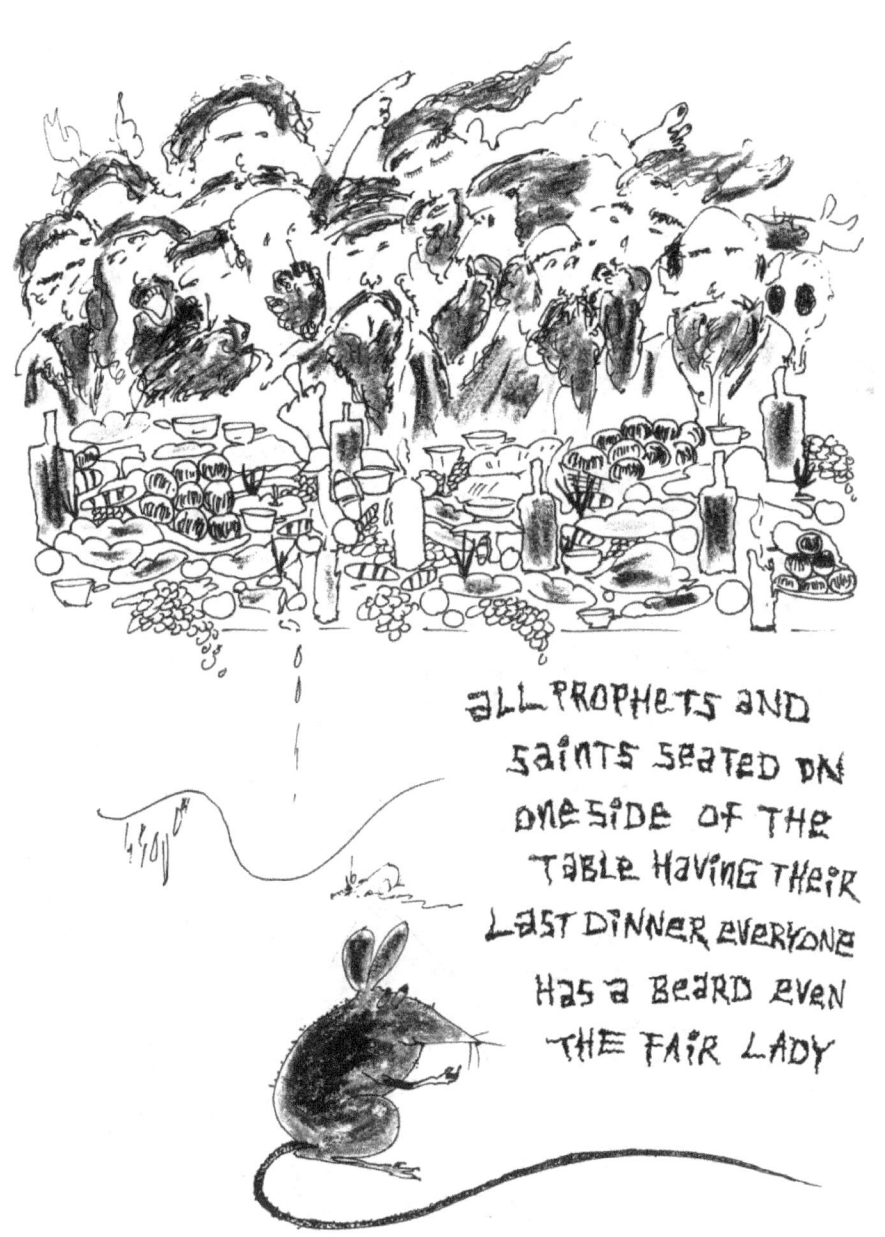

NOT HO CHI MINH

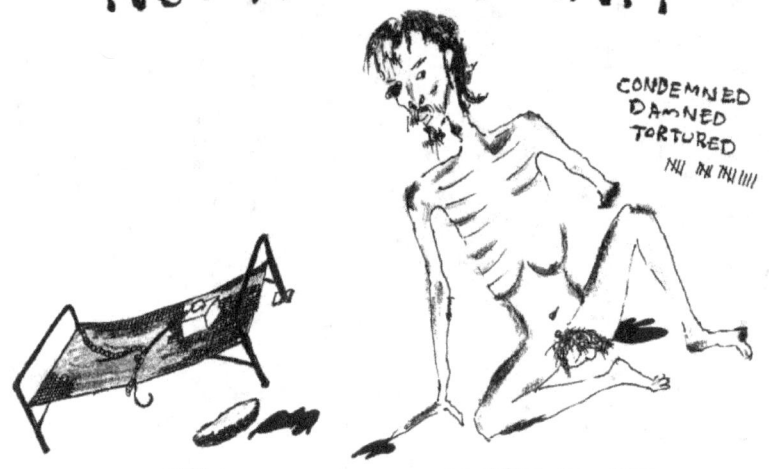

CONDEMNED
DAMNED
TORTURED
𝍸 𝍸 𝍸 ||||

THIS COMPUCHEAN WAS BOOKED
FOR WRITING POETRY
HE WAS THROWN INTO THE KILLING FIELDS
WHERE HE WAS EXCRUCIATED
LIKE HELL HE SUFFERED
HE DIDNT SURVIVE SO
COULDNT PUBLISH A DIARY

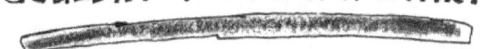

THE ARTIST WHO DREW THIS PIC SURVIVED
HE WAS EMPLOYED BY POLPOT TO DOCUMENT THINGS
MENG SAYS HE OWES HIS LIFE TO HIS ABILITY TO DO ᵛPAINTINGS
REALISTIC

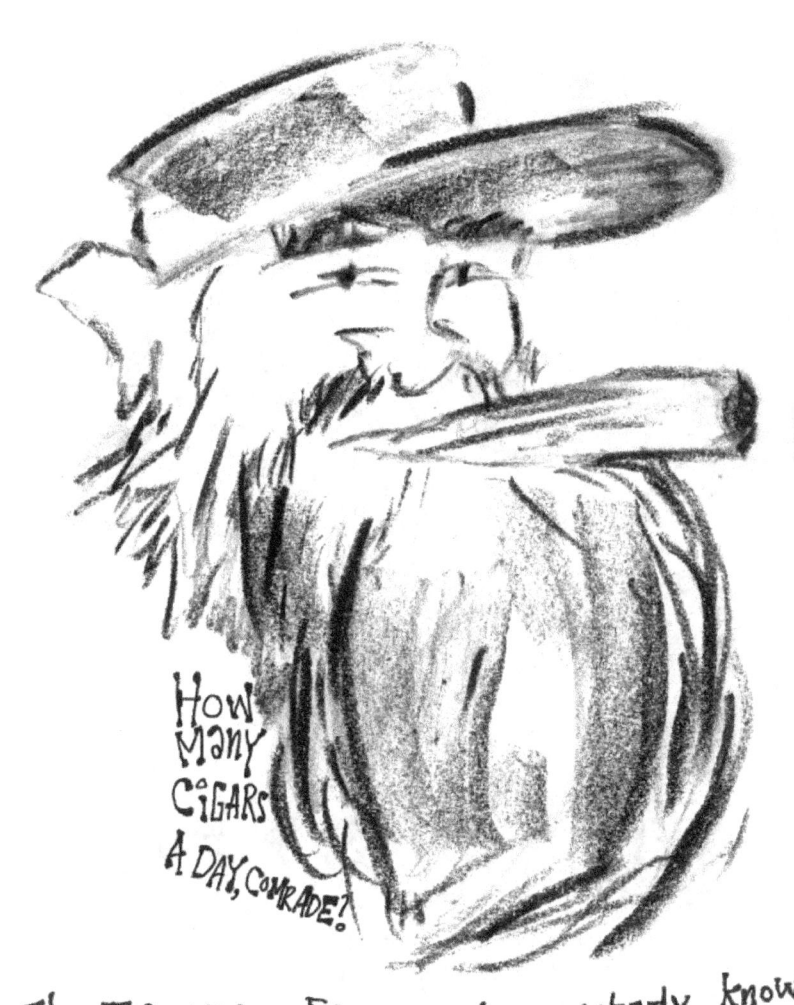

The Cigar is fine and everybody knows that. We neednt've spent time on propagating the idea. Instead we shdve cultivated hemp widely and exported it to rich countries, thru proper channel or otherways.
DOWN WITH CAPITALISM!

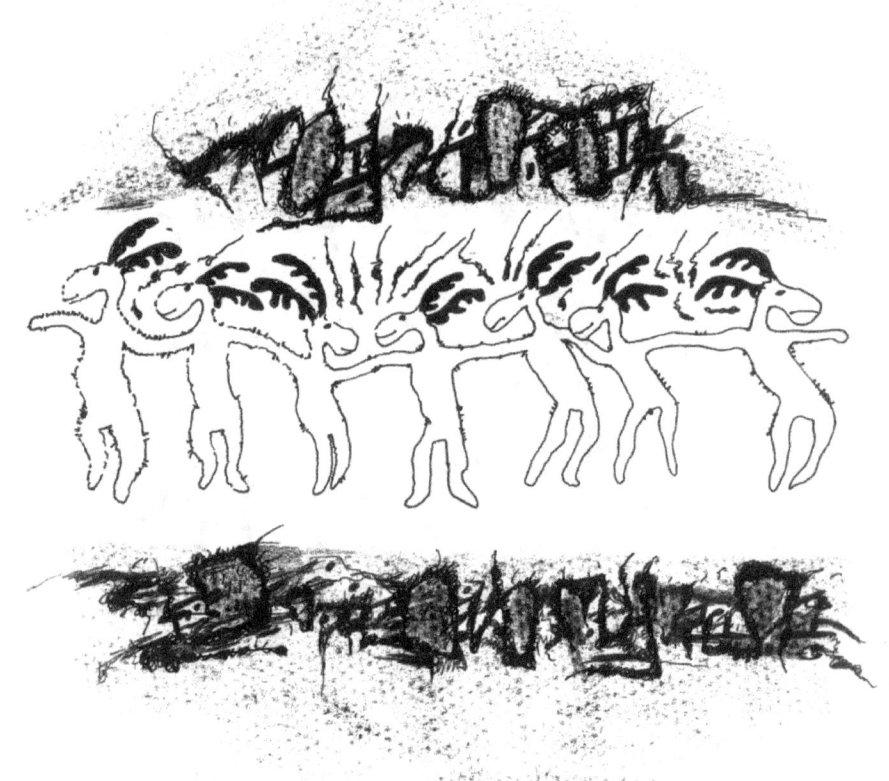

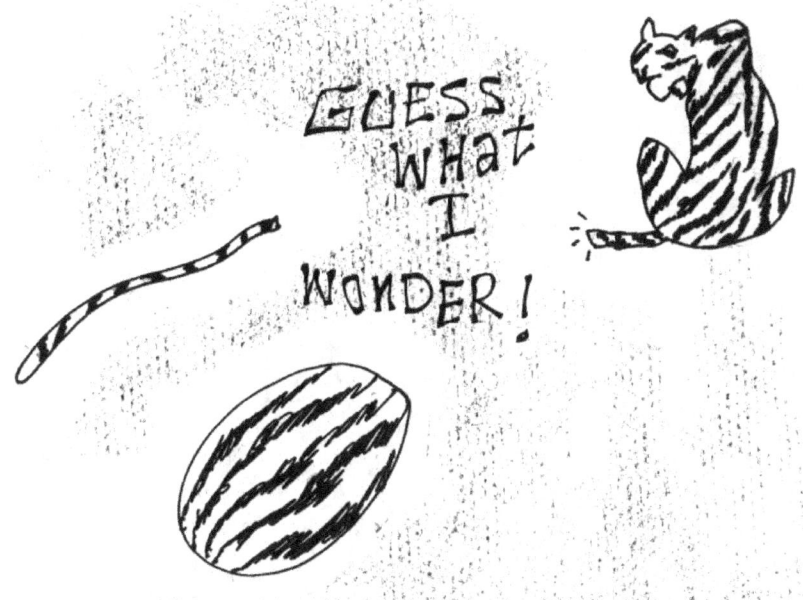
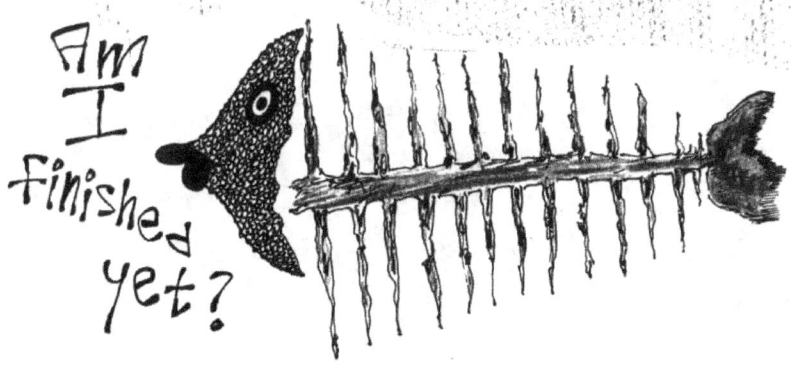

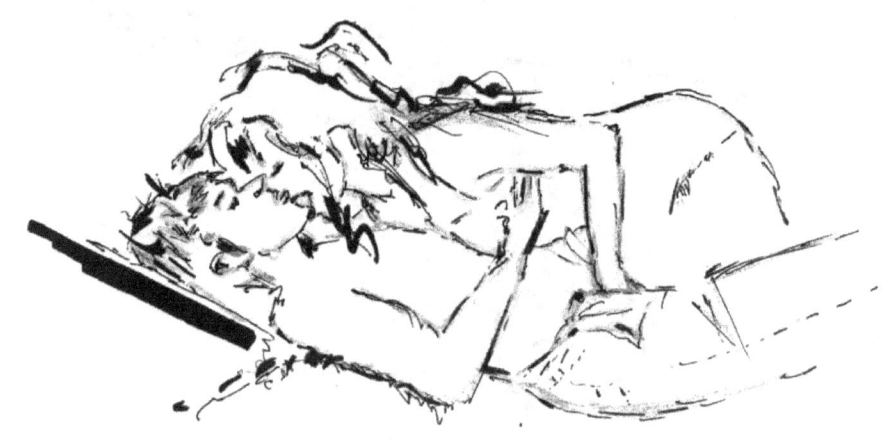

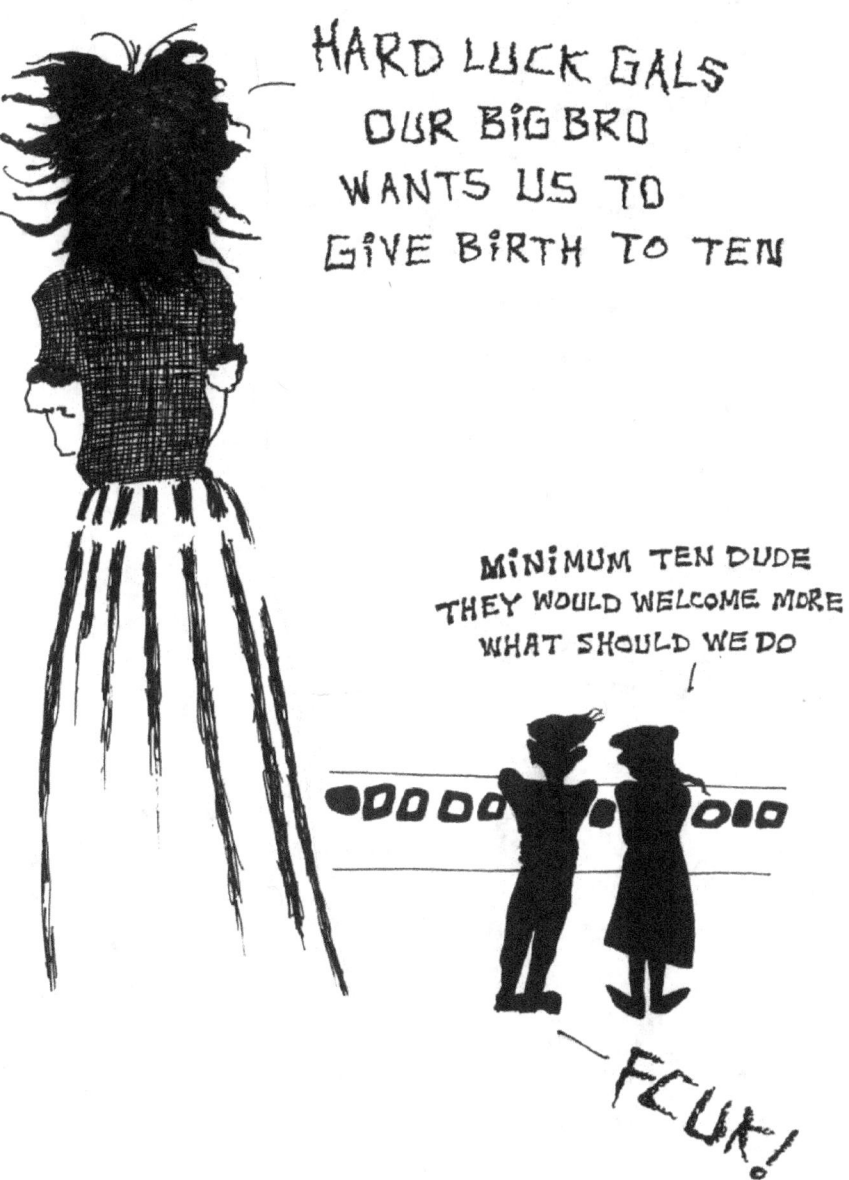

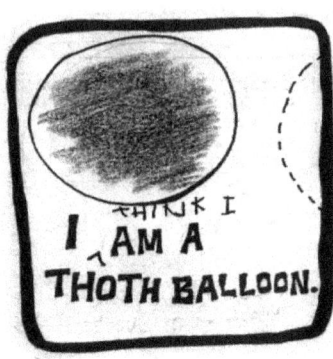
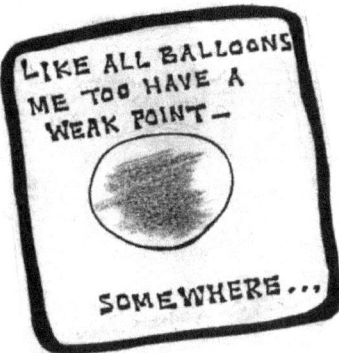
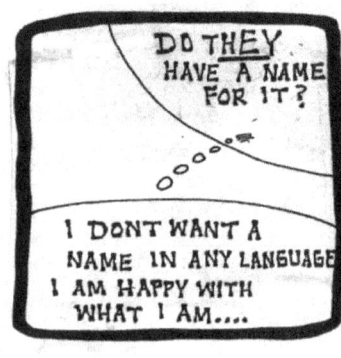
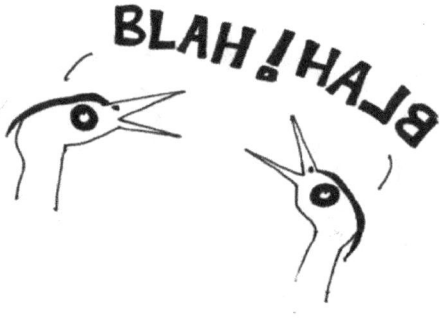

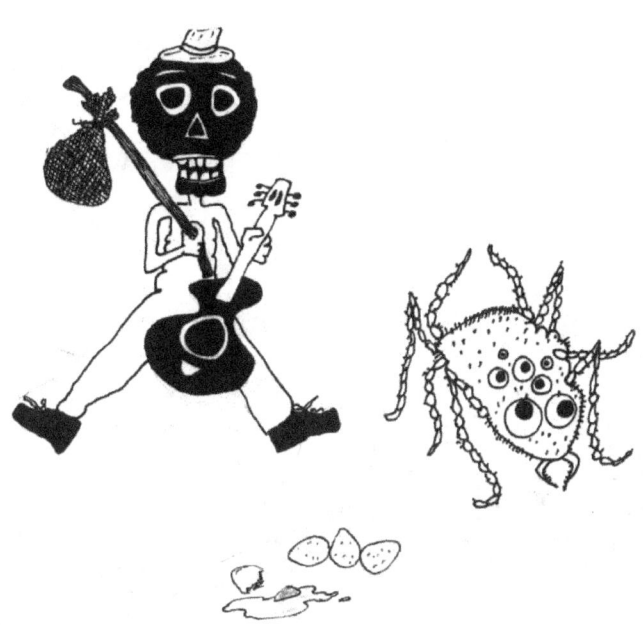

dysaphia
dyslogia
dysosmia
dyspersia
dysmorphia
dyskinesia
dyscalculia
dysarthria
dyschezia
dysphonia
dyscrasia
dyslexia
dysuria
dysphoria

dystocia
dysesthesia
dysrhythmia
dysgraphia
dystonia
dysphasia
dyslipidemia
dysthymia
dysphagia
dysmenorrhea

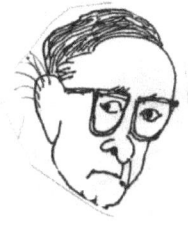

PUT THEM ALL TOG
IN ORDER TO FORM
DYSTOPIA

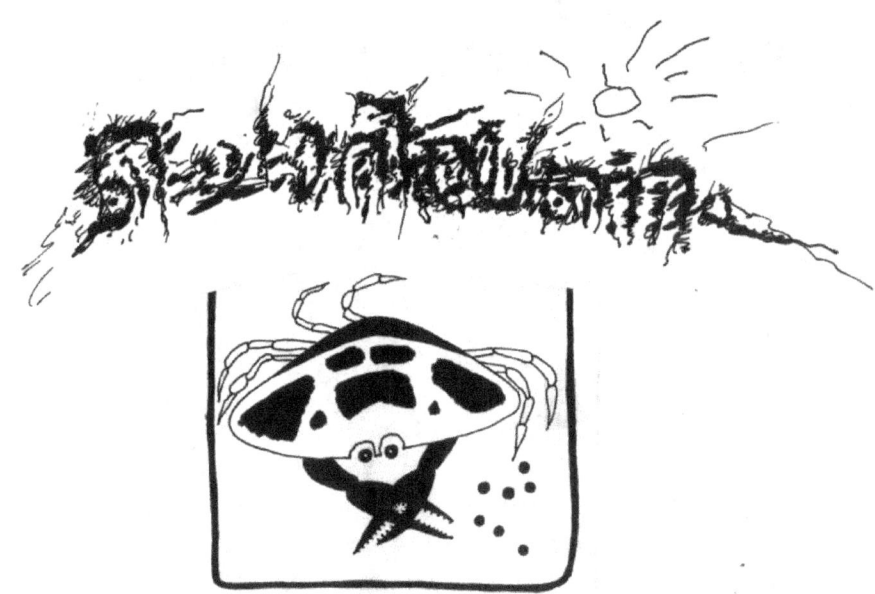

what is undone cant be redone
am i becoming
a lil bit superstitious

FOUL OWL THAT PROWLS

UVULA IS PINK WHATEVER MAYBE THE RACE

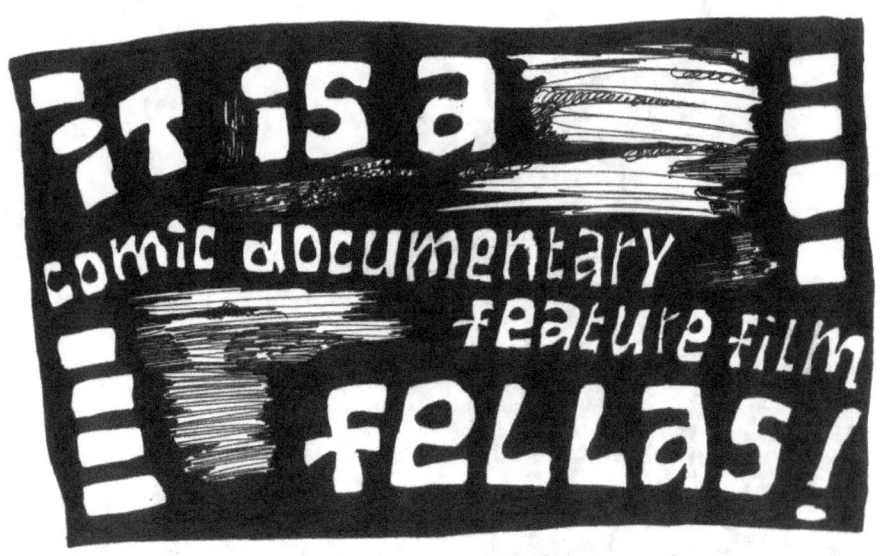

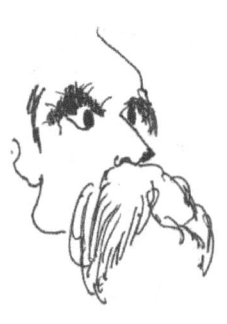
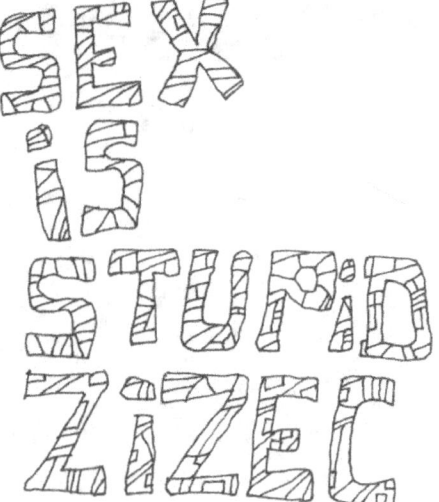

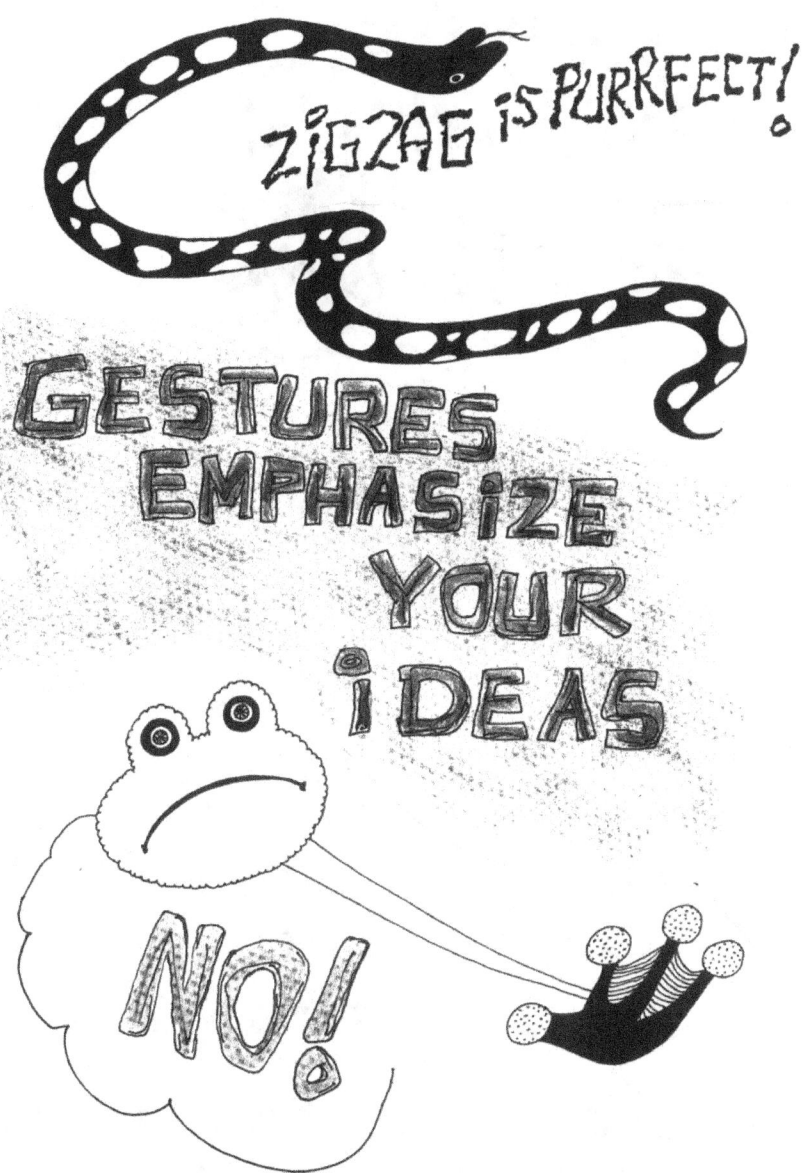

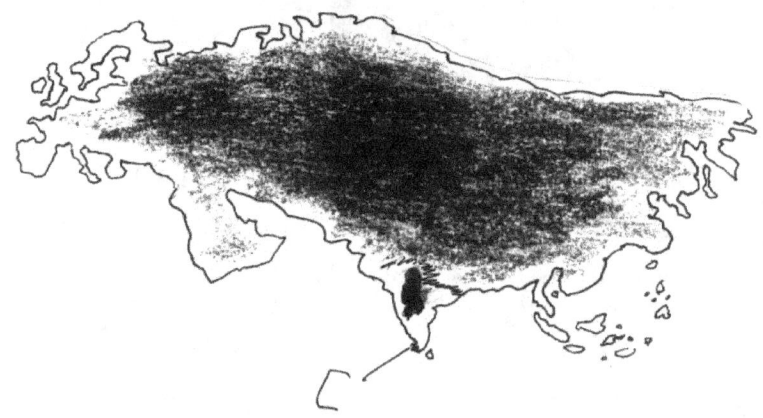

THE SUMMIT TAKES PLACE
OR FALLS OUT
AT SPOT C

THE APOLOGY OF A MAP SHOWN ABOVE
IS A ROUGH SKETCH DERIVED
FROM MEMORY PLEASE BEAR WITH ME

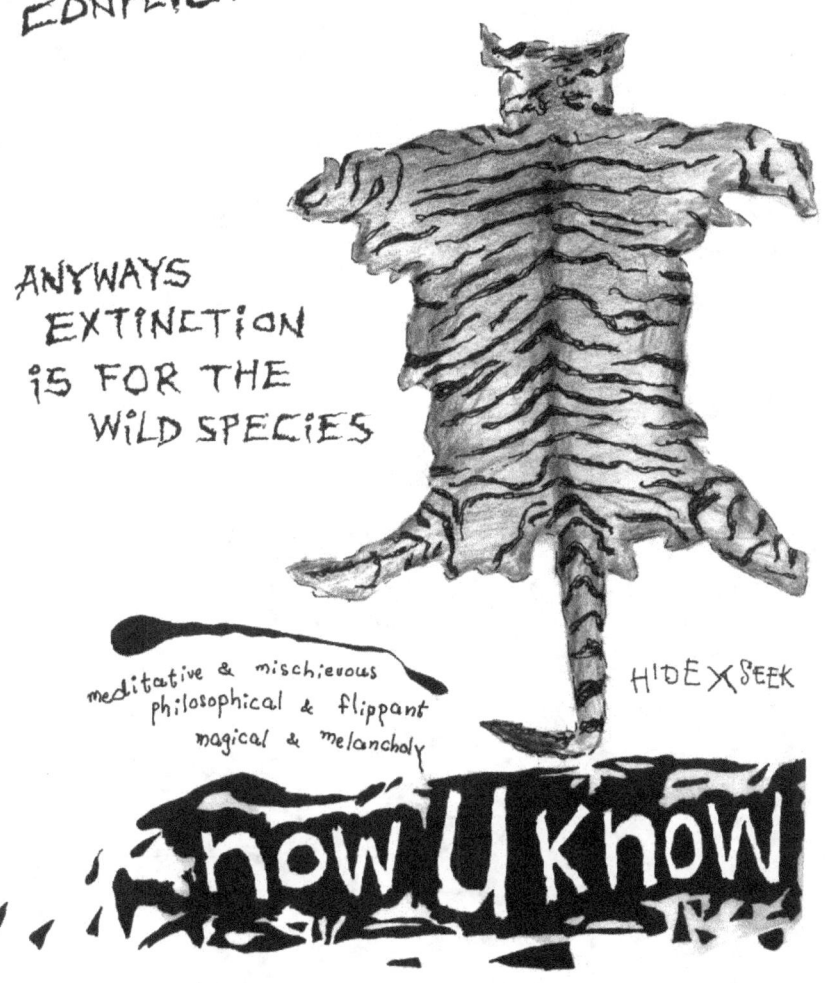

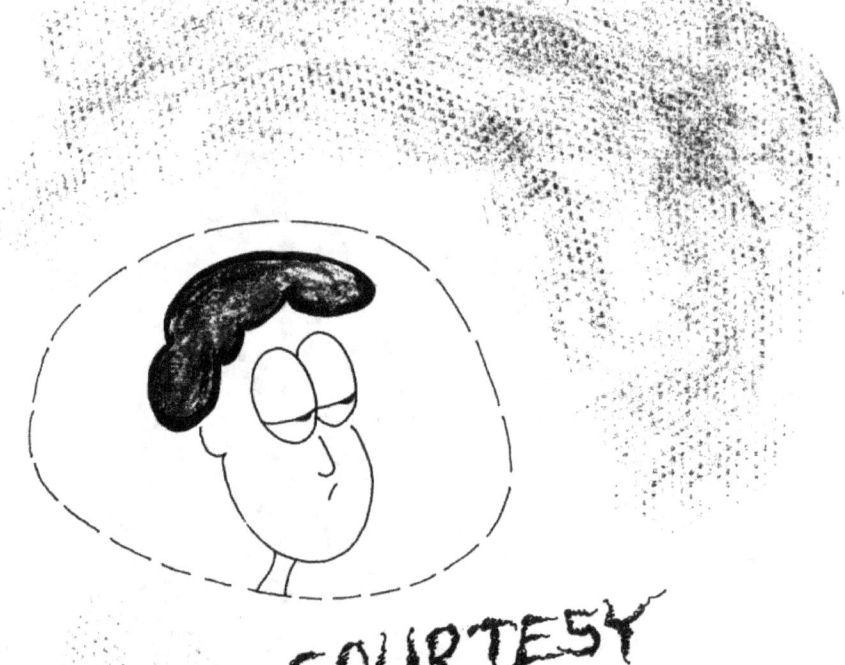
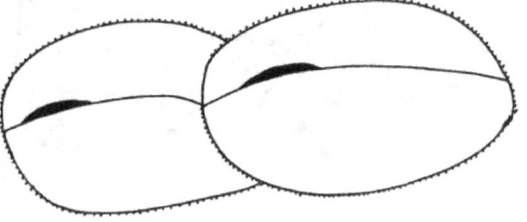

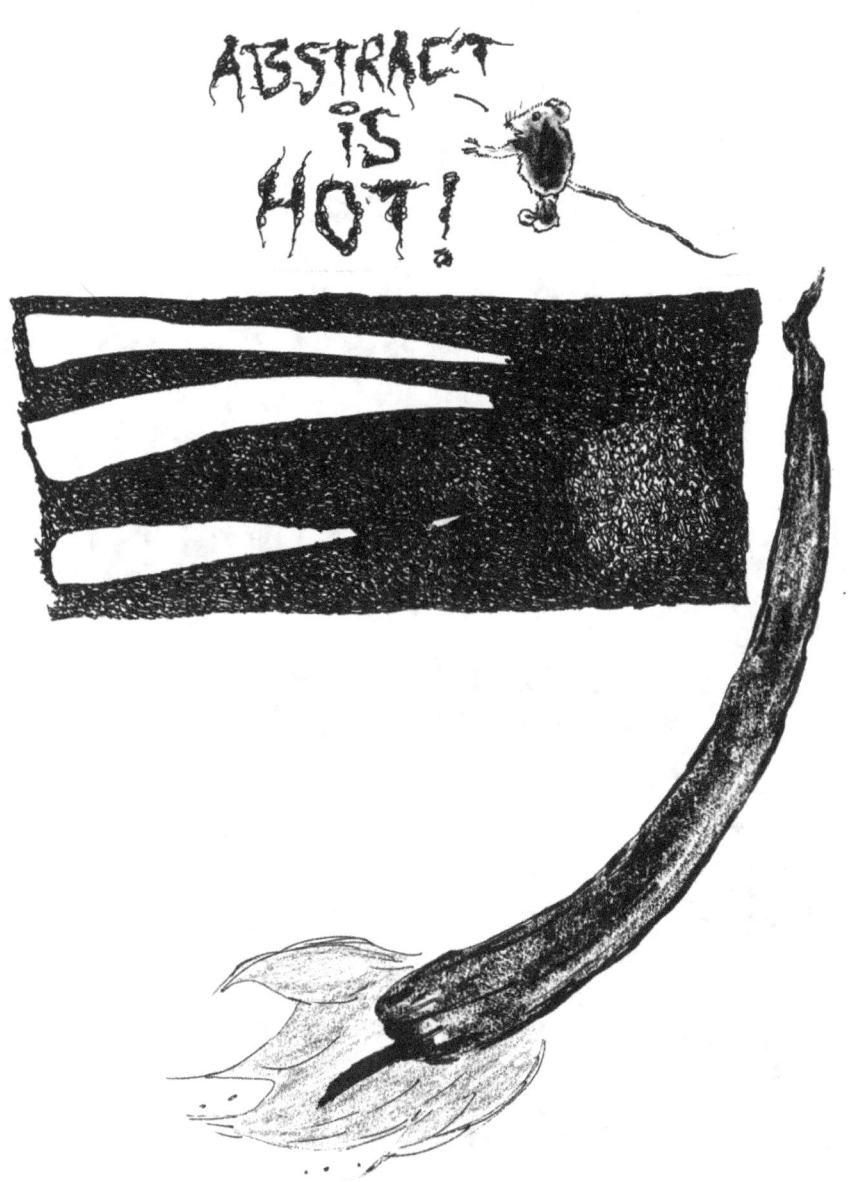

WHaT DOES iT MEaN

TO GET FaNCY

WiTH AN ELEPHANT

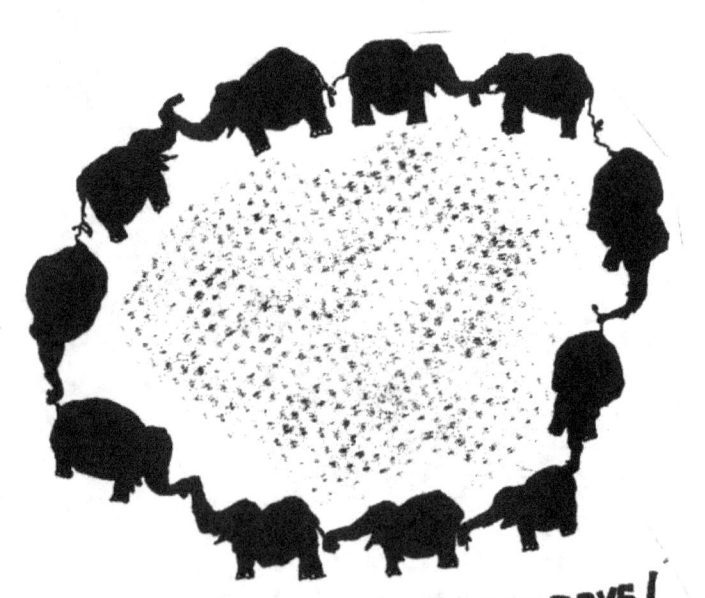

OH, THOSE MERRY-GO-ROUND DaYS!

spectators shout slogans
at me like
stop your pseudo art
to which i pay no heed

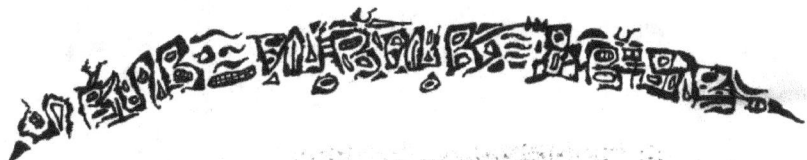

I WOULD LIKE TO DIE AN AMATEUR

UNBEKNOWNST TO US

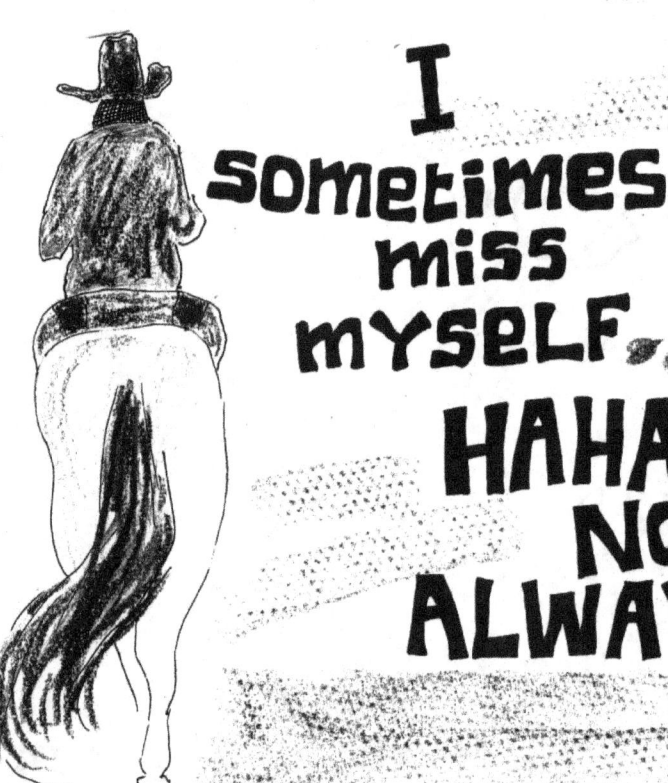

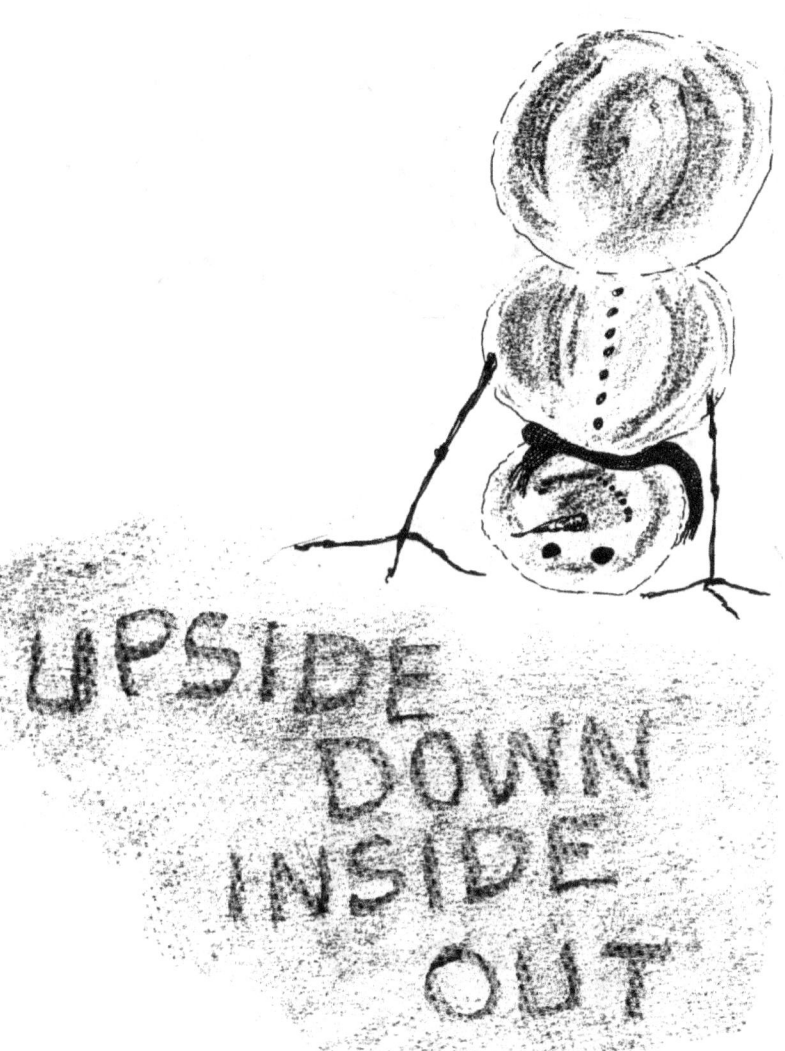

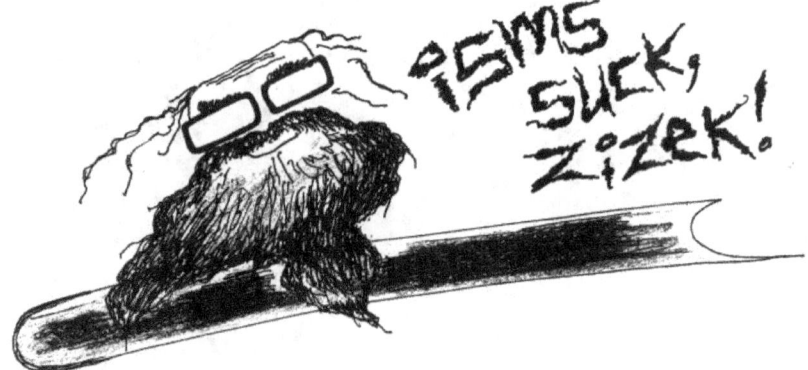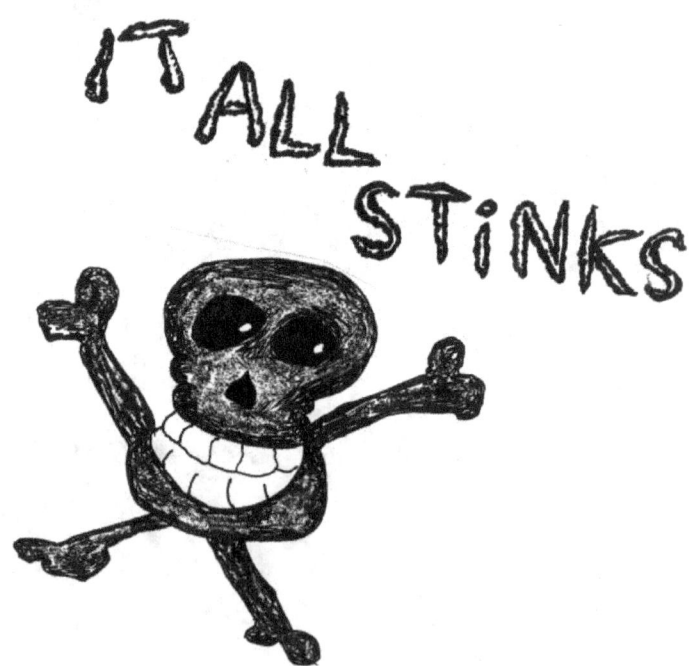

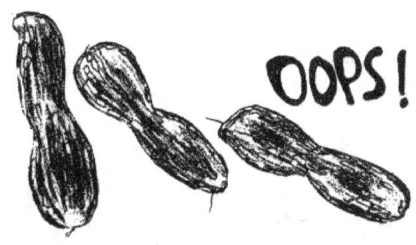

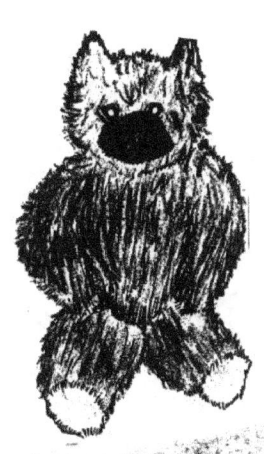

ORIGINALLY MEANING NUTS!

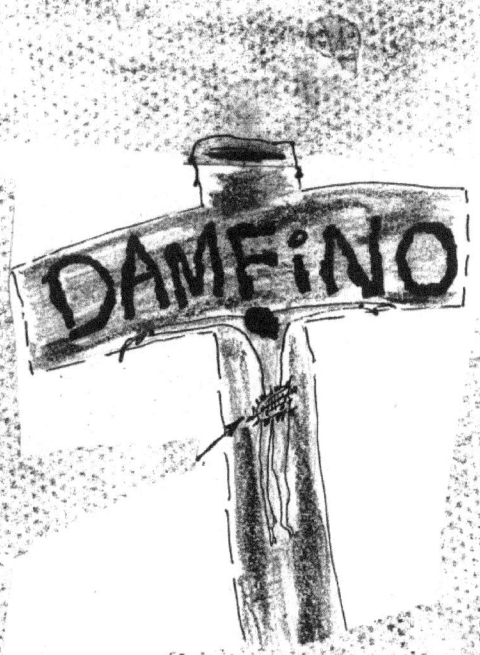

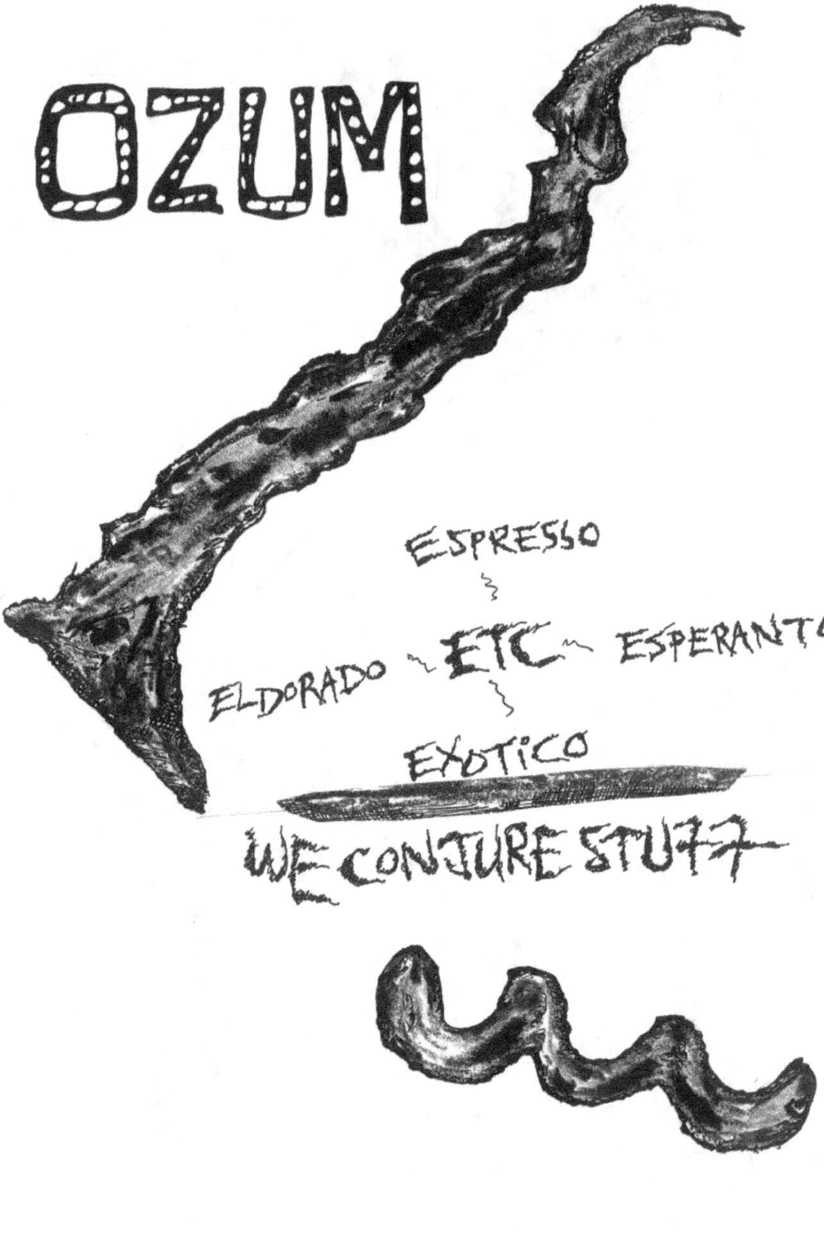

OZUM

ESPRESSO

ELDORADO ~ ETC ~ ESPERANTO

EXOTICO

WE CONJURE STUFF

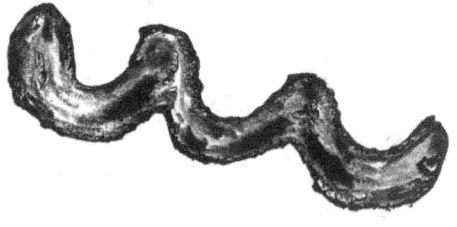

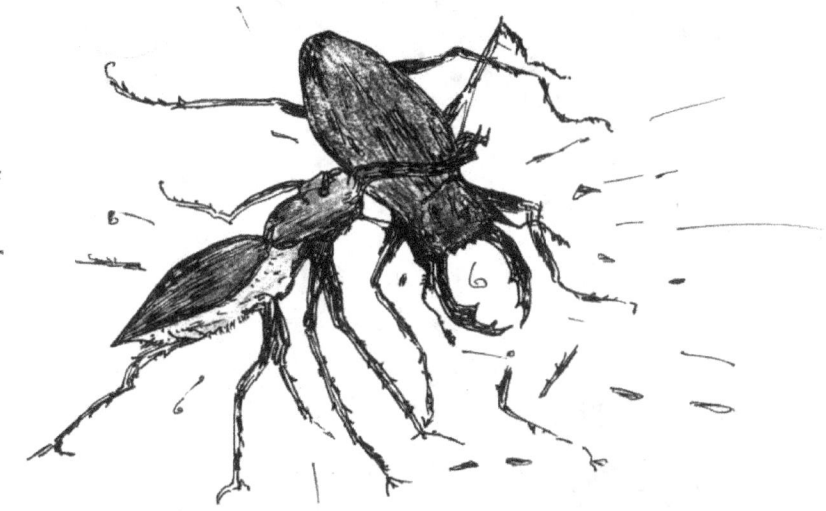

ORGASM IS OVER
INTERSEXUALITY: DOES A TEXT EXIST?

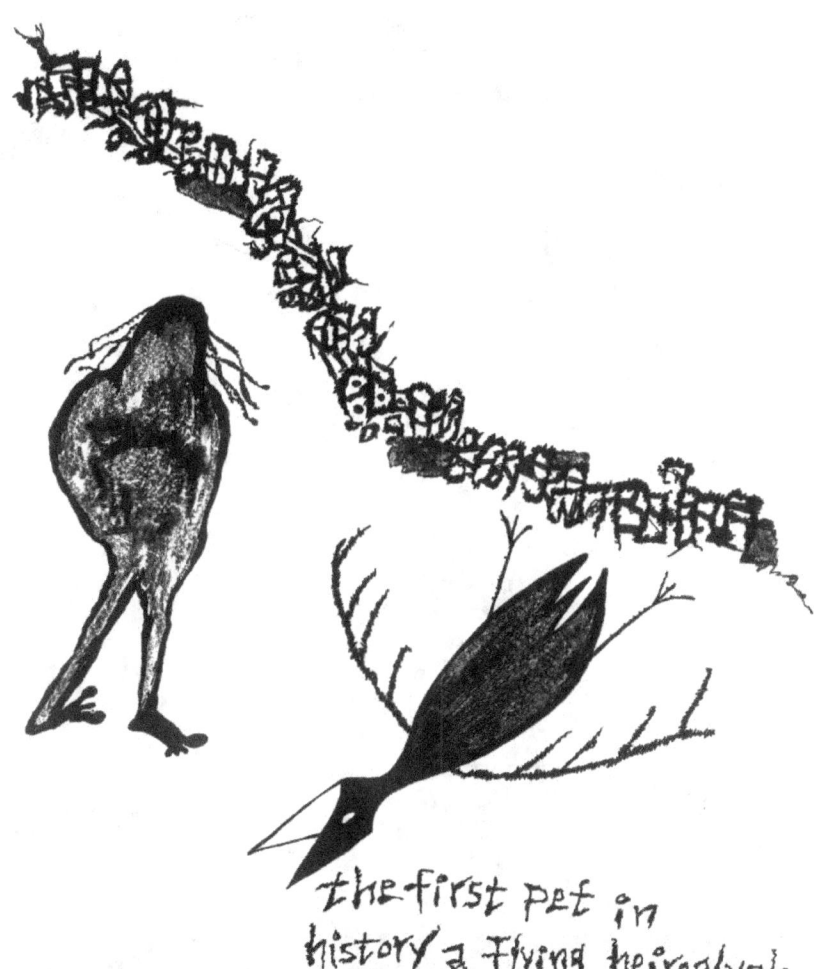

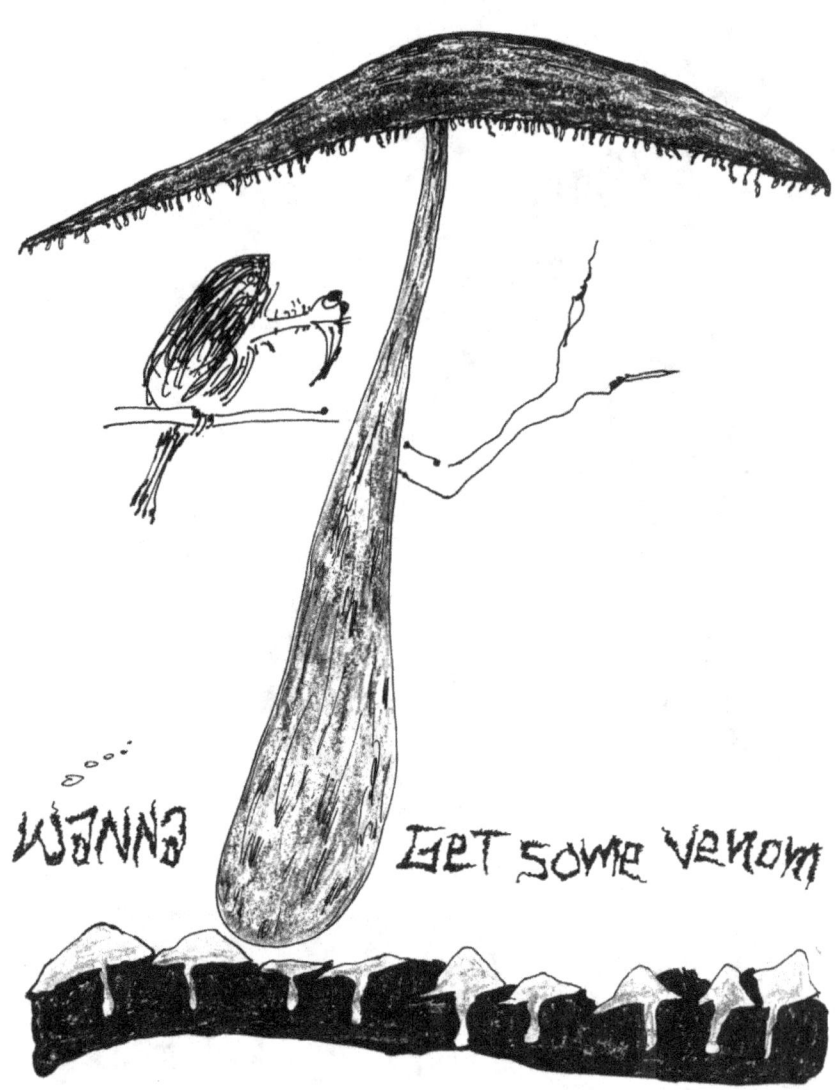

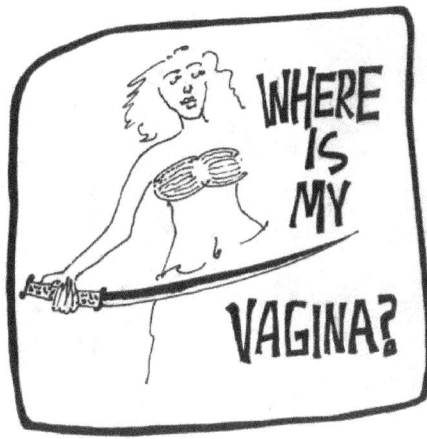

venom always was a
a love potion

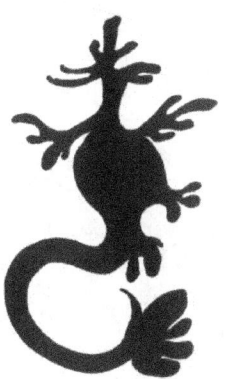

vagina originally means ___

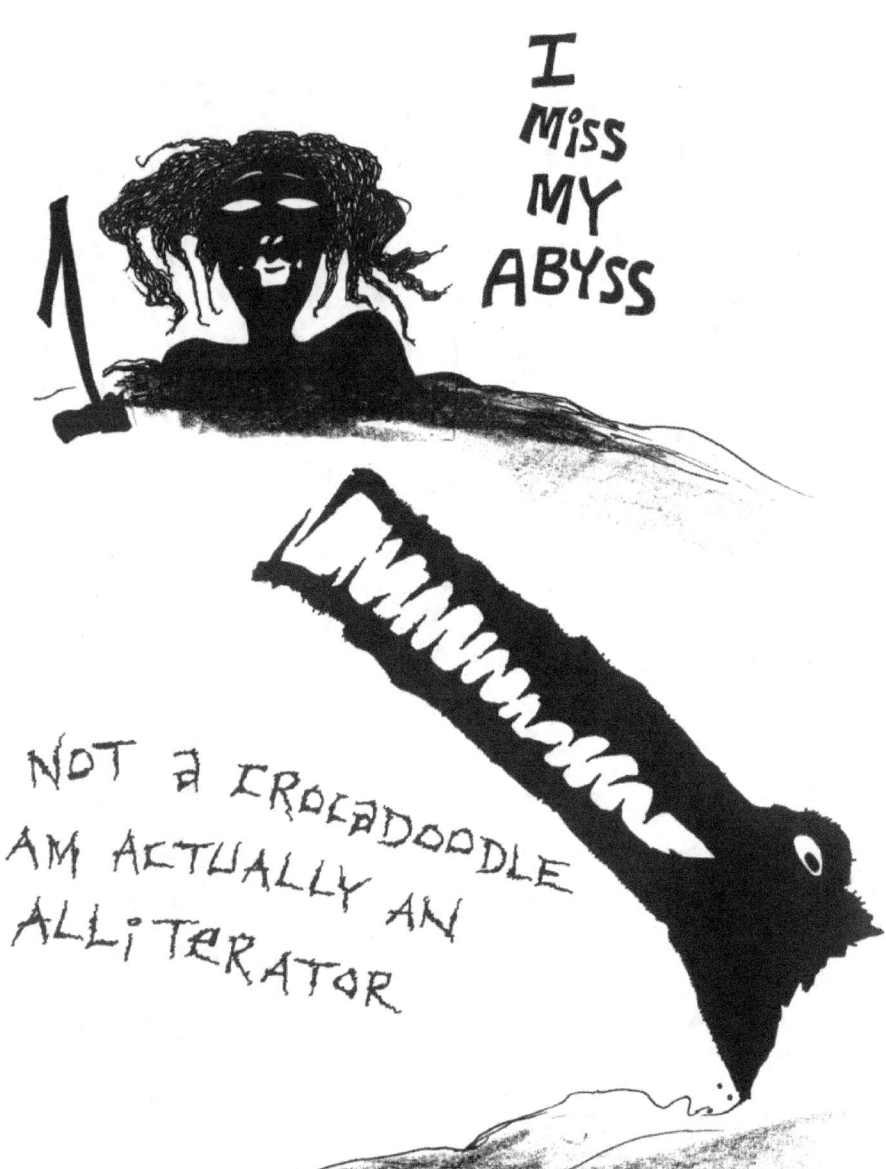

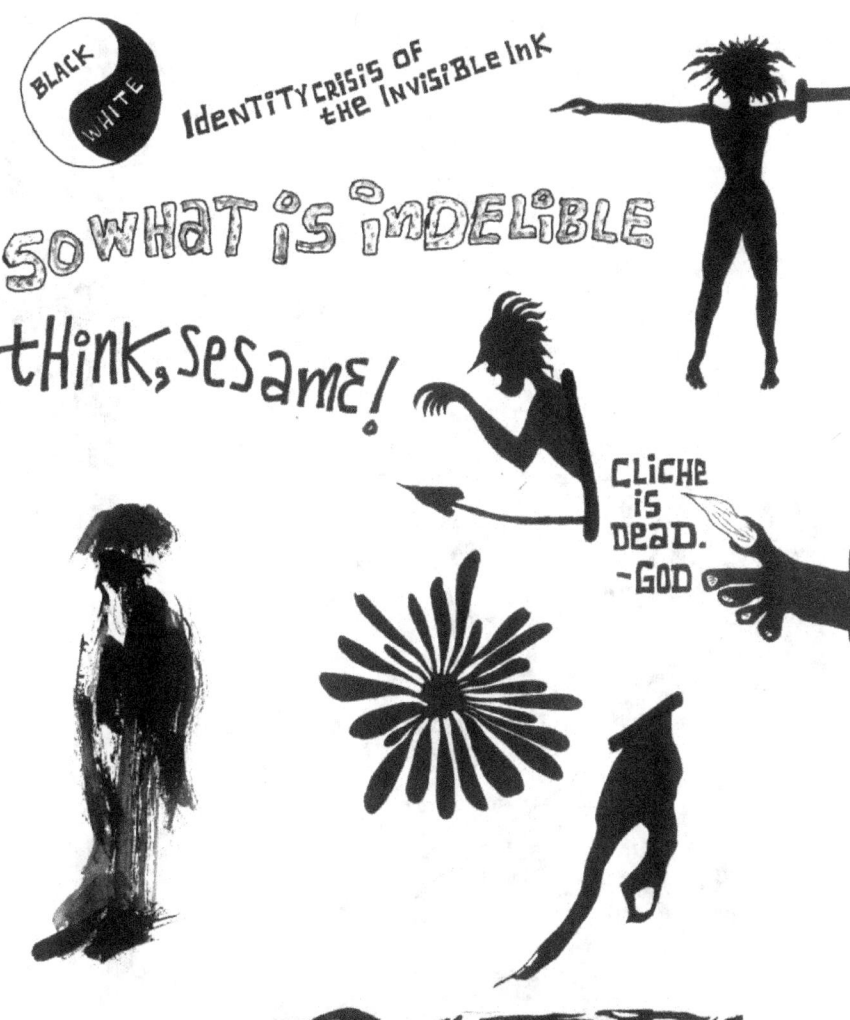

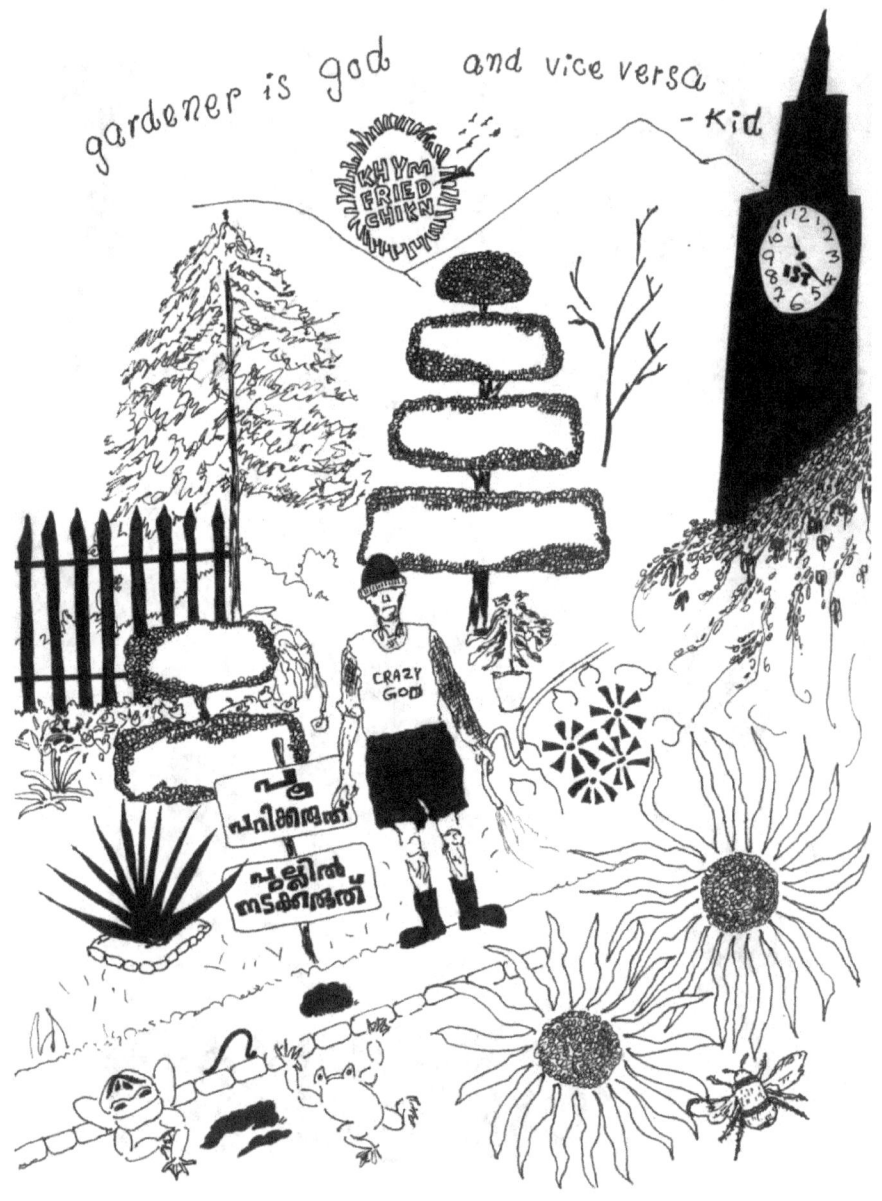

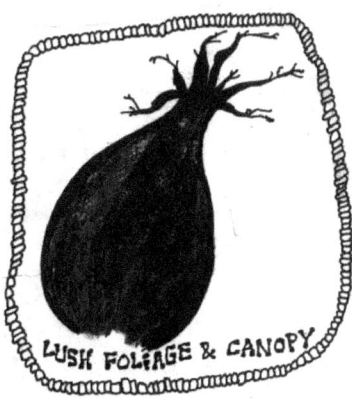
LUSH FOLIAGE & CANOPY

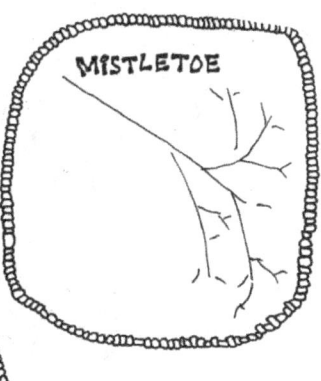
MISTLETOE

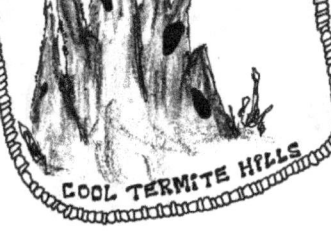
COOL TERMITE HILLS

the perfect garden

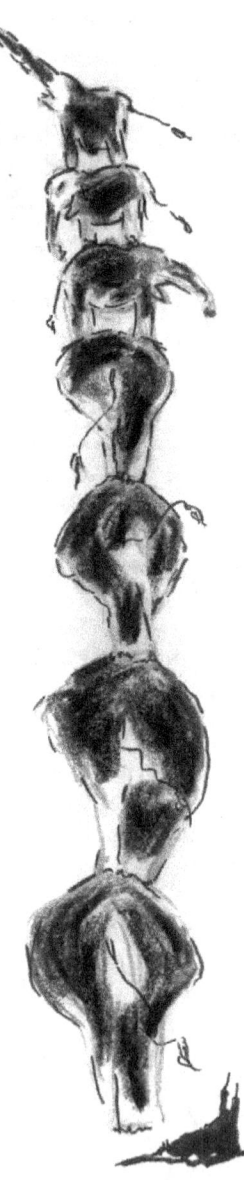

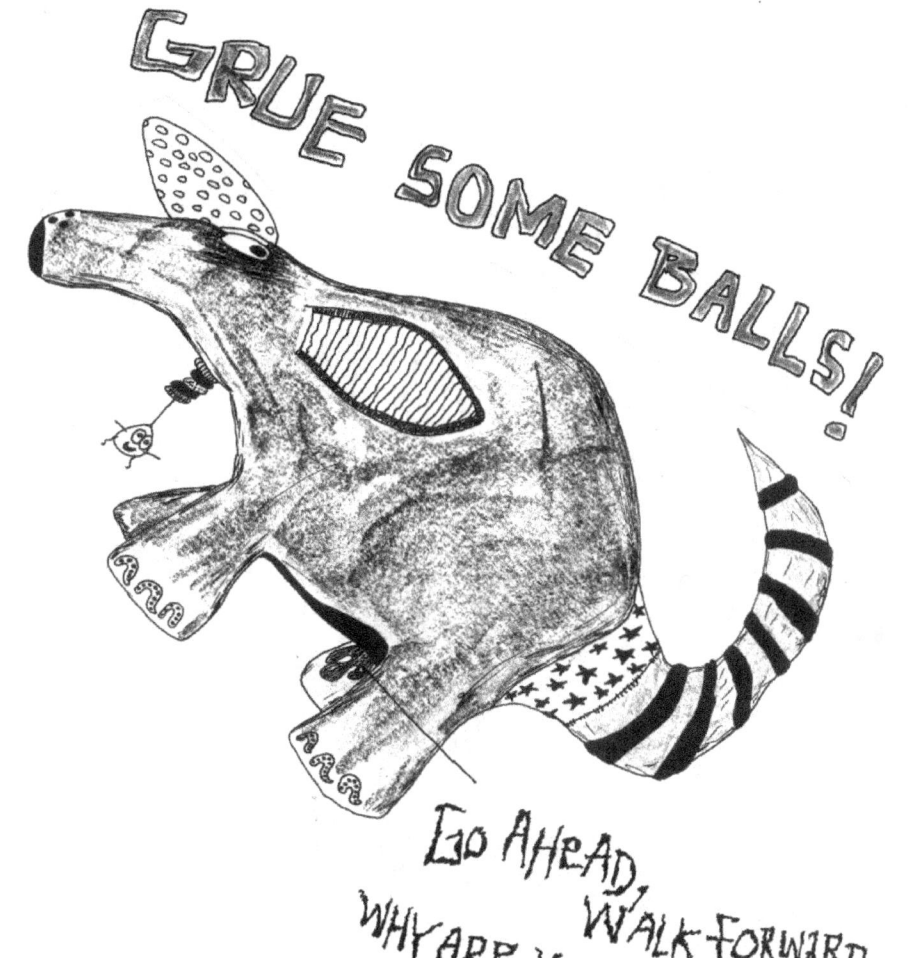

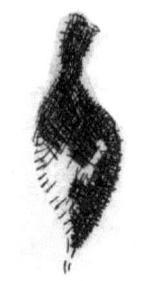
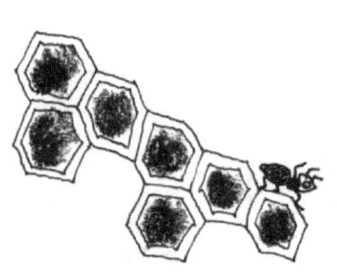

SHE CALLS ME HONEY

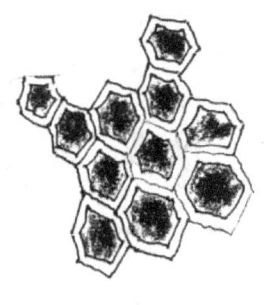

WHILE i SERENADE

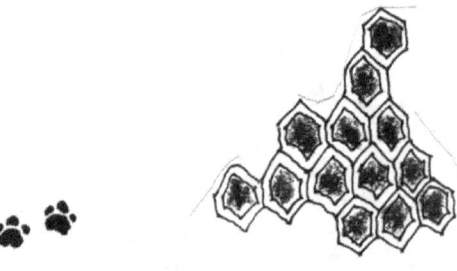

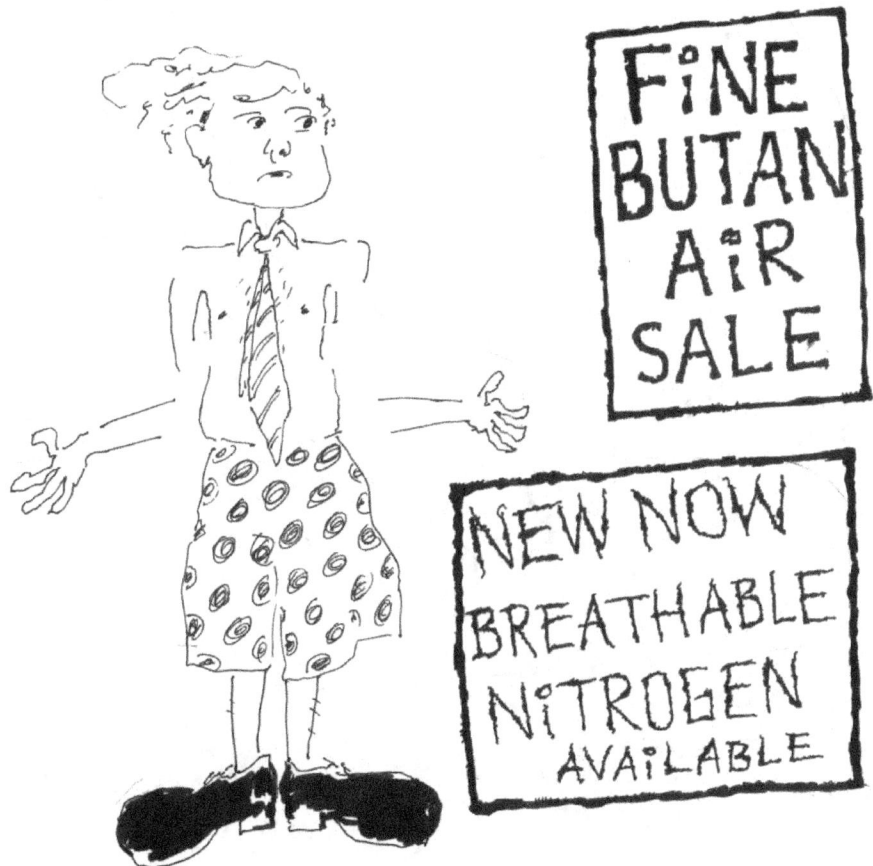

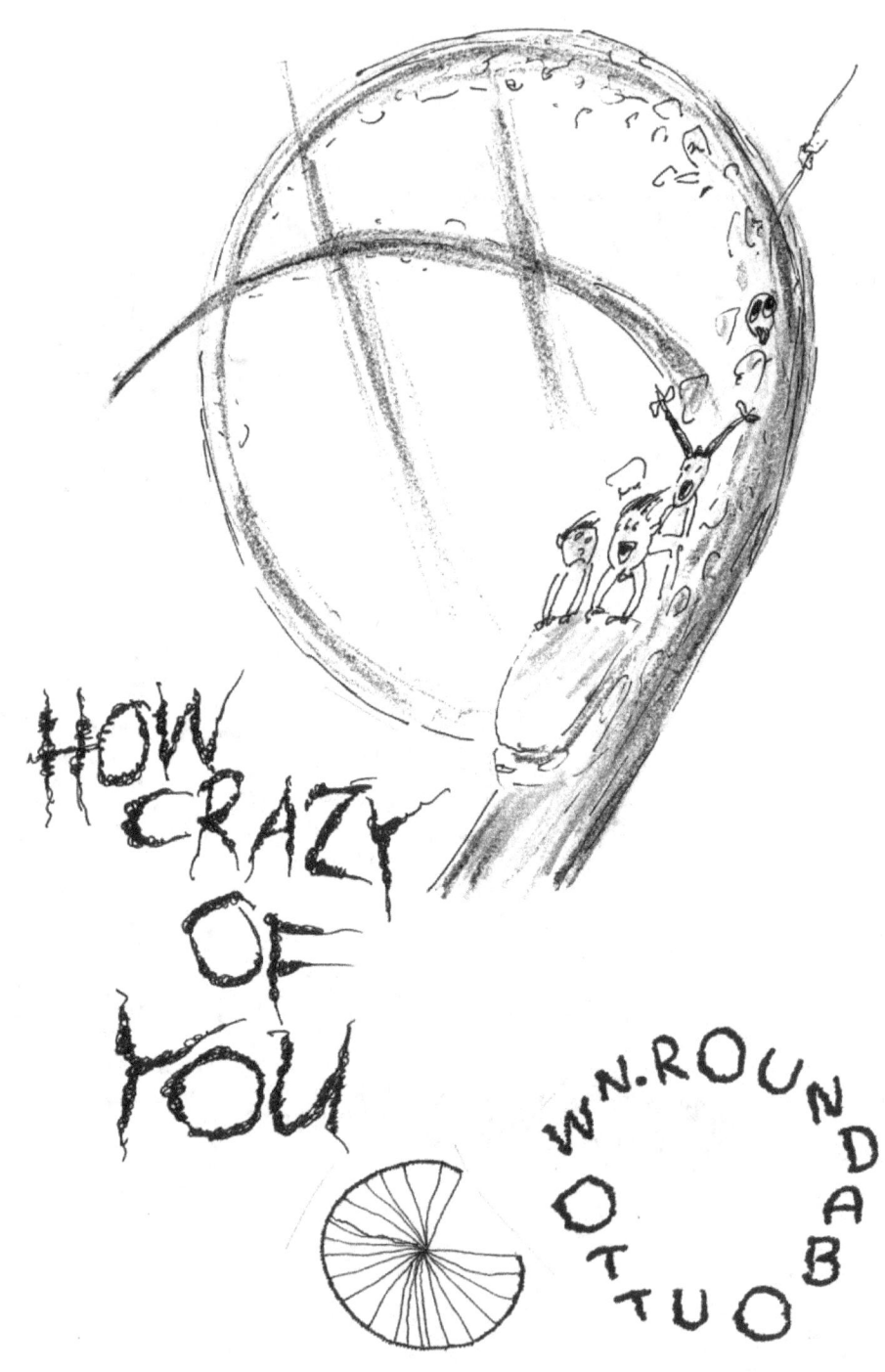

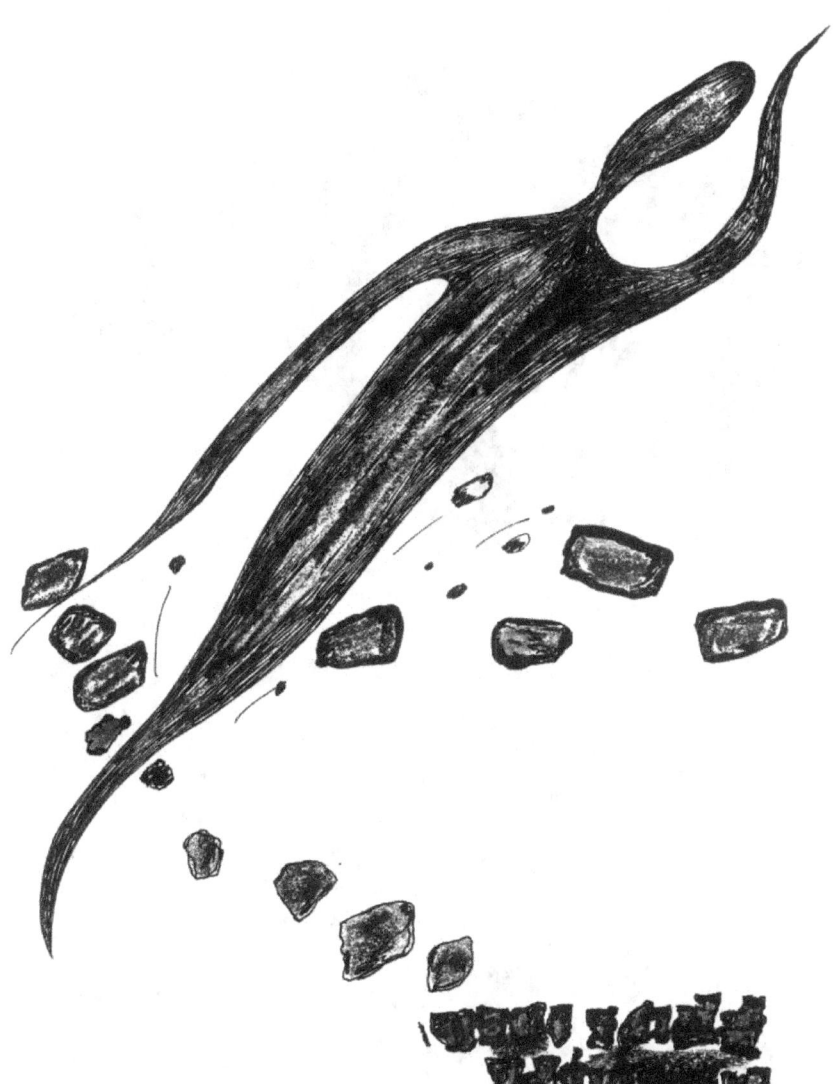

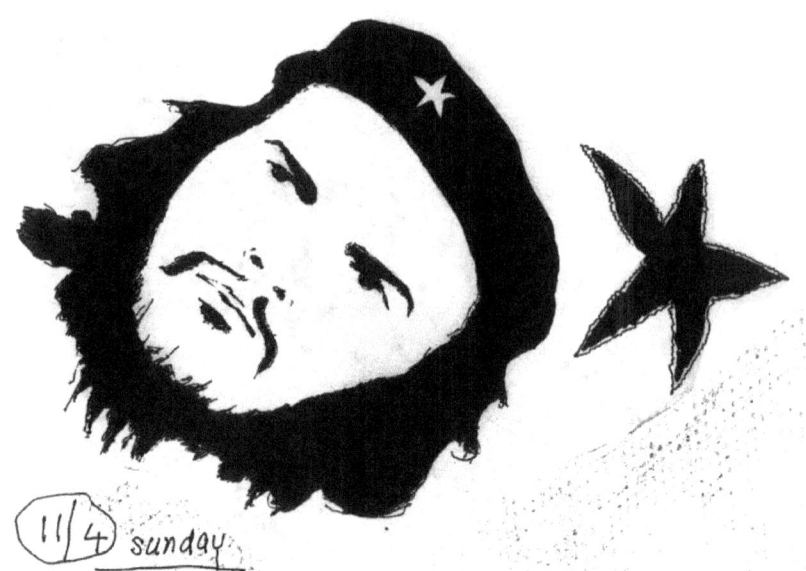

11/4 sunday

- Guevarism.
- Hail Che / Long Live Revolution.
- Guerilla warfare, foco etc.
- El Che Guevara (1928-1967).
- 'I am Che. Dont kill me. I have failed.'
- The classic portrait — the most reproduced pic in the history of photography.
- CHE = HEY in spanish.
- Ernesto Guevara de la Serna.
- 'the quintessential postmodern icon signifying anything to anyone and everything to everyone.'
- Suffered from severe asthma.
- Viva Che / buried alive.

When you know
there are some
popular comic strips
in which they portray
your fav hero che
as a bloody
vampire like nosferatu

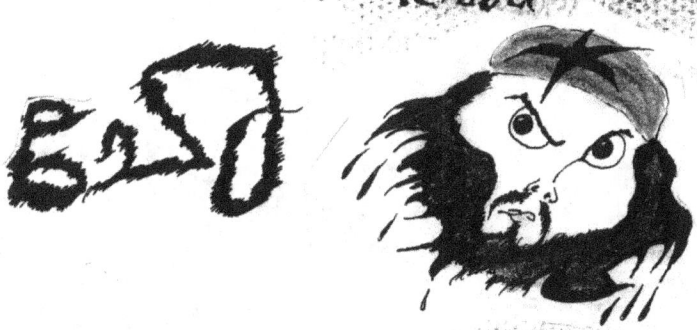

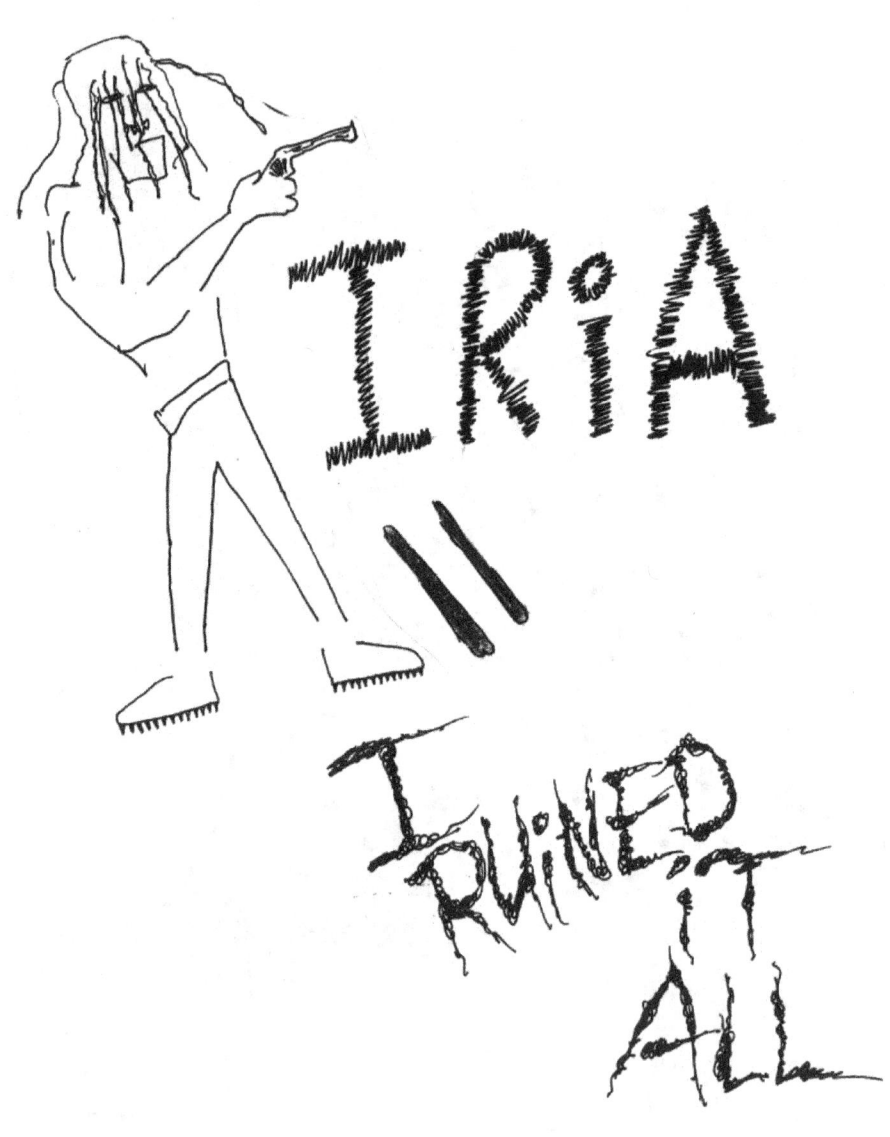

CALLIGRAPHY AND WHATNOT

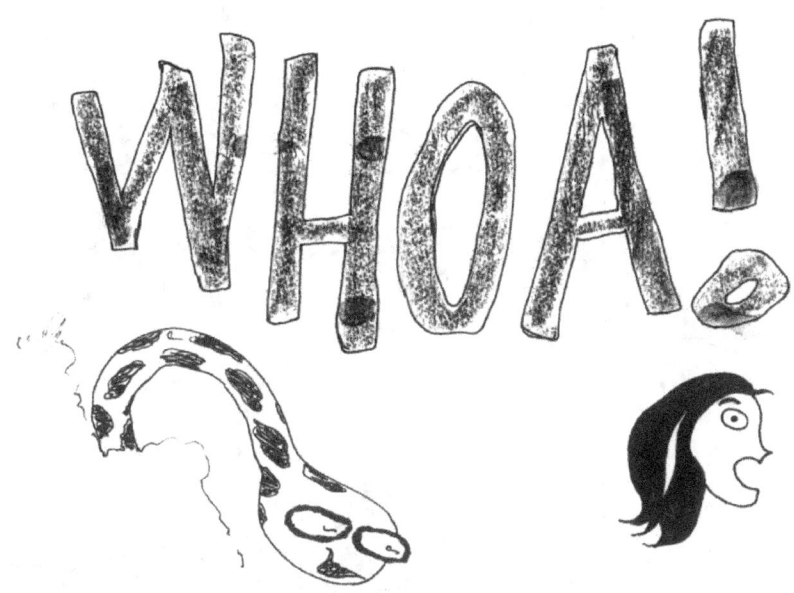

WHAT IS AMUSING IS THAT FOLKS DO NOT FIND THIS BOOK TITLE AWESOME

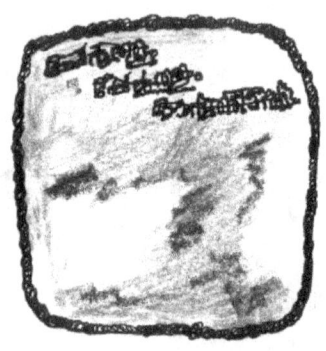

WE ONLY HAVE M!X3D F33LiNG?

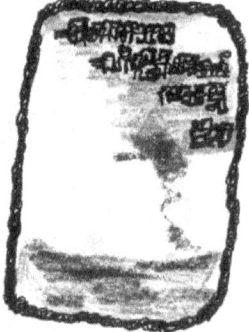
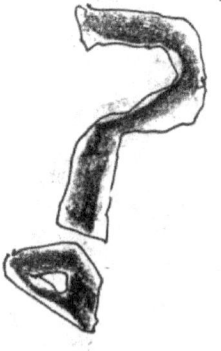
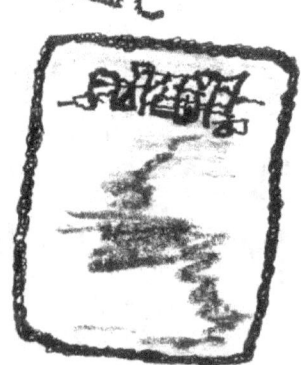

what is meant by LIBIDO

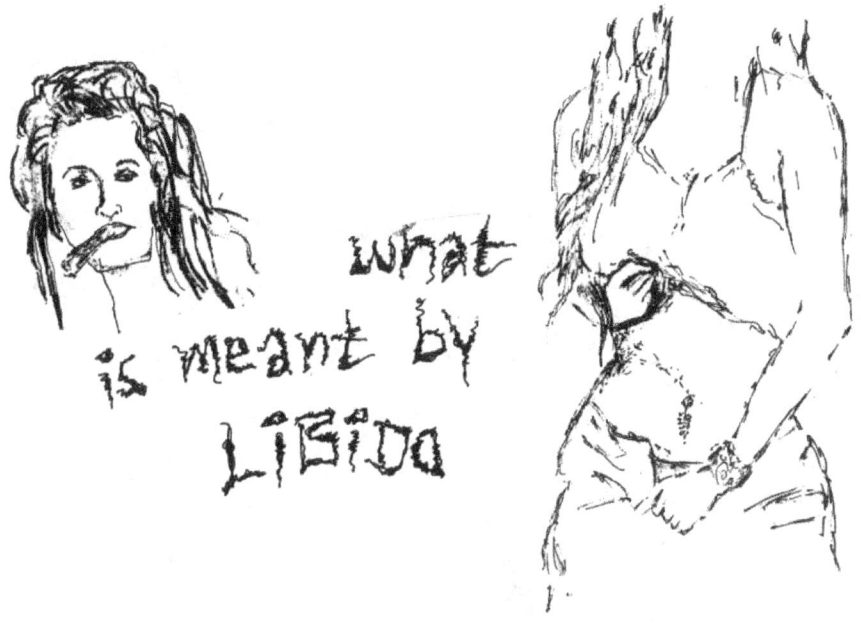

does it have a history too

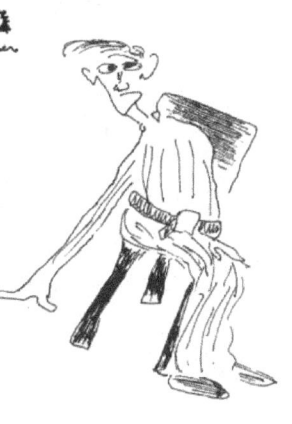

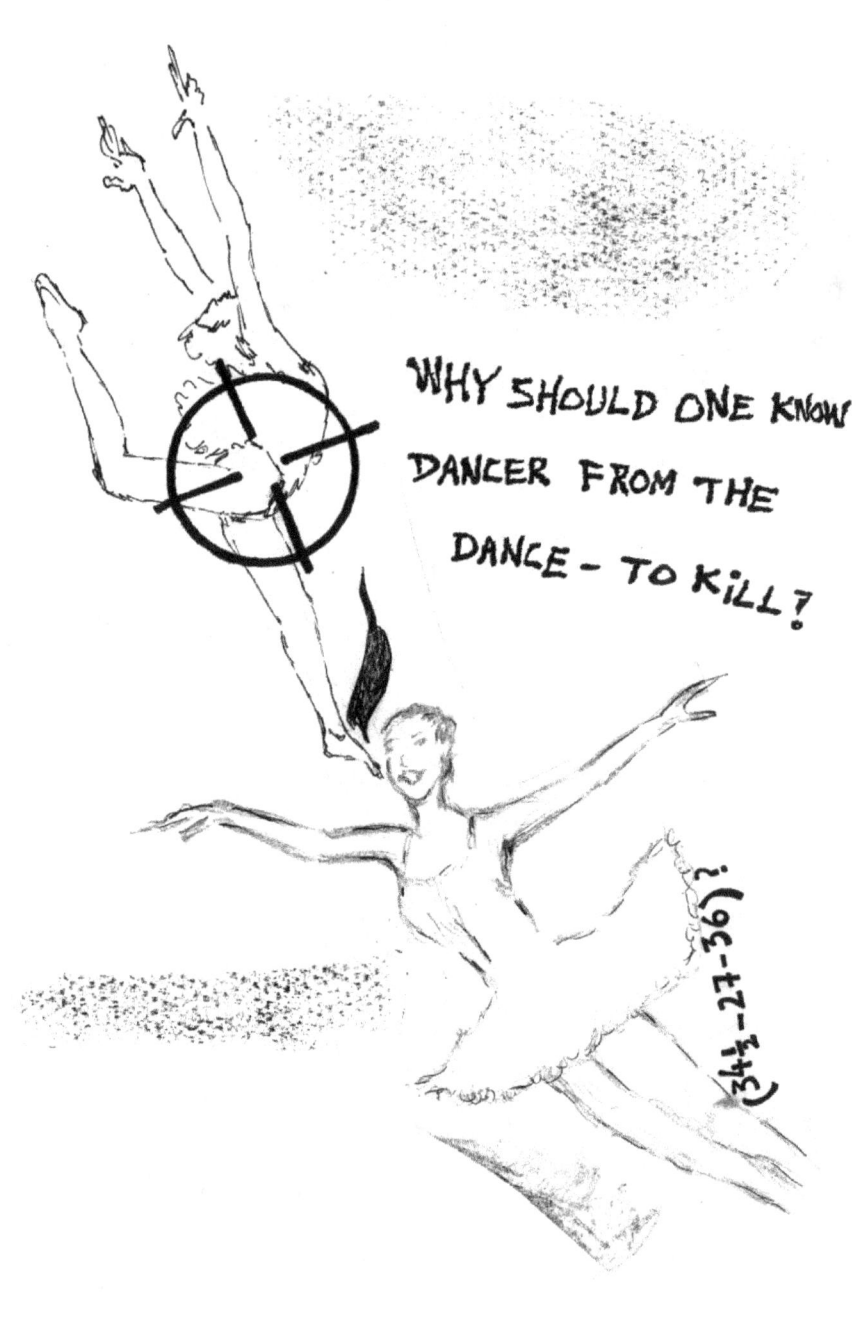

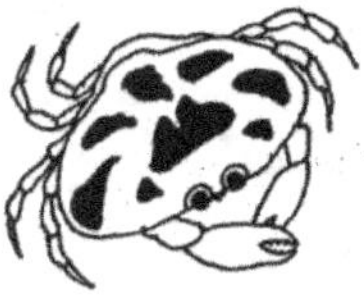

DO TABUS TEMPT YOU,

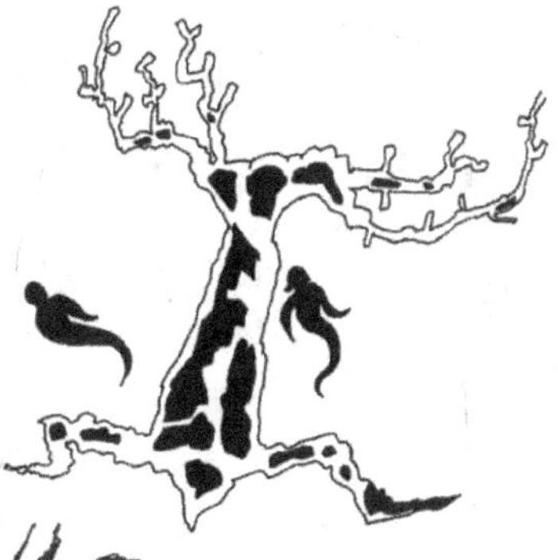

OH, HOW i WOULD LOVE TO

SUCCUMB!

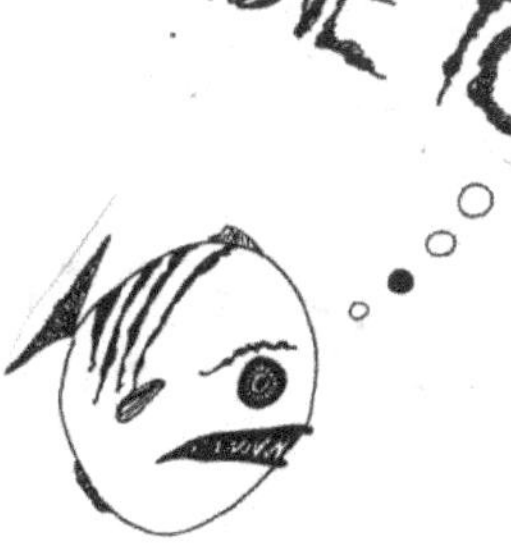

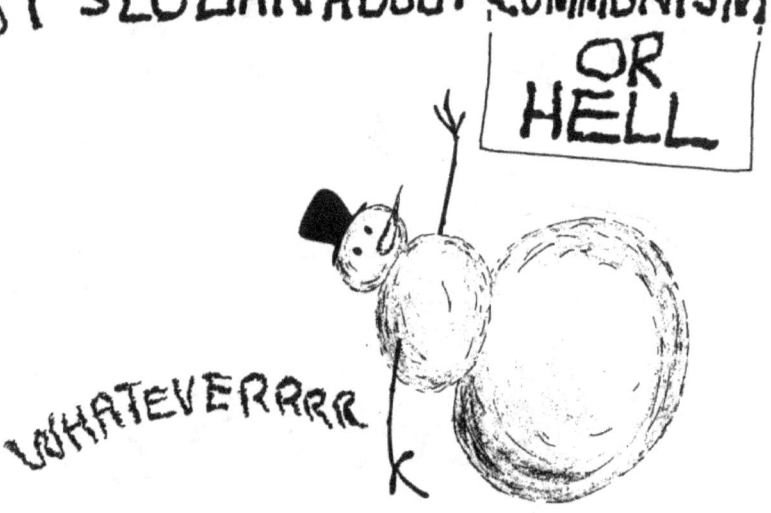

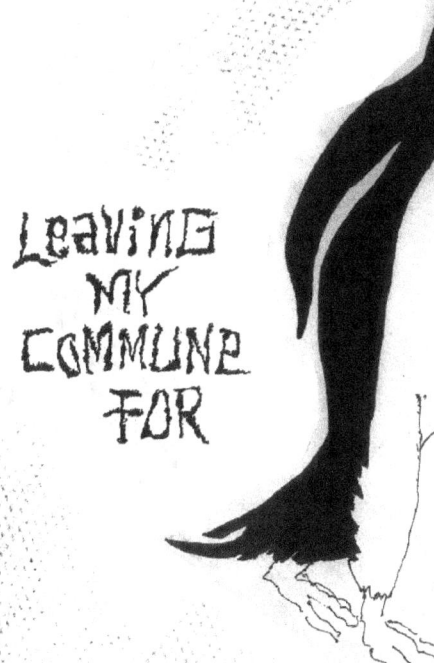

BYGONE

LEAVING MY COMMUNE FOR

BLUEBLOOD BUTTERFLY BUREAUCRAT BOWTIE

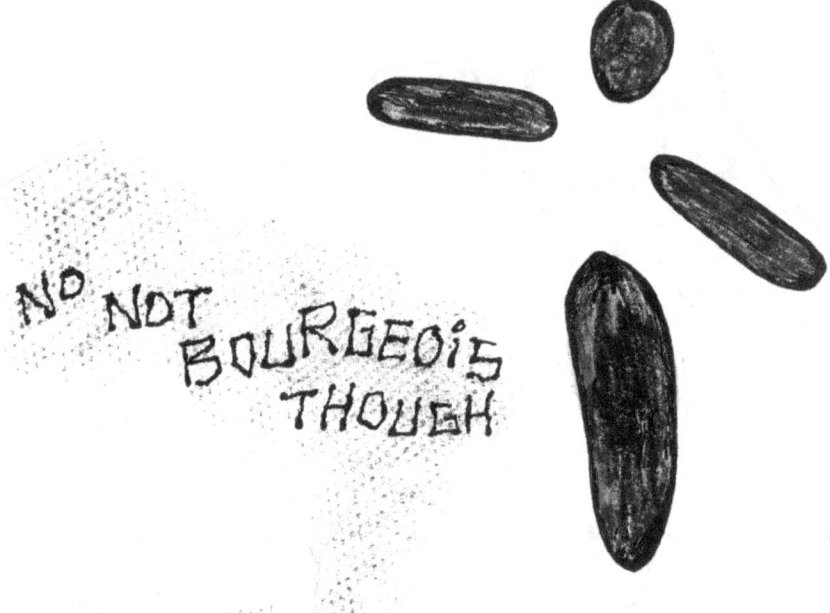

NO NOT BOURGEOIS THOUGH

nota bene:
I aint Petty, mediocre and Lukewarm.

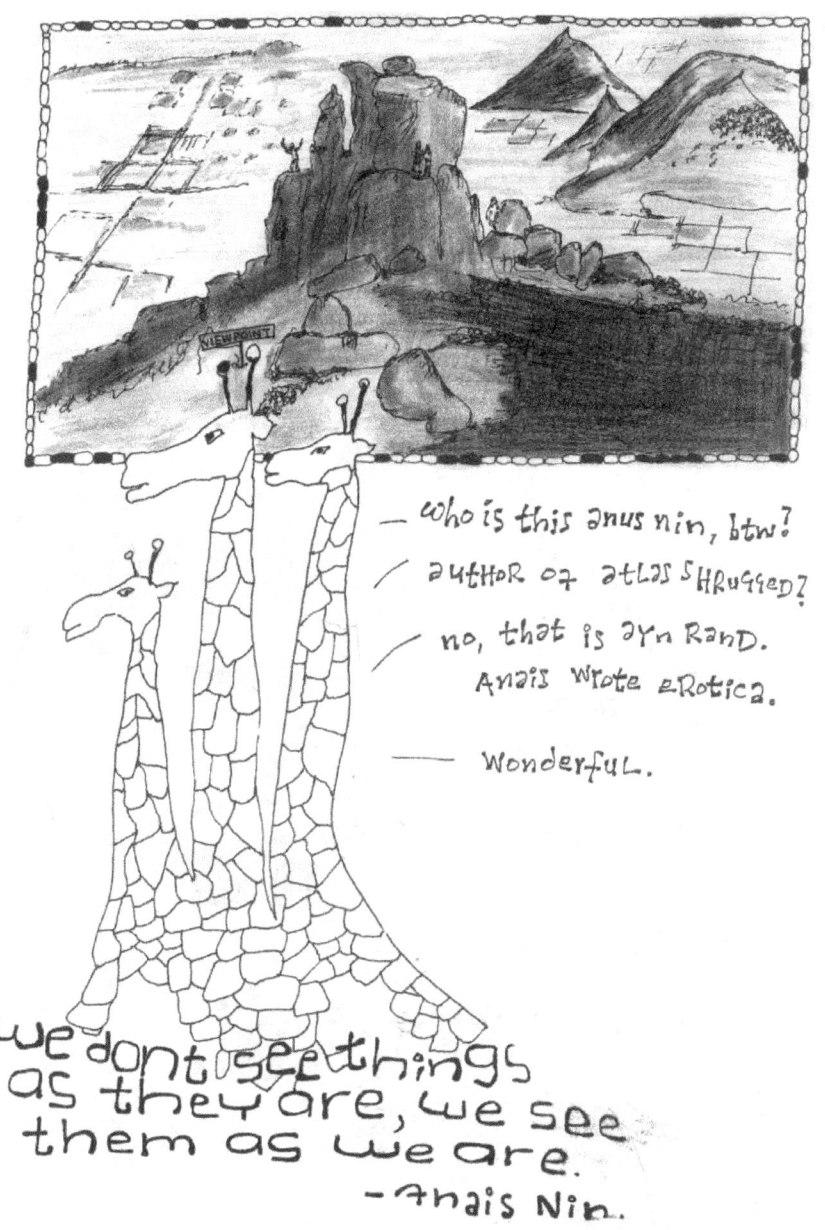

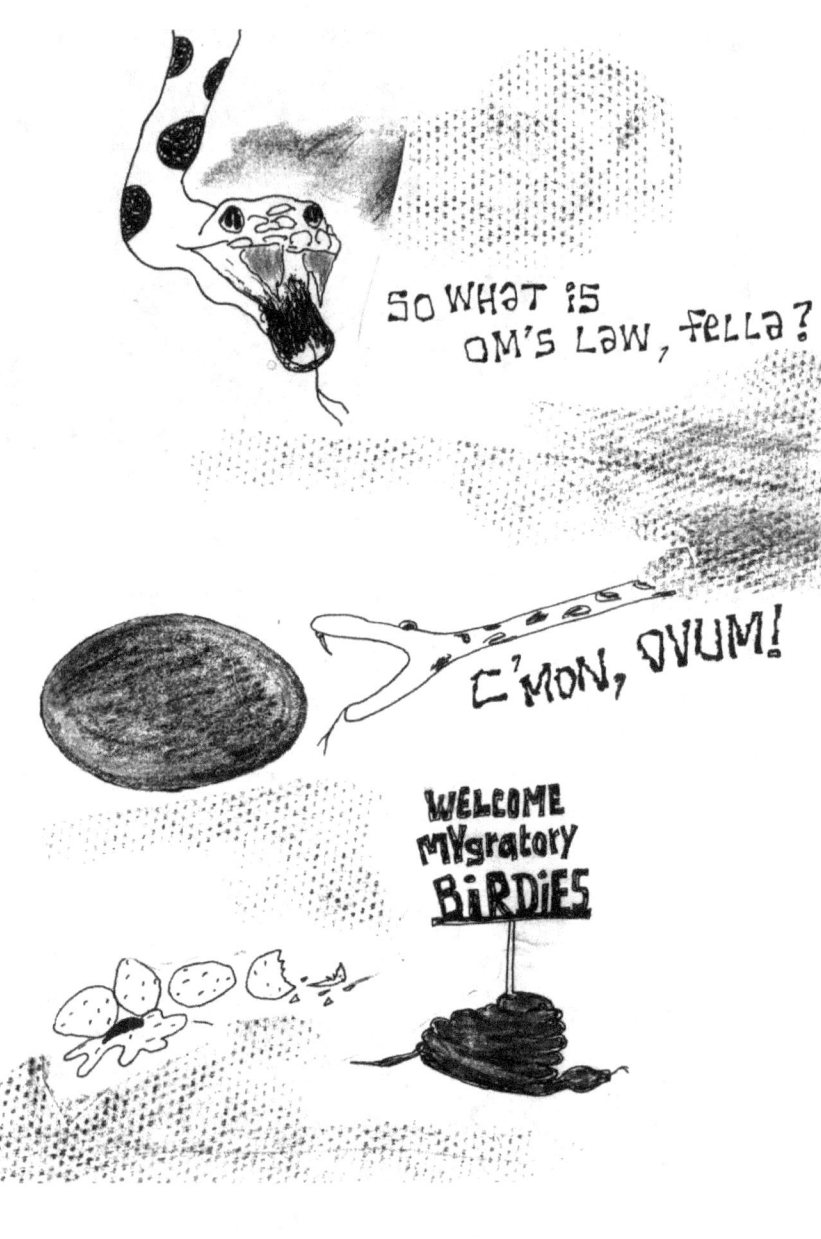

If a theory somersaults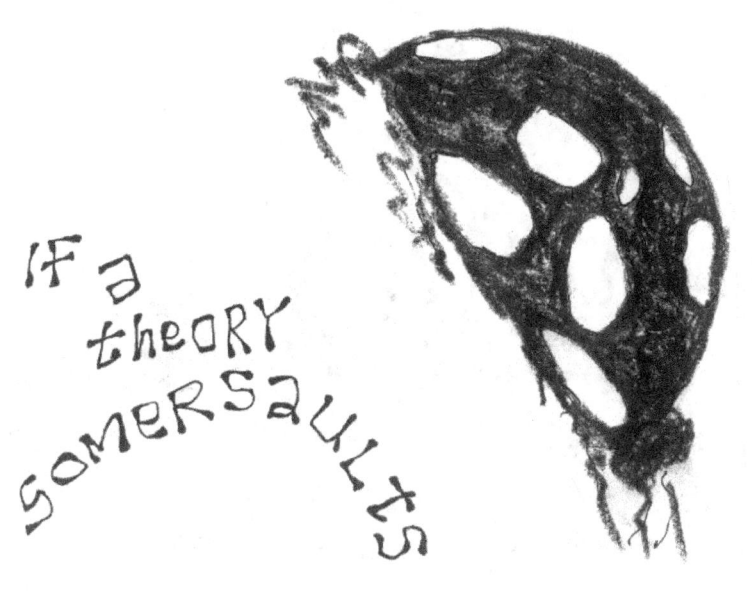

what happens to 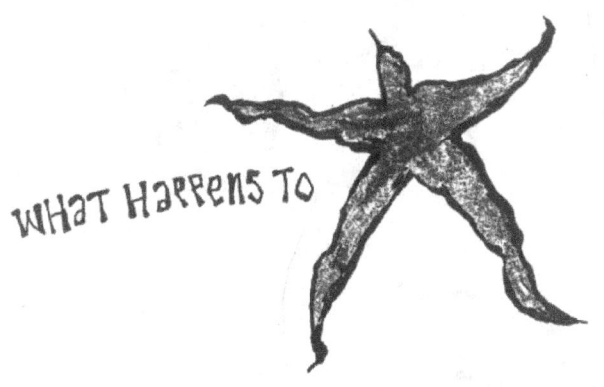 the original hypothesis

and all of them enthusiasts, obscurantists and ventriloquists

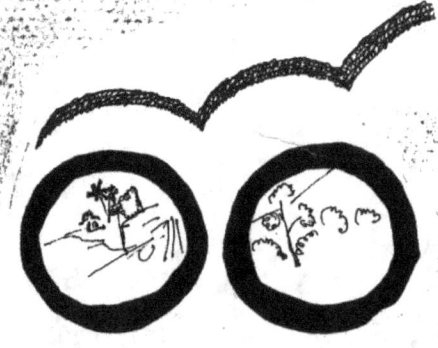

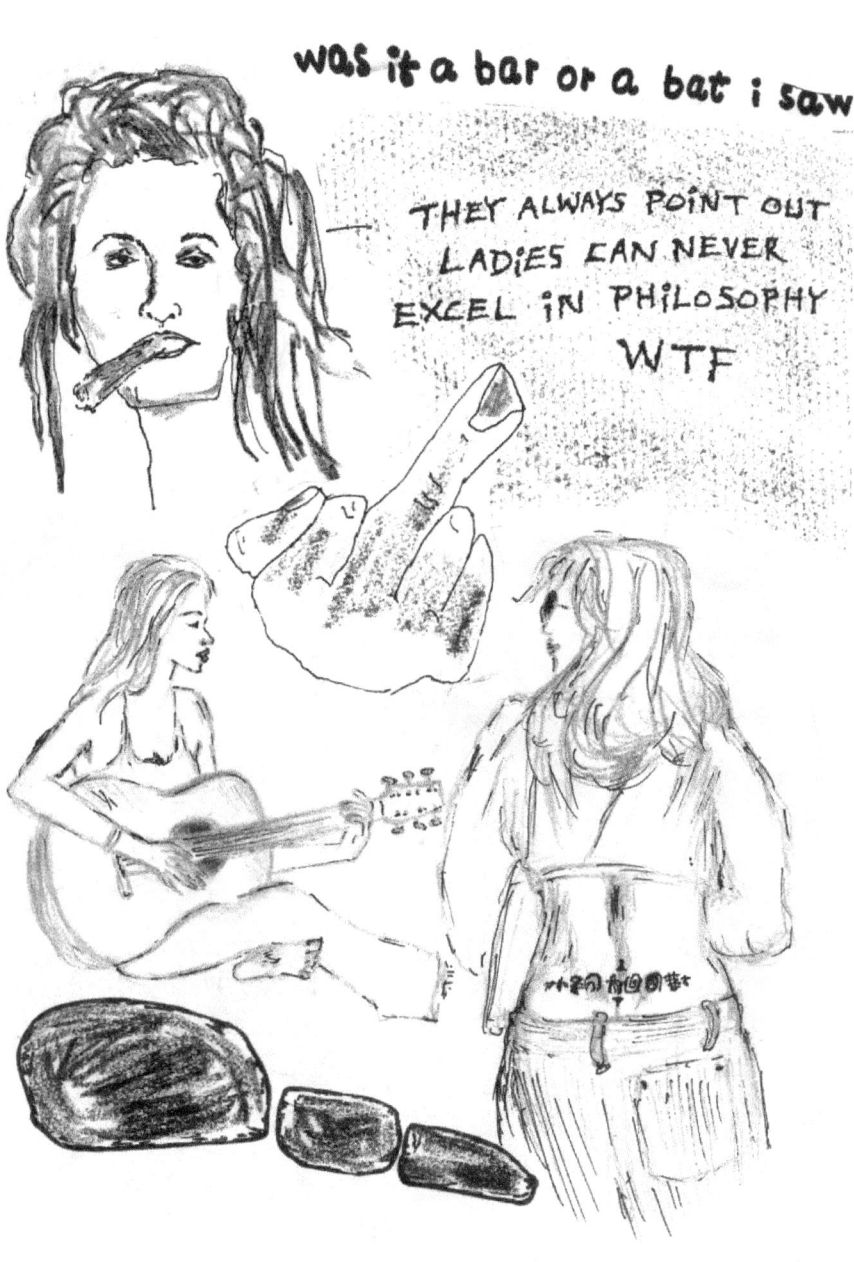

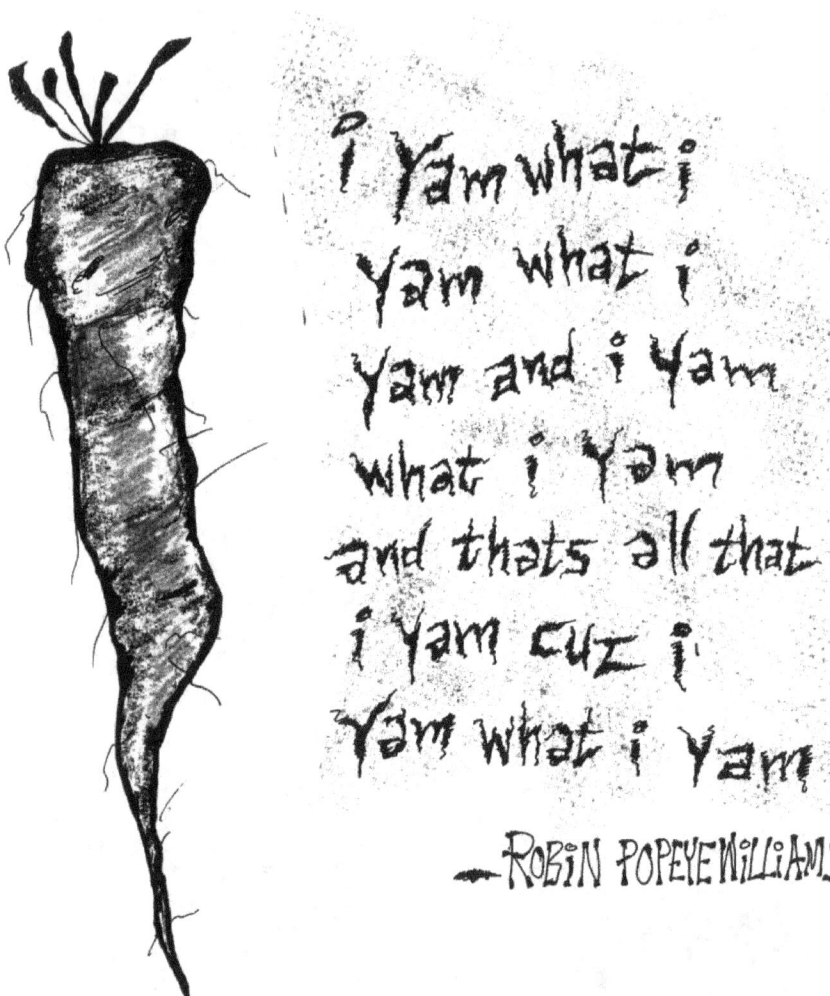

i Yam what i
Yam what i
Yam and i Yam
what i Yam
and thats all that
i Yam cuz i
Yam what i Yam

—ROBIN POPEYE WILLIAMS

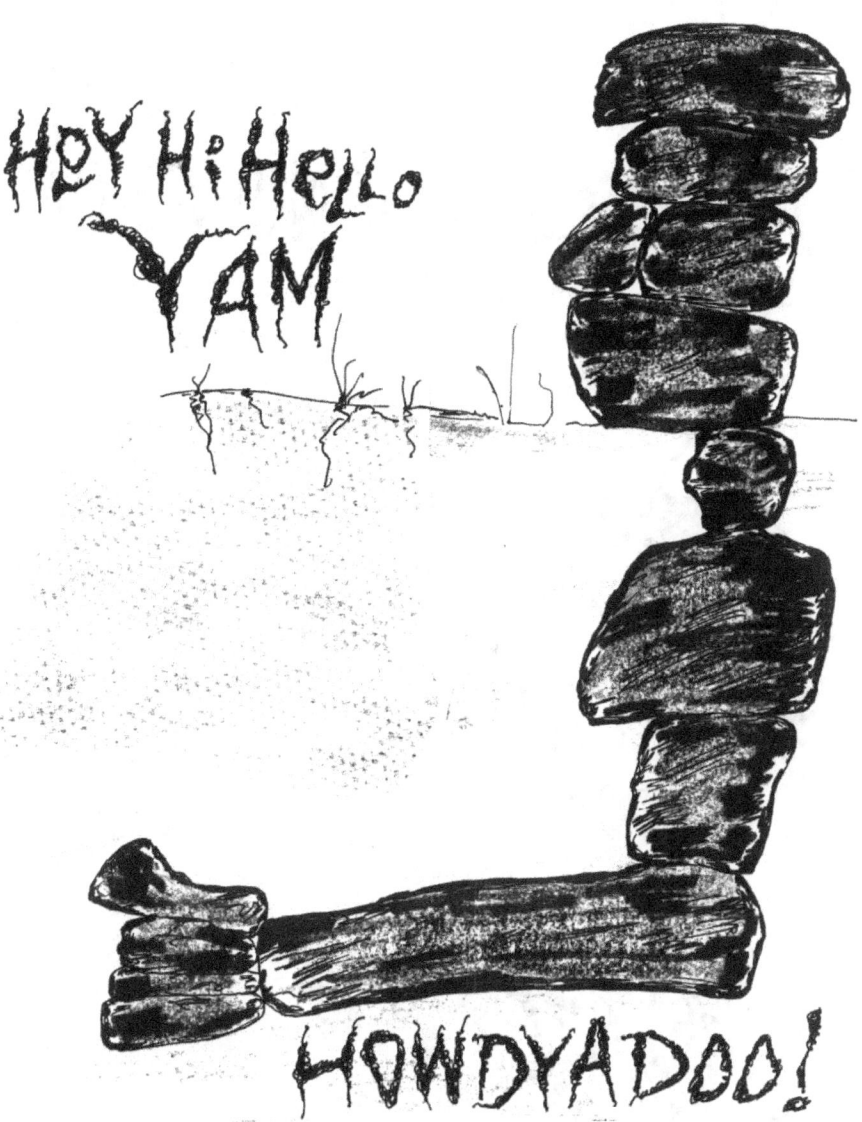

APOCALYPSE KNOWHOW

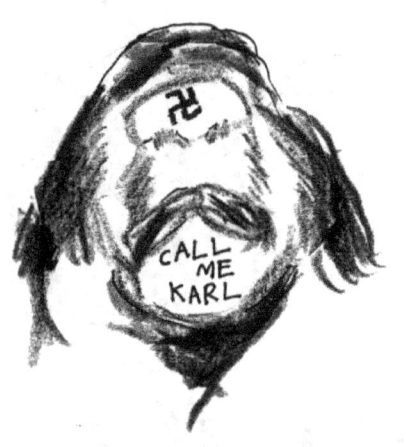

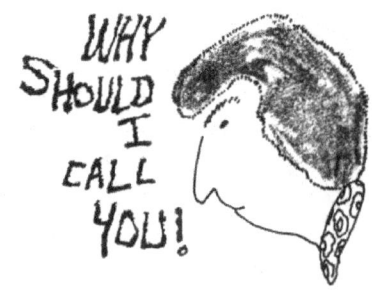

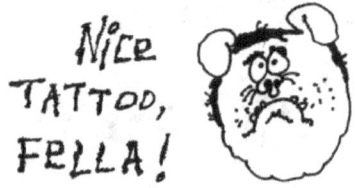

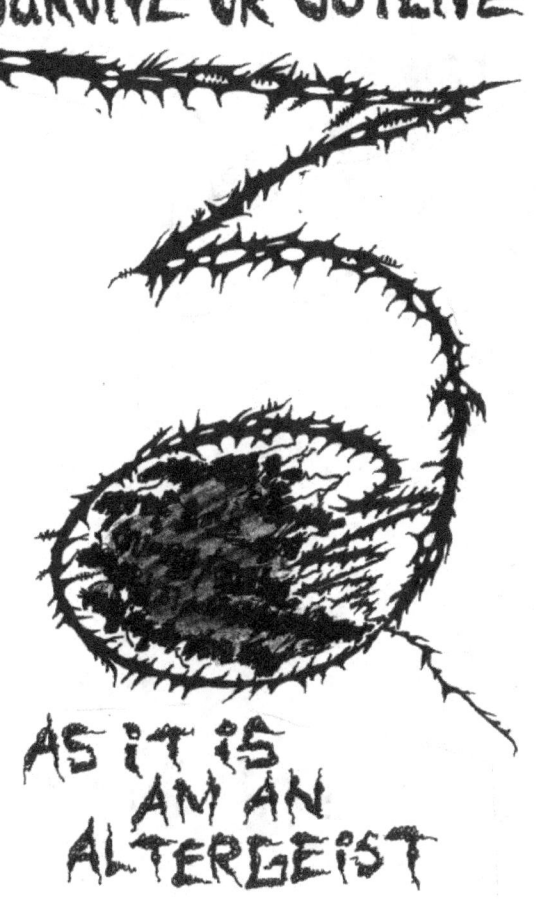

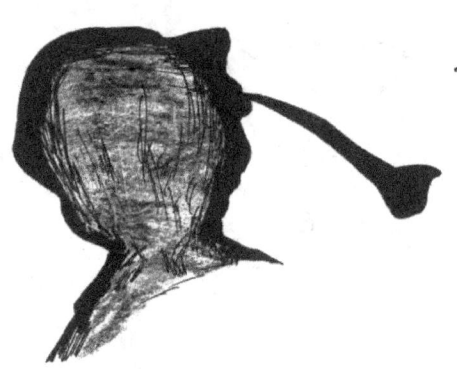

then when lilacs would bloom at last...

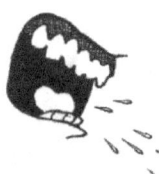

SCREW YOU, WORLD!

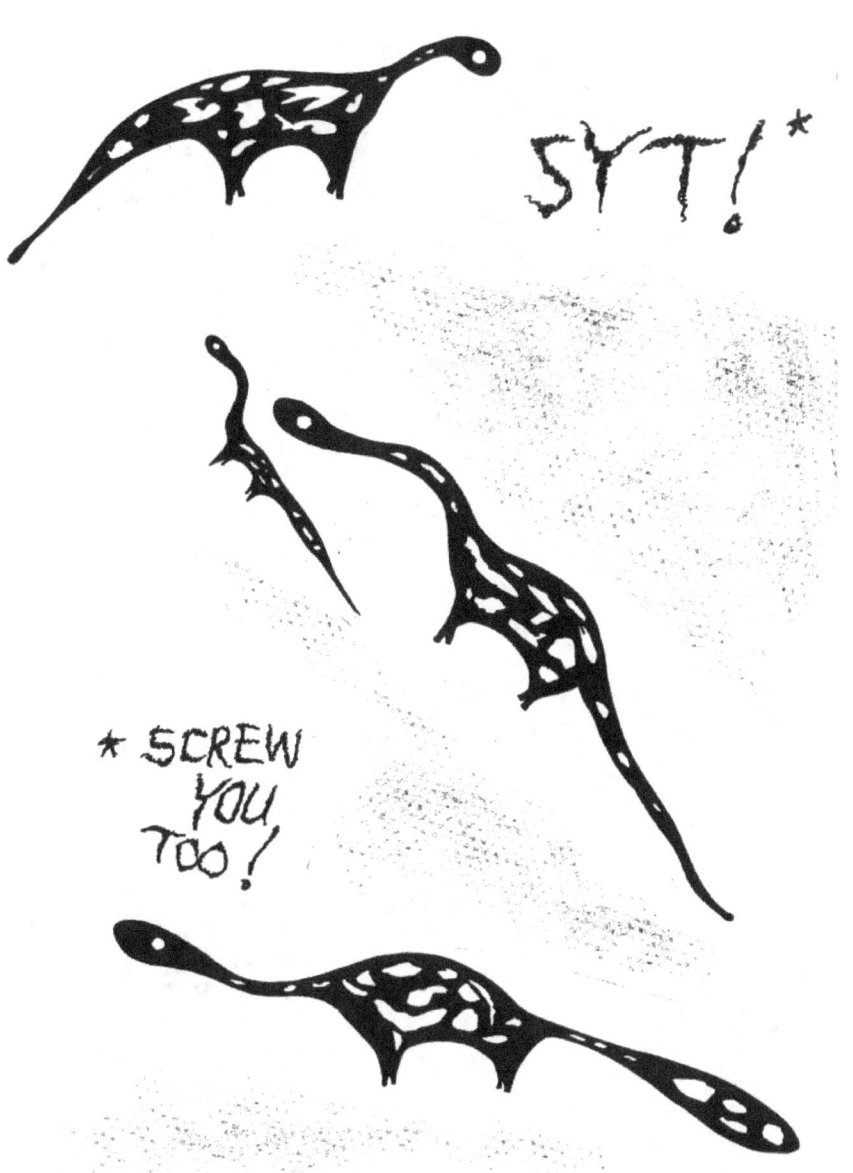

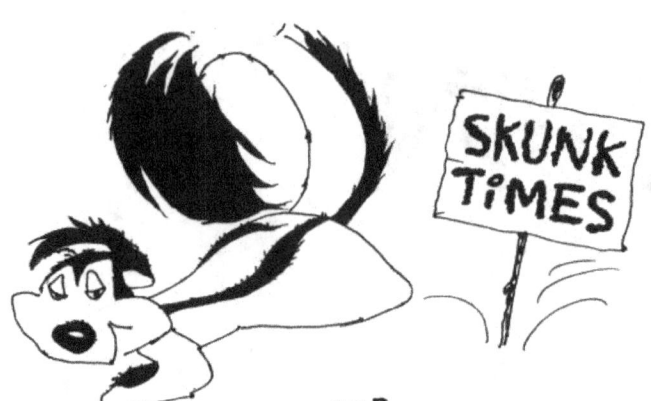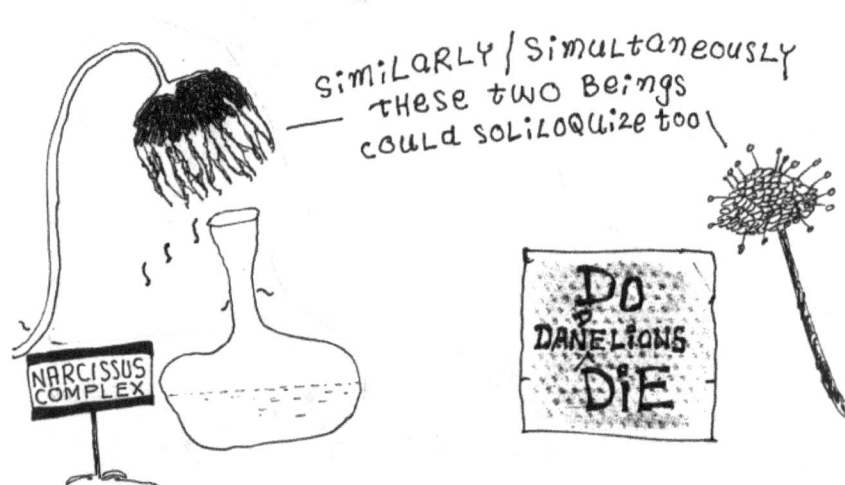

YOU TOO, AUTHOR!

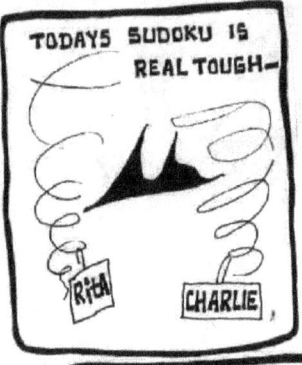

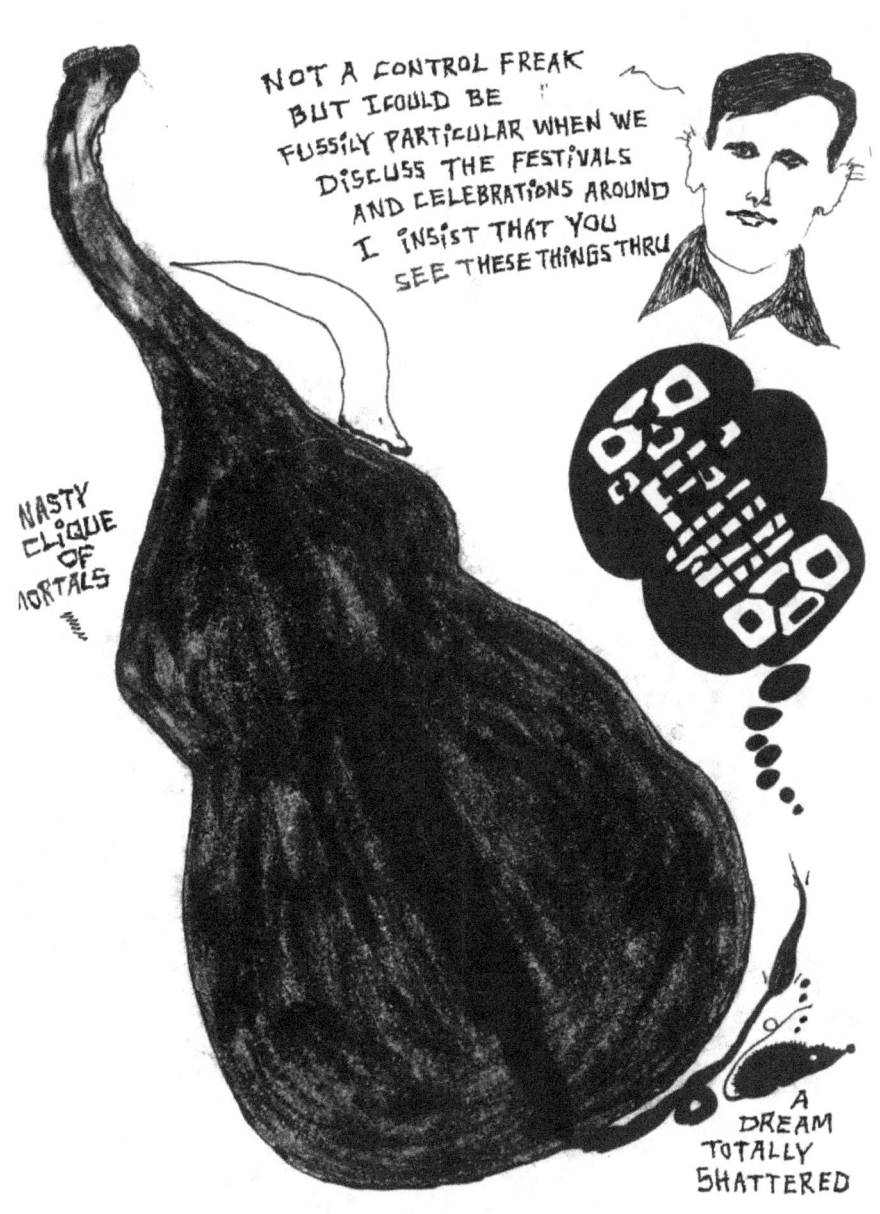

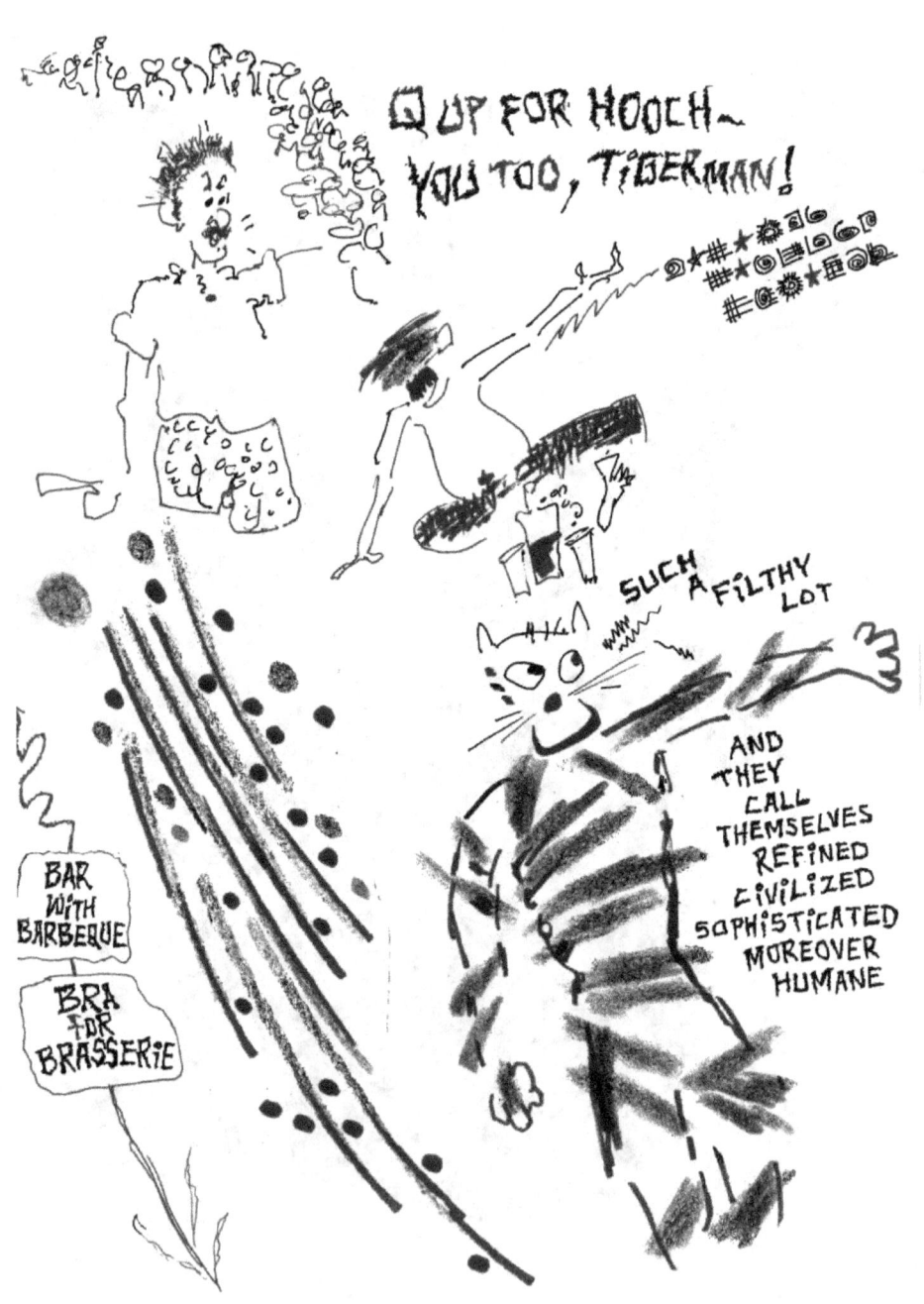

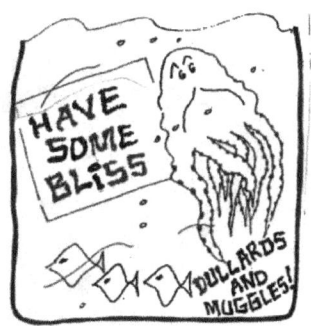
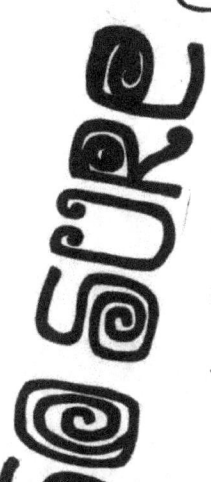
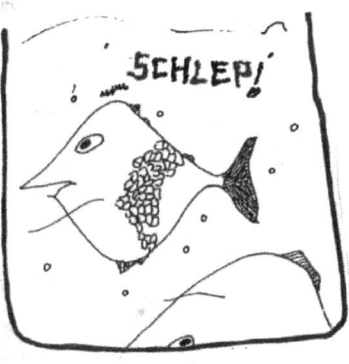
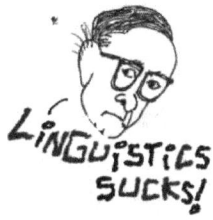
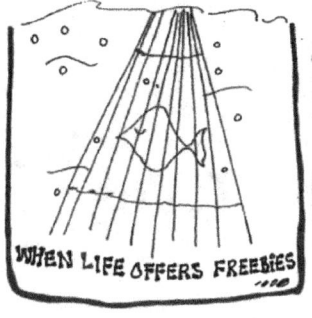

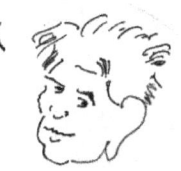

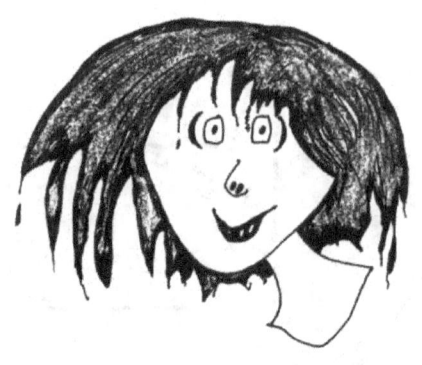

PEACE FOR ALL
SAYS SHE THOUGH
IT ONLY IS A
BOWLFUL

TIPSY
BABY TOPSY TURVY
SO WHO (33) IS GETTING CRUCIFIED NOW

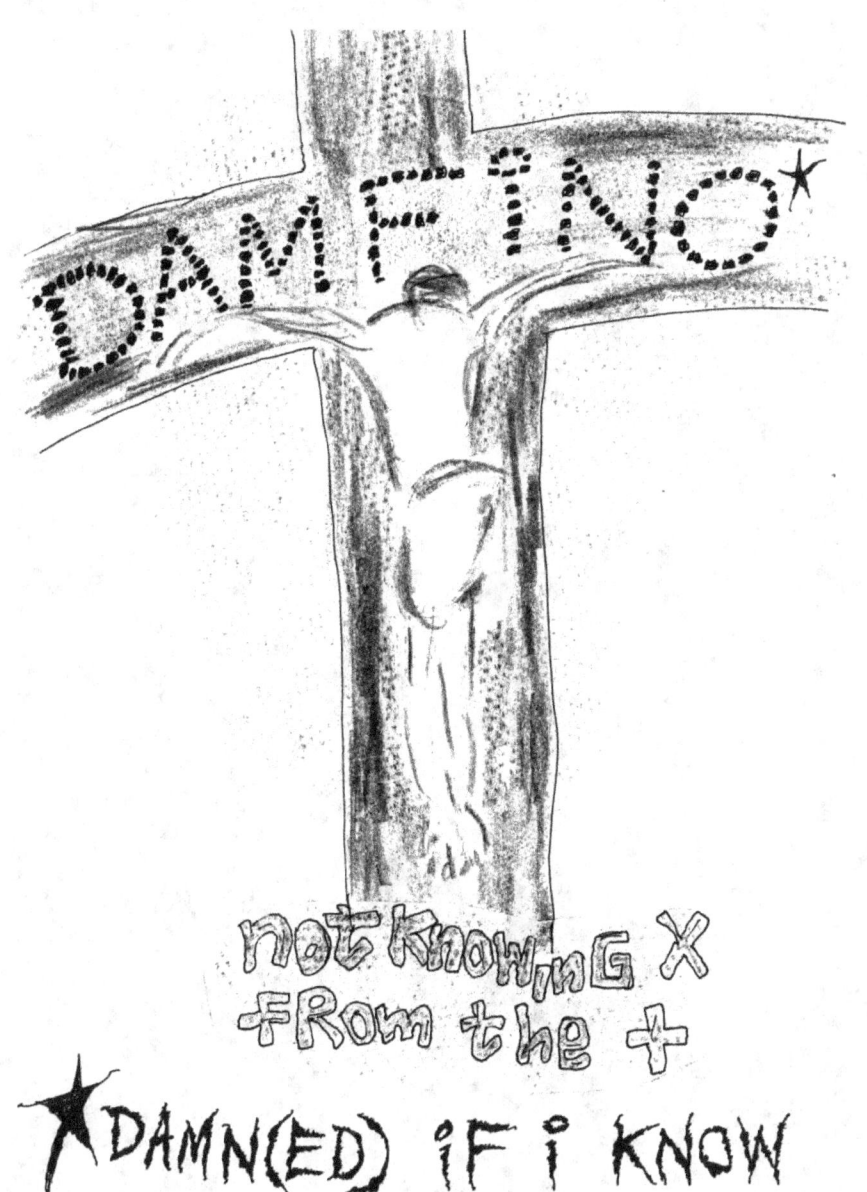

www.ingramcontent.com/pod-product-compliance
Lightning Source LLC
Chambersburg PA
CBHW071024240526
45469CB00006BD/2083